SHAKESPEARE'S AMERICA, AMERICA'S SHAKESPEARE

SHAKESPEARE'S AMERICA, AMERICA'S SHAKESPEARE

MICHAEL D. BRISTOL

ROUTLEDGE
London and New York

First published 1990
by Routledge
11 New Fetter Lane, London EC4P 4EE
29 West 35th Street, New York, NY 10001

Data converted to 10/12 Baskerville by Columns of Reading
Printed in Great Britain by Richard Clay Ltd
Bungay, Suffolk.

British Library Cataloguing in Publication Data

Bristol, Michael D.
Shakespeare's America, America's Shakespeare:
1. American culture. Literary aspects, History
I. Title
973

Library of Congress Cataloging in Publication Data

Bristol, Michael D.
Shakespeare's America, America's Shakespeare:
Michael D. Bristol.
p.   cm.
Bibliography: p.
ISBN 0-415-01538-3. — ISBN 0-415-01539-1 (pbk.)
1. Shakespeare, William, 1564–1616 — Appreciation —
United States.
2. Shakespeare, William, 1564–1616 —
Criticism and interpretation — History.
3. Theater and society — United States.
4. United States — Intellectual life. I. Title.
PR2971.U6B7   1989
822.3'3 — dc19   89–6057 CIP

ISBN HB 0-415-01538-3
BP 0-415-01539-1

Kate
Joe
This one's for you, kids

CONTENTS

ACKNOWLEDGEMENTS

This project, since it is concerned with Shakespeare, could not have been completed without the collaboration of many other individuals. My research assistants, Joe Masrour and the indefatigable Jim Nielson provided enough material to completely overwhelm this project at its inception. In tackling the extremely complex problem of research libraries I have benefitted from discussions with Kendall Wallis, Doris Bristol, Lena Orlin, Georgianna Ziegler, and Dan Traister. Michael Warren, Mette Hjort, and Stephen Orgel have provided helpful suggestions on the issue of textual editing. It is a pleasure to thank those who have been willing to discuss the politics of literary culture with me, sometimes at considerable length, especially Peter Stallybrass, Eileen Eagan, Kate McCluskie, Don Wayne, Howard Felperin, Walter Cohen, and Don Hedrick. Jean Howard and Terry Hawkes have been astute and sympathetic readers of the manuscript and their advice has helped to shape the final version of the book. My most important collaboration, as always, has been with Doris Bristol, whose refusal to foster illusions makes me think more clearly.

The Social Sciences and Humanities Research Council of Canada has given support in the form of a research time stipend, which has greatly facilitated the completion of this project. I am also grateful to the Graduate Faculty and the Department of English of McGill University for financial assistance and for allowing me sufficient time to carry out this research.

INTRODUCTION

Shakespeare is an American institution. His position as the representative of durable literary value has been affirmed as a natural fact within the United States for a considerable time. The plays are required reading in high school classes and in the curriculum of universities. In addition Shakespeare defines a field for a wide range of research and critical writing. The expansion of Shakespeare studies as an academic specialization and the dissemination of knowledge of his works is interpreted as evidence of cultural maturity in a society very much preoccupied with its own youthfulness and with the absence of a nature-like, immemorial tradition in literature and in social practice. Indeed, most accounts of the history of Shakespeare's reception in America presuppose an identification of his work with cultural goodness, wise teaching, and civilization. On this view every expression of interest in Shakespeare, both amateur and professional, is interpreted as an unambiguous sign of cultural advancement.

Interest in Shakespeare's writing is by no means confined to schools and institutions of academic research. The plays are also important in the entertainment industry. Festival theaters from New York to Ashland, Oregon produce a full repertoire of Shakespeare's plays for a wide and varied public. Perhaps even more important than serious productions, however, are the parodic versions of the plays performed by characters in certain popular television series.[1] In addition, Shakespeare characters escape formal constraints to make freelance appearances in advertising. Romeo, Juliet, and especially Hamlet have a lively afterlife in these settings. Shakespeare himself is also used in this way, and this is by no means a matter of all play and no work. In the world of practical affairs Shakespeare has real importance, for he is, among other things, the

1

greatest apartment salesman of our time.[2]

In the United States, Shakespeare exists as a complex institutional reality that cuts across many different levels of culture and many contrasting domains of social practice. But the reasons for such an authoritative and central position for Shakespeare are not at all self-evident or self-explanatory. Shakespeare's centrality in American culture might be construed as a kind of anomaly in that it entails respect and admiration for an archaic world-consciousness deep inside the American project of *renovatio*. Why should a society whose founding actions entail radical separation from all institutions of hereditary privilege be devoted to a writer whose primary themes are the pathos of kingship and the decline of the great feudal classes? The pre-eminence of Shakespeare might be interpreted in light of a conflict between nostalgia for traditional European social experience and revolutionary determination to constitute a new and historically unprecedented social and cultural dispensation.[3]

The identification of Shakespeare with an institutional apparatus requires some further clarification here. Shakespeare exists in the form of concrete semiotic materials, in books, in theatrical performances, and in filmed productions of the plays. It is in this sense that Shakespeare is institutionally produced or socially constructed; what we experience as his work is shaped by the organization of these means of cultural production. Shakespeare's popularity with a wide sector of the American public, for example, is clearly related to the availability of inexpensive, conveniently formatted texts that can be purchased almost anywhere. This fact makes Shakespeare a familiar presence throughout the USA. It would be difficult to establish whether this level of popularity is a reason for the availability of paperback texts, or whether it is a cultural effect of that availability. What is undeniable, however, is that Shakespeare is represented by very considerable allocations of productive resources and fixed capital assets.

The existence of a large-scale apparatus of reproduction certainly facilitates the dissemination of Shakespeare's work, and constitutes its meaning, at least in part. There is, however, a more fundamental sense in which Shakespeare may be defined as an institutional reality. In addition to its familiar notional sense, institution has a complex range of meanings that are pertinent to this definition. The verb, to institute, is from Latin *instituere*, which means to establish or to inaugurate. Shakespeare's status as an origin or foundation, that is, as an *institutio*, has been recognized by various cultural authorities. The idea that Shakespeare is a founder or creator of a specifically American experience of individuality and of collective life is articulated by Ralph Waldo Emerson, who described him as 'the father of the man in America'.[4] The broader suggestion that Shakespeare's *oeuvre* represents the moment of emergence of individualism has been articulated by Brecht, and more recently by scholars such as Catherine Belsey.[5] Emerson, however, makes the argument in its strong form, namely that Shakespeare is actually an institution-maker, the man who 'wrote the text of modern life' (Emerson 1968:211). In this sense the institutional reality of Shakespeare precedes and helps to define the more visible forms of the apparatus of cultural production.

There is a related meaning for institution that has equal pertinence for the problem to be explored here. The term is related to the idea of a statute, and thus an institution may be understood as an organization, a structure, or as a codification of social practice. Institutions are 'the more enduring features of social life'.[6] In this sense Shakespeare has been recognized as an institution within American society for a very long time. His works are included in the general curriculum of socialization because they are a codification both of norms and of practical consciousness within a political economy based on individualistic social ideals. Shakespeare as an institution or significant practice in the United States thus has long-term continuity in that it helps to valorize those ideals.

The argument to be developed in this book is that the interpretation of Shakespeare and the interpretation of American political culture are mutually determining practices. In order to analyze this relationship, considerable attention must be given to the institutional ethos that governs the reproduction of Shakespeare. The notion of an institutional ethos refers to the set of consciously held beliefs about the value of Shakespeare and the purpose of studying or just enjoying his works. The scholars, editors, and curators studied here have all been selected because they articulate such an institutional ethos explicitly. They also reveal the operation of an institutional pathos, or structure of feeling prompted by underlying social contradictions that Shakespeare presumably helps to reconcile. From within that structure of feeling the writings of Shakespeare are often celebrated as remedial and therapeutic, reconciling or transcending conflicts within the social landscape

3

depicted in the plays. In fact, contradictions that appear in the plays often coincide with strains and divisions in the context of their reception. This discovery, (or is it a projection?) of social contradiction in the fictional world of the plays is an important function of the Shakespeare institution.

The present project assumes that the institutional and the social life of Shakespeare is what really matters. It further assumes that a critique of institutional practice *vis-à-vis* Shakespeare is possible, although such a critique cannot proceed on the basis of some *other*, really real or natural Shakespeare as the normative standard for evaluating the institution, its social and political orientation, or its function. A critique of institutional practices is very different from an *exposé* of institutional follies, since such an *exposé* presupposes knowledge of an essential Shakespeare prior to any institutionaliz-ation. It is not my intention here to present a derisory account of institutional Shakespeare as a kind of carnival dummy to be ridiculed and thrashed, so that a triumphant essential Shakespeare may be restored. Shakespeare scholars often express unhappiness over the institutional realities in which they must carry out their work. But sentimental yearning for an essential Shakespearean presence has itself been the institutional position *par excellence*. To chastise institutional Shakespeare from within those institutions entails both an obvious epistemological circularity and an unsup-ported claim of privilege.

Neither Shakespeare nor institutional practice stands outside historical and social determination. If Shakespeare's plays hold some knowledge in reserve that exceeds the present horizon of those historical determinations, then a critique of currently existing institutional realities can have some real pertinence. Critique differs from more affirmative types of scholarship, however, in its defensive or antithetical orientation to the powerful and possibly irresistible literary material it seeks to understand. This requires both an acknowledgement of the researcher's position within a culture already constituted by Shakespeare, and an attempt at emigration from that cultural ground.[7] Since the choice of topic here already signifies a fascination with Shakespeare, it is clear that such emigration can scarcely expect to locate a frontier, let alone cross it. In undertaking a critique of Shakespeare then, I necessarily proceed on the understanding that I am implicated in and defined by the very institutional reality I propose to analyze.

Shakespeare enters into the consciousness of everyone in the culture, whether or not they have read any of the plays. We understand Shakespeare as subjects that have already been Shakespearized (Emerson 1968: 204). There is thus something aberrant in conceiving the notion of a critique of Shakespeare, since such a notion implies that Shakespeare might be something to become emancipated from rather than something to be emancipated by. This very fact, the tyranny of Shakespeare's goodness, is an indication of just how powerfully situated this material is within the ensemble of social and cultural relations in contemporary society. A project that seeks to identify Shakespeare with an institution will necessarily appear negative, and even destructive in the present political atmosphere. The reason for this difficulty is that the usual goal of research and criticism in relation to Shakespeare has typically been to rescue his authority from institutional distortions accumulated through its history. The existence of such pre-institutional authority as well as its socially binding character have been perhaps too readily assumed. The hypostatizing of Shakespeare's authority is, however, related to the pattern of cultural interests that such authority helps to conserve.

The critics, editors, and scholars whose work has been selected as the archive for this analysis are, without exception, men. The work of women scholars such as Rosalie Colie and Madeleine Doran has certainly been as valuable as anything done by their male peers and contemporaries.[8] Since the institution of Shakespeare has been created largely by and for men, however, their work occupies a somewhat anomalous position. Although it was primarily orthodox, both in its methods and its results, this work articulated distinctive interests that anticipate an emergent and heterodox feminist orientation. The absence of women from the illustrative material here is intended as a strategic omission. Shakespeare's writing was achieved within a candidly patriarchal dispensation, and it has continued to be constitutive of that dispensation. The institutional pathos I have attempted to describe here may be understood as an array of specifically masculine subject positions. These positions can be defined as the uneasy coexistence of an isolated, exceptional subject with a totalizing and fundamentally alien structure of social discipline. From within this experience neither the contradictions of bourgeois culture, nor the possible horizons of any radical social transformation can become visible.

Feminist theory locates a strong critical standpoint from which research might negate and undo this dialectic.[9] Feminist critique, like literary criticism, is concerned with articulating the relationship between a cultural object and a knowledge-seeking subject. Unlike literary criticism, however, feminism understands such a knowledge-seeking subject not as a neutered private sensibility responding to specifically aesthetic experience, but as a public and political agent or subject implicated in historical struggle. Such an agent necessarily exists within an historically specific ensemble of social relations elaborated over stretches of time that exceed the horizons of any individual. This critical, knowledge-seeking subject cannot be conceived of in voluntaristic terms as fully autonomous, free of prior social determination. Nevertheless such a subject can be a knowledgeable social agent. The possibility of a genuine knowledge is derived from the recognition or making visible of a patriarchal order. That order misidentifies a culturally produced inequality as a natural difference. In feminism the category of gender difference is identified as an organic social variable.[10] On this view, gender difference appears in every cultural setting, but the specific coding of that difference is determined within the symbolic order. There are no ungendered subjects because gender difference has always been constitutive of the general protocol of social relations within patriarchy.

The statement that there are no ungendered subjects runs counter to the assumption of humanist scholarship, namely that general human interests are enshrined in a tradition that transcends all historical conflict. Feminism is a rejection of the idea of transcendence predicated on a category of *Man* that purports to represent generic humanity. Would a fully implemented feminist *praxis* really be 'the end of civilized life as we know it', as some of its opponents have claimed?[11] As a type of critical theory, feminism is a refusal of any of the prevalent meanings for the notion of civilization that have contemporary currency in so far as these notions perpetuate reified conceptions of a general human interest.[12] Despite its radical aims, however, feminism cannot be wholly transformative and utopian in its practice. Some feminisms and many feminists are in fact objectively revisionist in that they contribute primarily to stabilizing existing conditions. Even in its weaker variants, however, feminism is a rejection of an essentially sado-masochistic form of existing cultural policy. In other words feminism is the refusal to make

6

aesthetic or imaginative pleasure out of actual historical pain.

Feminist Shakespeare scholarship differs from other variants of feminist literary criticism in its demand for answerability from a male author.[13] In all the variants of feminist criticism, as in other types of critical social theory, it is imperative to work against cultural tradition and to reveal its ideological character rather than simply to promote loyalty to it. Typically feminist scholarship does not really interpret a text, but rather expostulates with and sometimes denounces its object. These activities and practices are frankly oriented towards a utopian future in which the currently existing institutional pathos has been utterly transformed. The critique of tradition must be concerned, however, not only with the disclosure of false consciousness, but equally with hegemonic ideology's functional approximation of and even equivalency to historical truth.

The feminist project is not a continuation of 'business as usual' in the field of cultural studies. It simply is not possible to do justice to this intervention by attempting to assess 'feminist interpretations' with reference to the criteria of business-as-usual literary scholarship, as Richard Levin has done in a recent article.[14] The recent 'breakthrough' of an outspoken and even outlandish feminism is related to a much wider mobilization of resistances outside the highly specialized world of Shakespeare scholarship. But neither feminism nor any other oppositional project will succeed in overturning a deeply entrenched hegemonic order just because it is oriented towards a utopian transformation of existing conditions. In keeping with the principle of methodological pessimism typical of an older critical theory, I have adopted a primarily negative orientation in this study.[15] I have been concerned with the complex links between Shakespeare as a cultural institution and the larger dispensation of bourgeois political economy. It is obvious that such institutional arrangements are not feminist, or socialist either for that matter, and to undertake a critique by assuming the correctness of these utopian orientations actually reveals very little of the internal contradictions within those institutions. The critique of Shakespeare as an American institution cannot be a simple affirmation of an alternative ensemble of cultural values, any more than it can be an affirmation of present institutional and social realities. The present volume is intended as a contribution to an oppositional practice and to the possibility of an alternative political culture. A critique of Shakespeare only really matters, finally, against such a horizon and this horizon is, at the moment a very distant one.

This book is specifically about Shakespeare, though the meaning of the term, Shakespeare, is not construed here in the usual way. Since this study is mainly concerned with an account of particular institutional and discursive formations, it contains no readings of Shakespeare's plays, and scarcely any consideration of specific interpretations at all. Scholars who specialize in the study of Shakespeare continue to be preoccupied with the task of separating good interpretations from bad ones. This project assumes that such a separation is possible, but without making any claims one way or the other as to its urgency. Whatever might be the social function of good, as opposed to bad, interpretation, it is clear that the criteria for making such discriminations cannot be articulated either by producing new interpretations or by reproducing old ones. The issues raised in this discussion cannot be analyzed in and through the medium of textual analysis, since it is precisely the sociological and thus the epistemological status of textual analysis that is in question. It is, perhaps, a scandal to speak of Shakespeare without attending to any of Shakespeare's poetry, but this tactic is necessary if the relationship between interpreting Shakespeare and interpreting American political culture is to be made clear.

This study is an attempt to look at the formation of an implicit cultural policy in and through the practice of Shakespeare scholarship. That cultural policy has been oriented towards the integration of the individual into the dispensation of bourgeois political economy. I will be concerned both with the continuing function of Shakespeare in stabilizing this dispensation, and with significant shifts or moments of strategic reorientation within the institutions of scholarship and criticism. This analysis thus explicitly connects literary analysis as it pertains to Shakespeare with the formation and dissemination of ideology. Since ideology is an equivocal term, however, it is necessary to exclude certain usages in order to make clear what a critique of ideology is attempting to undo.[16] To begin with, the term ideology has an invidious and unsavory character. Ideology is always 'other'. It is the term we apply to the articulated self-understanding of any cultural or social group whose goals and objectives we dislike. Denunciatory usages of this kind are natural enough, but not very helpful in the present context. Nor is the obverse sense in which ideology means simply any more or less systematic and widely held world view. To refer to cultural differences, mental habits, or the diversity of world views as ideologies simply evacuates the critical force of this important concept. I take the position that ideology differs both from knowledge *and* from deliberate or malicious deception. Ideology is false consciousness or distorted communication that nevertheless has a functional equivalence to truth.

Many ideological *exposés* have tended to concentrate on the element of error or untruth in the positions they analyze. But this type of ideological *exposé* usually does not explain why essentially false beliefs can appear plausible to those who adhere to them. Nor do they give any indication how ideological convictions can be in contradiction with social reality and at the same time enable the groups who possess these convictions to function adequately within that social reality. The concept of ideology as I understand it is closely related to certain basic tenets of Durkheim's sociology of religion.[17] Religious belief, even in its most fantastical manifestations, is never entirely a case of simple mass delusion. This analysis stipulates the objective cogency of both the doctrines and the ritual practices of the believers, in this case Shakespeare scholars. These beliefs and practices do indeed represent a fundamental set of truths about the world of these believers, although this truth is not expressed in the self-understanding of the members of the religious community. For Durkheim the veneration of a ghostly entity and all associated doctrines are a misrecognition of the actual social foundations of the entire religious apparatus. The sacred is a powerful and at the same time powerfully disguised transformation of the social order that structures the activity and provides for the solidarity of its members. This is a solidarity constructed in the domain of the imaginary, but it is not a mass delusion.[18] It may, however, be a differentiated structure that is contrary to the interests of many or even all the members of that solidarity. On this view the social bond is maintained, not through a homeostatic equilibrium achieved by individual agents pursuing their own interests, but by a fundamentally irrational though affectively binding displacement of the objective structure of social relations with a purely imaginary construction of myths and symbolic practices.

Durkheim's position stresses the affectively binding character of religion as a form of socially distributed *eros*. Marx, on the other hand, was more concerned with the irrational and thus oppressive dimension of those structures. This concern is worked out in Marx's famous discussion of religion as both an expression of real misery and a protest against it.[19] The image of religion as an 'opiate' does not simply denounce religion as a mere palliative and still less as a malicious deception. Opiates do, after all, alleviate pain. Religion is regarded as a contradictory phenomenon, in which a powerful truth (the perception of social injustice and the desire for redress) is united with an equally powerful untruth (God exists and He will redeem all injustice in some other world). This is, I believe, the paradigmatic instance of an ideology. In other words, the ideological is what makes possible the integration of functional and of dysfunctional elements within social reality. This may also be understood as the integration of aesthetic with anaesthetic functions within the sphere of cultural production.

The institution of Shakespeare has a quite specific history in Britain.[20] Although there is obvious overlap and exchange of views, Shakespeare has had a substantially different history as an institution in North America.[21] The first section of this book will analyze what Emerson called the Shakespearization of America, a phenomenon I understand as a massive transfer of authority and of cultural capital to American society. To understand that transfer of authority it is necessary to consider at some length the problem of tradition as a social agency and as a medium for sustaining collective life. It is also important to understand concrete logistical aspects of this transfer, and thus consideration must be given to the building of libraries and research facilities as well as to the activities of editors and textual scholars. The second section of this book is concerned with the circulation of a discourse on Shakespeare, and with the relationship of that discourse to broader cultural policy themes within the United States. Much of that discourse, from the time of the First World War right up to the present can be related to a dialogue between neo-conservative culture criticism, and its ecumenical, centrist antagonist in advanced liberalism. This analysis will show that our system of relations with Shakespeare is a reading of our situation-bound existence within bourgeois political economy. The hypostatizing of Shakespeare's authority has been and continues to be a quasi-religious practice. This is true both in relation to the erotic submission to that authority required by the traditional humanist hermeneutics of reconstitution, and in relation to more recent apostasies and indecisions of various post-structuralist orientations.

Part 1

SHAKESPEARIZING AMERICA
THE INSTITUTIONAL INFRASTRUCTURE

Chapter one

DOING SHAKESPEARE: THE POLITICAL ECONOMY OF SCHOLARSHIP

The complexity of Shakespeare's positioning within the context of North American culture is suggested very forcefully in the strange case of Charlie the Tuna. This animated cartoon figure has been used for many years as the focus in the advertising campaigns of a nationally distributed brand of canned tuna. In one of the perennial favorites in this campaign Charlie appears clad in doublet and hose, carrying a rapier. It is Charlie's desire to be recruited by a certain tuna company, and so he proposes to 'do Shakespeare' to show that he has good taste. To do Shakespeare, Charlie explains, 'I beat guys wit' 'dis sword whilst hollering poetry'. Alas, the tuna company is unimpressed by good taste; it only wants tuna that tastes good. 'Sorry Charlie!' He never understands the distinction between 'good taste' and 'tasting good' or between doing Shakespeare and getting processed into canned tuna. Because of this, he will remain a 'lovable loser' whose inadequacies keep him outside the dispensation of the industrial corporation, though marginally serviceable to its interests.

Charlie the Tuna is important for two reasons. First, he makes it clear that Shakespeare has some kind of normative force within American culture. Doing Shakespeare signifies cultural advancement since it places Charlie on the side of 'good taste' even though it has nothing to do with 'tasting good', that is, with Charlie's market-worthiness. Second, although Shakespeare has a culturally norma-tive aesthetic value, it would appear that he is also a figure of considerable emancipatory potential, since 'doing Shakespeare' saves Charlie from the fate of the tuna that taste good, that is to be butchered, cooked, and canned.

The tension between 'good taste' with its consequent exclusion and marginalization, and 'tasting good' with its consequent absorption into the apparatus of production and consumption has not been diminished by the enshrining of Shakespeare as a figure of indubitable cultural authority. Shakespeare scholars have always been constrained to experience the conflict between the governing imperative of bourgeois aesthetics – that is, the autonomy and expressive unity of the artist and his work, and the governing imperatives of bourgeois economic and social practice – that is the rationalization of the socio-cultural order and the extension of social discipline more and more deeply into the ethical sphere in response to a demand for greater productive efficiency.[1]

In the United States, more so probably than in Britain, Shakespeare has been identified with general or universal human interests, or to put it another way, with social and cultural goodness. Although Shakespeare is himself characterized as never dogmatic or authoritarian, the doctrine of a copious and benevolent Shakespearean creativity has been advanced with considerable dogmatic and authoritarian rigor. This insistence on placing Shakespeare on the side of social goodness, however one may understand social goodness, is a manifestation of the general unwillingness among American culture critics to settle accounts with Shakespeare and with their European past. Instead, various modes of idealization have been elaborated within the practice of scholarship as mandated by a broadly liberal and humanistic cultural dispensation. This dispensation has not been characterized by a high degree of consensus or unanimity, and there are in fact numerous variants of humanistic scholarship that differ on both ideological and on methodological grounds. Nevertheless, humanistic scholarship can be defined as sharing a background consensus in terms of its primary institutional goal-values.

THE HUMANIST EROTICS OF READING

Traditional humanistic scholarship has placed its hopes in a hermeneutics of reconstitution, intending through this strategy to keep faith with tradition.[2] Debates within humanism are concerned mainly with the form such a hermeneutics will take, and with the relative validity of historicist or formalist orientations to literary texts. There is a background consensus here, however, that defines scholarship as a disinterested love for the various products of literary tradition and for the institutionalization of that love in a substantive educational curriculum consisting of great works. This position entails a normative distinction between loving Shakespeare and using him as a cultural commodity. Scholarship is committed to the intact classical body of the Shakespeare text, and to the absolute primacy of Shakespeare's cultural authority over that of his interpreters. The central imperative of humanism is not a search for determinate knowledge, but rather a submissive empathy with the transcendent source of aesthetic experience.[3] That empathy, or love, must be kept chaste, and remain disinterested. In other words, there can be no intrusion of purely modern concerns or interests, no violation or degradation of the intact body of the text.

The desire to keep faith with tradition by professing love for Shakespeare is obviously related to the idea of modernity as a faithless condition, or at least one in which a tradition is in the process of vanishing from the cultural landscape.[4] This view interprets modernity as an experience of loss or grieving, so that scholarship in the humanities appears as a kind of nostalgia. More specifically it is nostalgia for presence or for the unselfconscious affiliation with or assent to the constraints and the imperatives of a customary social order. Such a dispensation requires that the disciplines of the humanities emerge as hermeneutic sciences. These sciences contrast with the natural sciences in that the human sciences are tied to particular psychological requirements. The humanist needs tact and sympathy in his relations with the distant contexts that were actually lived by his forbears. In addition, he needs a well-stocked memory and a willingness to submit to authorities.[5] Scholarship is thus linked to the 'remembrance of things past,' and to the feeling of sadness for the loss of a spiritual homeland.[6]

Love for Shakespeare is frequently proposed as a necessary consolation for this loss. But what exactly does it mean to speak of love for Shakespeare and in what sense should this figure be regarded as lovable? The discovery of a predicate for the subject 'Shakespeare' is the end point in all the variants of humanistic scholarship. In pursuing this objective, however, the meaning of the author's name is left undefined. Shakespeare, it would appear, is a concept that does not bear much looking into. An important reason for this is that the term is used equivocally, with at least three quite distinct meanings that are frequently confused. To begin with, Shakespeare is the name of a specific historical individual, William

Shakespeare of Stratford, who was, among other things, an actor and playwright. That historical Shakespeare, living and working within the social life-world of late sixteenth-century England, certainly saw his world from the position of an historically situated subject. There would obviously be some value to research that attempted to reconstruct the world-consciousness of such a subject. Although a surprising amount is known about the historical Shakespeare, most biographical research has had an anecdotal and reverential orientation, so that the horizons of an historically specific Shakespearean consciousness remain on the whole vaguely delineated.

The second meaning of the term Shakespeare is the idea of Shakespeare as an author, an idea characteristically formulated according to the literary model of 'the man and his works'.[7] The relationship of Shakespeare as author, both to his works, and to the historical William Shakespeare who enjoyed an early retirement in Stratford is extremely complicated. The unity of 'Shakespeare: the man and his works' is typically grasped in such terms as integrity, complexity, development, and so forth. Ironically, since most of the surviving records of Shakespeare's life are those preserved in Stratford, it has been difficult to map his practice as an author on to a detailed account of his life experience during his London career. In any case, there is no theoretically compelling reason to posit an identity between an author-function and any historically contingent individual. This general principle has very particular applicability to the problem of understanding just what the expression 'Shakespeare' means.

It is probably correct to say that the historical William Shakespeare of Stratford is *not* the 'author' of his 'works' in the sense generally intended today by these notions. This by no means implies that some other, unknown individual is the 'real' author; in fact the perdurable existence of an anti-Stratfordian camp has made it extremely difficult to state the problem in a lucid way. The point is first, that Shakespeare the author has been retrospectively constituted in order to establish an institutional basis for the expressive unity of 'Shakespeare: the man and his works'. Second, the actual modes of human creativity that first generated the theatrical scripts of *Hamlet, King Lear*, or *The Tempest* were in all likelihood collaborative and improvisatory, but in any case were not the institutionally recognizable forms of individualized literary/artistic production or 'genial creation' taken to be natural under present conditions.[8]

It is not always clear in the interpretive usage of Shakespeare's name whether the historical individual or the 'man and his works' is intended. The confusion is compounded in the extremely casual identification of these two categories, whereby a biographical construct like 'gentle Will' is implicitly held to be fully identical with and perfectly expressed in 'the body of the text'. And there is a further complication. Behind the equivocation between a conception of an historical individual and an author there is a third sense of the term Shakespeare, and it is this sense that is characteristically invoked in the conventional interpretive usage. The authoritative force of these statements depends on an implicit assumption that 'Shakespeare' is a reference to some kind of socio-cultural or spiritual origin, source, or presence. This ghostly entity is evidently benign and, although extremely complex, ultimately trustworthy. Meanings that can be discovered in and thus authorized by 'Shakespeare' have a quasi-religious function in that they are meanings that may be internalized to inform the spiritual/psychic life of readers or auditors. It is this last meaning that constitutes the love-object of traditional humanist scholarship.

Shakespeare is the name of a tutelary deity or cult-object. The present project – though it is certainly not a celebration of bardolatry – is not based on a derisory and dismissive repudiation of this phenomenon. On the contrary, I maintain that cultic veneration of Shakespeare has powerful objective cogency, though not for the reasons usually cited by Shakespeare scholars. Something certainly exists that compels the attention both of an attentive theatre-going audience and a large community of professional scholars and researchers. That something is not really a ghostly entity, or spirit, even though it functions as an authoritative presence. However, the quasi-religious structuration of presence, text, and the general pattern of affirmation reproduced in the ascription of various cultural values to Shakespeare suggests a way both of resolving an equivocal usage and of initiating a critique of Shakespeare.

The 'sacred character' of the Shakespearean scripture accounts, at least in part, for the very considerable cultural and even spiritual authority allocated to the poems and plays that make up the canon of his work. It is precisely this sacred character that a critique of Shakespeare would have to account for. There is scarcely any point in merely pointing out that the discourse and the practice surrounding Shakespeare are quasi-religious activities organized and regulated by a cadre of scribes and priests. There is even less point in suggesting, either directly or through a tone of high irony, that this religion is some sort of vast cultural error or delusion.[9]

Any discussion of a quasi-religious practice must recognize the objective cogency of both the doctrines and the ritual behavior of the believers, because these belief systems do indeed represent a fundamental set of truths about the world. Love and service devoted to a ghostly entity is, however, a misrecognition of the actual social foundations of the entire religious apparatus. The sacred character of the Shakespeare text is a powerful and at the same time powerfully disguised transformation of the social order that structures the activity and provides for the solidarity of its members.

The existence of an institutional apparatus and of a wider surrounding socio-political context in which research takes place is generally acknowledged by humanist scholars. But this surrounding context is viewed primarily as a source of error in the practice of interpretation, especially when 'modern theories' are permitted to regulate or even to inflect the reproduction of meaning. The intellectual achievements of the twentieth century do not help to advance knowledge; instead they are characterized as forms of cultural violence. Interpretations that privilege a theoretical discourse are described as 'forcing' or 'violating' the text. This language implies that a text has a natural or obvious meaning, and that the task of scholarship is to remove obstacles to the disclosure of that natural meaning. It is possible to say what a Shakespeare play means, and thus to use the text itself as the norm for distinguishing good interpretations from bad ones, but only on the condition that we have not been blinded by cognitive prejudice induced by unreflective acceptance of our own historical situatedness, or our own 'modernity'.

Humanist scholarship does not provide any analysis of this problem of situatedness, any more than it provides a coherent theory for the analysis of historically distant contexts themselves. There is certainly no sustained analysis of the 'modernity' that can fatally prejudice research. In effect this is a renunciation of knowledge in favor of a deeper, more intuitive empathy with trans-historical general humanity most fully revealed in the canonical literary texts. Humanistic scholarship has tended summarily to reject interpretations in which a given set of theoretical assumptions overtly govern or determine the interpretive results, on the grounds that the results are 'dictated' by those theoretical assumptions. I have always found this attitude bewildering, in that it appears to require a distinction between responsiveness to a text on the one hand, and argumentative coherence on the other. What, one is moved to ask, would determine the conclusions of an argument if not the governing principle, thesis, or set of assumptions from which the argument proceeds? Can an 'argument' be simply a sequence of *ad hoc* statements; is interpretation nothing other than a strictly opportunistic canon of discourse? Marxist or psychoanalytic theories are bound to produce 'overdetermined' and probably 'one-sided' interpretations of literary texts if they are to make any sense at all. But this is not the real basis for the humanist's disaffection with contemporary theories.

Traditional humanist scholarship's quarrel with modern critical and interpretive theories is an expression of loyalty to the lost cultural homeland, and of the understanding that there is no contemporary theoretical achievement that will permit a return to that homeland. Sympathy and careful attention to the primary texts are proposed as the alternatives to the intolerant claims of theoretically motivated research programs. Humanism's disclaimer, the assertion that 'we have no theory' is an equivocation between a broad, genial eclecticism and a far less tolerant, quasi-positivistic view of the canonical text. The text offers its obvious meanings to a readership divided between humbly faithful 'lovers of Shakespeare' and wayward critics rationalizing their own self-interest within the research agenda of a determinate theory. What this produces is a complex defensive strategy that promises to forestall both ideological closure (possibly a coding for Marxism) *and* the radical dispersal of meaning (possibly a coding for post-structural orientations such as deconstruction).

In a humanist erotics of reading, once the work's own meaning has been identified and amplified, the task of interpretive scholarship is completed. Discussion of the validity of that meaning does not form part of the legitimate discourse. As an example of this strategic orientation, it might be helpful to consider a play like *The Taming of the Shrew*. This text *appears* to represent the subordination of women in an approving way, and even to suggest that a certain brutality in achieving that subordination is both edifying and amusing. If a reader were to object that the play constitutes a legitimation of

21

patriarchal violence against women, humanistic scholarship will provide an explanation that affirms the play's meaning. The explanation may proceed in accordance with a traditional historicism that clarifies Elizabethan belief systems in respect of gender and sexual difference, or it may proceed in accordance with a formalist account of the play's irony. But in either case the objecting or critical reader will be placed in the position of 'not understanding something'. Critical discussion of the general validity of a belief system is deflected back towards the reader's capacity not just to understand but to assent to the text's message. Simply put, readers can misinterpret, but *the play cannot be wrong*. In the case of *Taming of the Shrew* an offended reader or audience member appears to have two choices, depending on which kind of explanation of the play is advanced. Historicist explanations of Elizabethan belief systems concede the overt patriarchalism of the play's message, but require a disengaged aesthetic response as the sign of a sophisticated understanding. Explanations of the play's irony simply deny that patriarchalism is present in the text's 'real' message, and so denigrate the critical response altogether. In either case humanism entails not only the demand that the text be loved, but that it be loved 'on its own terms'.

Humanism is conservative rather than critical, both in its denial of the problematic of historically distant contexts and in its nostalgia for various forms of archaic repression. In addition, humanism has made an historical commitment to large-scale, centralized agencies of organized power *which it knows to be inimical to its deepest interests*. Humanism has made this unhappy commitment because in the end humanism is haunted by the much deeper fear it has of a popular element, a radical and levelling collective will that poses a constant threat to the humanist project. Although there is an element of discomfort in this complicity with a coercive apparatus, the possibility of orderly social existence is predicated on the management, or the regulation of a marginal and excluded element. Aesthetic experience and aesthetic education provide the crucial mediation between the constraints demanded by the structuration of political power and the desires of individual subjects. The richest and most complex of those mediations are sedimented in the works of Shakespeare. By internalizing this experience, the individual subject can facilitate his or her own self-integration within an already given ensemble of social constraints.[10]

SHAKESPEARE AND AFFIRMATIVE CULTURE

It has been part of the profession of faith of humanist scholars that Shakespeare 'tells us more about the human condition' than any other author. It is this sympathy with the generic human condition, the ability to transcend the parochial aspects of historically specific culture that supposedly accounts for Shakespeare's international reputation. This is the aspect of humanism that Jonathan Dollimore identifies as essentialism.[11] But unless we already know what the human condition is, there is no way to ascertain whether or not Shakespeare is telling us the truth about it. Humanism actually specifies a content for the generic human condition that Shakespeare's plays reveal; the human condition is an ambiguous one and therefore the most sophisticated cognitive strategies are those that transcend partisan interests of every kind. In its weaker variants this celebrates a profound indecisiveness, even vacuousness, discovering in Shakespeare orientations to experience that are politically neutralized and culturally innocuous.

However one may feel about this traditional politics of literary culture it is evident that it entails a subtle and at the same time a very thoroughgoing form of ideological processing. Marcuse has described this as 'affirmative culture':

> Its decisive character is the assertion of a universally obligatory, eternally better and more valuable world that must be unconditionally affirmed: a world essentially different from the factual world of daily struggle for existence, yet realizable by every individual for himself 'from within', without any transformation of the state of fact.[12]

Shakespeare not only belongs to this domain of a universally binding and eternally better world, his work in fact epitomizes this world and stands as its most compelling instantiation. There are historical peculiarities in this, in that Shakespeare's work comes into being in that highly suspect institutional *mise-en-scène* of fluid, shifting, and meretricious representation, the theater. The lifting of this historical stigma and the assignment of Shakespeare to the sphere of literary culture has been fully achieved relatively recently as part of a larger socio-cultural movement, in which market relations become more fully differentiated from other forms of symbolic exchange.

The 'real world' of market relations and the 'unreal world' of the theater have a long history both of antagonism and of secret complicity. Initially both the 'placeless market' of rationalized commodity exchange and the theater were perceived as sites of transgression and anomie, inhabited by unstable 'artificial' persons whose existence posed a threat to the stable hierarchies of a pre-capitalist social system. As the 'placeless market' becomes the hegemonic system of exchange and its form of artificial person becomes legitimated in jurisprudence, the theater is marginalized, though not entirely banished. The exchange of meanings and of identity that occurs within a theater is assigned to a subordinate position within the larger sphere of political economy, where it is permitted to function either as a business in its own right, or as the 'privileged' sphere of high culture. This then gives rise to a highly significant division of intellectual labor, in which the economic and the cultural are given separate and exclusive status. This disciplinary separation of economy and culture, like the corresponding separation between a real world of market relations and a fictive world of theatrical representation, helps obscure contradictions within the market itself.

> Cultural studies owe their birth, after all, to the concerted efforts of nineteenth-century Anglo-American thinkers to reserve a portion of their collective world of meaning from incorporation within the price system; these writers strained to keep the 'priceless' aspects of culture at a safe remove from a symbolic system (money) the operational principles of which they were otherwise content to leave unchallenged. . . . Aestheticism and economism effectively cartelized the social world by dividing cultural exchange and market exchange into separate disciplinary jurisdictions. As a consequence, the juncture of these two aspects of life vanished from view, and the deep and unacceptable division *within* market culture re-emerged as the deep but eminently acceptable division *between* the market and culture.[13]

It should be clear that the disciplinary assumption of a domain of the specifically literary, consisting of autonomous wholes within a larger, autonomous universe of literary works, is the formal expression of this intellectual division of labor or 'cartelization'. Until fairly recently, the 'priceless' domain of literary meaning has been set apart, not only from political economy as such, but also from the symbolic exchanges characteristic of political economy, that is from ideology.

When Shakespeare is proclaimed to be 'beyond ideology' or when it is discovered that he is 'not for an age, but for all time' he is in fact positioned within the dispensation of affirmative culture. The celebration of a world of priceless meanings that exist in a horizon 'beyond ideology' is a mode of resistance to the imperialism of market relations. This is the real meaning of Charlie the Tuna's rejection by Starkist. Unfortunately it is also a denial of the institutional and social reality in which both Shakespeare and the people who read his work are embedded. Such a view is an ideology in the strong sense, that is a widely disseminated discursive system that exercises real power over people's lives and at the same time makes critical scrutiny and interrogation of the conditions in which those lives are actually lived impossible.[14]

An important part of this socio-cultural agenda is advanced in the way literary scholars take a dim view of institutions and of routine institutional life. This expression is intended here in a double sense. First, there is a characteristic attitude of disapproval implied towards institutions, which are held to interfere with more natural, authentic, and direct concern with the cultural 'thing itself'. But, second, there is a deliberately cultivated sociological blindness demanded by the idea of the autonomy of the domain of art or of the individual art work, a blindness that amounts to a specific denial of the institutional situatedness of both the object and the subject of literary understanding. This 'othering' of literature and of literary study has certain distinct advantages. Literature is 'elsewhere' or maybe just 'out of it'. From this position of exteriority it constitutes a refusal of existing conditions. Art, and especially the art of Shakespeare, is conceived as the sphere of reconciled wholeness, expressivity, libidinal satisfaction, and thus opposed to the tyranny of GNP and the state apparatus. But the emancipatory desire of such an erotics of reading is never linked to the idea of a social agency. On the contrary, the energy of free expressivity is privatized, and thus recaptured for the purposes of an inimical power structure. The literary imagination initially positioned outside routine institutional life reappears at the center.

The centrality of Shakespeare within the literary culture has been mandated by humanistic cultural policy and sustained throughout a spectrum of ideological contention over determinate meanings of individual plays. There may be disagreement over how to interpret

Macbeth and even over what is to count as a legitimate issue in the interpretation of *Macbeth*. Nevertheless there is a kind of background consensus and this is perhaps most sharply indicated in the way that Shakespeare, as an authoritative source, is used by critics and interpreters as an unquestioned point of departure for a wide range of general psychological and political assertions. Expressions that take the form of 'Shakespeare + predicate' are used regularly to confer authority on a spectrum of formulations concerning the nature of individual experience, as well as the organization and purpose of collective life. These expressions suggest that the plays are discursive sites at which a variety of both public and personal issues are to be elaborated. Exegesis and critical scholarship on Shakespeare's *oeuvre* would thus seem to have an immediate connection with social and political practice. It is characteristic of most institutional scholarship, however, to disown and to deny the aspects of practice and of contingency in its own discursive projects. This is because contingent social practice is in some sense incompatible with received notions of the art work as free or autonomous, as possessing a specifically aesthetic being-in-itself which it is the task of criticism to elucidate. It is in the light of this doctrine that the class of expressions 'Shakespeare + predicate' is held to disperse into a range of narrowly partisan and parochial claims, on the one hand, and on the other, into a smaller set of statements produced by those for whom the 'play itself' is the exclusive object of attention. The task of institutional scholarship, thus understood, is to distinguish a range of predications which are authorized by Shakespeare and remain in some sense for Shake-speare, from those predications which are no more than ideological appropriations. The task of separating the pertinent interpretations from the impertinent ones is a momentous one given Shakespeare's centrality, and his identification with social/cultural goodness. But that task of selection and exclusion is made deeply problematic given the auxiliary imperative of an ideological *quid pro quo*.

The conflicting tendencies built into the humanist dispensation lead to a situation of 'damned if you do and damned if you don't'. If Shakespeare is a multiple and polysemous phenomenon as it is now generally and somewhat dogmatically asserted, what grounds are there for excluding *any* proposed meaning? Liberal humanists are generally prepared to live with a situation of multiple Shakespearean meaning, providing affirmative culture with varying substantive content for a wide range of differing constituencies. Neo-conservative humanists, however, find this privileging of expressive autonomy and cultural dispersal intolerable. It is the substantive dispersal of Shakespeare's authority by liberal humanists that traditional humanist scholarship now has to struggle against. Because its exclusive claims to knowledge have been so severely challenged by various theoretical research programs, however, advocates of this dispensation must now base their own defense on the superiority of their affective affiliation with the literary and artistic material itself.

Traditional humanistic scholarship, we are now being told, is history. Although it continues to fight energetic rearguard actions against various opponents, the emergence of new interpretive constituencies and the resulting dispersal of authority within Shakespeare scholarship makes the historical disappearance of this cultural dispensation inevitable. Whether this ought to be regarded as a paradigm shift, a cultural revolution, or merely a changing of the palace guard is by no means clear. The project of reconstructing, reproducing, and disseminating the authority of Shakespeare remains strongly positioned within the politics of literary culture practiced both within academic institutions and in popular culture generally, despite the broad challenges to traditional scholarship that have been advanced in recent years. This is evident in the continued absolutizing of Shakespeare's cultural and spiritual authority in many of the new discourses, irrespective of the ideological content assigned to that authority. It is Shakespeare's centrality as such that must be defended, and this results in the elaboration of a consensus around the idea of a polysemous and fully non-partisan cultural authority, despite the obvious self-contradictoriness of such a notion.

The redefinition of Shakespeare's authority as somehow pluralistic reflects the ideological themes and the ideological dilemmas characteristic of late twentieth-century American society. It also permits very rapid accumulation of additional intellectual capital in that the universe of literary discourse becomes 'finite, but un-bounded'. As far as literary scholarship is concerned, hyperbolic expansion in the quantity of discursive currency is limited only by the spectrum of ideological positions available outside the discipline. As long as the background consensus is contained within a relatively narrow range, literary studies appear to have a paradigmatically stable core. In a more socially open and ideologically ecumenical setting, as in the United States after the end of the Second World War, the spectrum of legitimate ideological contention appears to broaden, and the rate of intellectual dispersal accelerates. This increased rate of dispersal makes it more and more difficult to specify a determinate content for the authority of a canonical author like Shakespeare.

KNOWLEDGE SEEKING AND THE PROBLEM OF DISPERSAL

One of the more conspicuous indications of Shakespeare's special importance in the politics of literary culture within late capitalist North America is the very large quantity of critical scholarship and commentary that continues to accumulate around his works. This is a significant manifestation of cultural concern, inviting social and theoretical commentary that goes beyond programmatic and normative reviews of literary interpretation. The sheer quantity of scholarship on Shakespeare is indeed prohibitively large, but apart from complaints about the difficulty of mastering this corpus, or even taking it in, there has been surprisingly little in the way of cogent theoretical observation of this phenomenon.

The amount of scholarship produced on Shakespeare has been relatively large in relation to that on most other authors for at least two hundred years. But it is not the relative quantity of interpretation that has been so striking in recent decades; it is rather the quite extraordinary absolute quantity that begins to seem more and more ominous. Thousands of new items appear each year, and, according to some bibliographers, the rate of increase still seems to be growing. It is obvious to most observers of this situation that the rapid accumulation of new books and articles on Shakespeare is related to changes and developments in the institutions that produce such materials, but actually very little is understood about these institutions and how they affect the quantity, to say nothing of the quality of critical scholarship.

Professional discourse on the question of how much scholarship there is and how much there ought to be has been quite casual, vague, and lacking in theoretical clarity. Much of this self-critical discourse derives from a traditional humanist research program, so that it is hardly surprising that this effort of self-understanding among Shakespeare scholars is weakly theorized. It has also been

28

divided in its judgements. At times the opinion is advanced that the increase in the quantity of writing about Shakespeare is a sign of burgeoning cultural vitality, of general and pervasive intellectual well-being across a wide spectrum of social groups.[15] On this view the abundant variety of approaches is evidence of a democratization in the institutions of scholarly production, which can now accommodate a diverse list of ideological orientations. Shakespeare's house has many mansions, it would appear.

The broad church view is not, of course, the universally accepted one. An opposing view describes the annual increase in the professional bibliography not as a sign of intellectual ferment and growth, but simply as overproduction. The argument is frequently made that the sheer quantity of new material produced every year exceeds the capacity of any individual scholar to take it all in. Even if this material were uniformly valuable and useful, the argument goes, reading it all takes up time that would be better spent in reading (or re-reading) Shakespeare's works. But the material is far from being uniformly valuable. Some of it consists of routine, repetitive projects devoted to reinventing the wheel, while some of it is idiosyncratic, far-fetched, the result of ideological prejudice or private folly rather than serious devotion to Shakespeare. Whether these jeremiads are jocular in spirit, or frankly grumpy and denunciatory, they necessarily entail a critique of institutional practice based on some kind of implicit normative standard.

Most accounts of overproduction identify an uncontrolled expansion of activity with the private vice and folly of individual scholarly producers.[16] Overproduction is the sum of many individual abberations caused by a drift of attention away from the object of interpretive commentary as such – in other words Shakespeare – and towards an increasing conformity with the imperatives of an institutional dispensation that replicates itself without any genuine and sustained commitment to its own generative *raison-d'être*. This is a morally objectionable phenomenon, in which institutionally mandated activity is opportunistic rather than disinterested, more a way of advancing careers than of either advancing knowledge or keeping faith with a valued tradition. The usual criterion for determining just what constitutes overproduction, however, is primarily a matter of administrative convenience. Too much means more than a busy editor can, or wants to read. But this is an *ad hoc* judgement that reduces questions of scholarly production and evaluation to the more or less routine problem of how to manage a scholarly journal. In the context of the present discussion, however, the issue of determining an appropriate level of scholarly production cannot be reduced to various *ad hoc* empirical considerations, but must be interpreted within a sociology of the institutions of research. Such an approach would focus on the decision-making apparatus within institutions, the allocation of prestige and of material rewards among the various individual practitioners, and finally, the complex matter of setting research agendas and of deciding what is to count as a legitimate disciplinary question.

If we consider Shakespeare scholarship, or for that matter any branch or subdivision of the humanities to be a knowledge-seeking activity, the question of how much activity there ought to be is related to a tension between the necessity of a paradigmatically stable 'normal science' and the desirability to that science of intellectual innovation. That same tension is reproduced in the distinction between the context of discovery and the context of justification. Normal science requires some element of innovation in the practice of individual scientists if the domain of what is known is to be extended and more fully explicated. At the same time normal science seeks to conserve the stability of its own paradigm, which is necessary as the framework for determining whether or not something is actually new and also valid. This makes the problem of how much research and the related problem of defining an optimum range for aberration and playfulness within scientific research extremely difficult to resolve.

Everyone who does any sustained research on Shakespeare is able to give testimony that the size of the bibliography is a gigantic inconvenience. Scholars can also describe the *ennui* produced by a body of writing that can be maddeningly repetitive and insanely dispersed *at the same time*. Still, the exasperation that one may feel cannot really provide any kind of helpful understanding of the problem. The question 'how much is too much?' must be rephrased as 'how do we know how much is too much?' or 'what grounds are there for determining when there is overproduction?' This is clearly related to the way the institution of scholarly production is organized, and what its goal-values are. Literary scholarship in general, and Shakespeare scholarship in particular are 'institution-ally ambiguous'. The practice of scholarship is only partially mandated by knowledge-seeking, and partially by the affirmation or

30

elaboration of tradition. Individual scholars feel themselves in a condition of uncertainty that results from cultivating a set of responses appropriate to a scientific community, but these are more often than not incompatible with the responses appropriate to a community of exegetes whose task is to oversee the orderly transmission of traditional meanings.

As a first approximation one might imagine that the apparent overproduction is actually a case of 'anarchy of production' caused by the unacknowledged coexistence of multiple intellectual systems with incompatible epistemological *and* social foundations. This situation might be similar to one in which both astrology and astronomy were still practiced under the rubric of a single, undifferentiated academic discipline. The confusion that would result could never be resolved by appeals for a return to 'good old fashioned star-gazing'. It would be necessary as a first step to attempt to distinguish in a much more critically detailed way the differences between institutions organized to pursue determinate knowledge of stars, planets, and other physical realities, and institutions organized primarily to interpret a traditional *arcana* that has no relation whatever to physical reality. The problem for literary scholars requires some kind of effort to articulate the intellectual and social conditions that would make possible some mode of literary knowledge and to distinguish that from the more or less diffuse institutional apparatus required for the affirmation of a quasi-religious tradition.

Scholarly research is neither an industry nor a priesthood, but a variant of the craft-guild. Scholarship, on this view, is roughly similar to the work organization of an *atelier* rather than an assembly line. Considerable authority for day-to-day decision-making, task selection, and scheduling is delegated to skilled practitioner/artisans for the accomplishment of larger practical objectives. This is fundamentally different from the vertically structured authority and the segmented task allocation characteristic of a factory. Scholarly research is, moreover, reputation-driven. As every literary scholar knows, no one does academic research for the money. The immediate objective for younger scholars is achieving job-security; for the more ambitious scholar, wider recognition and influence is sought. Ultimately the aim is to have significant power over research agendas – that is, determining what will count as a significant disciplinary question and controlling the allocation of professional recognition. The competitiveness that characterizes the relations between various individuals and the research agendas they promote is, ultimately, of extra-disciplinary concern. In the field of literary scholarship and of the humanities generally the question of research agendas is directly linked to issues of pedagogy and, even more widely, of general cultural policy. These extra-disciplinary factors have a direct impact on what seem to be purely disciplinary questions of method, approach, and paradigm articulation.

Literary scholarship, together with most fields in the humanities, has an extremely loose form of overall co-ordination. It has been suggested recently that the observable dispersal of literary studies at the present time is a consequence of paradigm crisis. However, dispersal may be more or less normal for these fields, given their overall lack of centralization and the absence of any co-ordinating administrative apparatus. Literary study is a 'fragmented adhocracy'. Despite the facetious tone of this expression, the characterization is not intended as a derisory or dismissive one.

> The dominant feature of these sciences is their intellectual variety and fluidity. They do not exhibit a stable configuration of specialized tasks or of problem areas, nor do they have strong co-ordinating mechanisms which systematically interrelate results and strategies ... where co-ordination of results does occur, it is highly personal and linked to local control of resources.[17]

Under these circumstances there will be a good deal of strife and contention ranging across many issues. Since there are relatively few mechanisms for the arbitration of disputes other than the persuasive force or personal charisma of individuals, groups will tend to diverge not so much on the basis of competing paradigms, but rather in accordance with their preferences, some of which will be extra-disciplinary. Despite the extensive and voluminous publication on the issue of theory over the past ten years, the social organization of literary studies does not in any way encourage the formation of a theoretical paradigm that would provide the means for integrating and co-ordinating the results of its multiple and dispersed research programs.[18]

The problem of how much scholarship is too much is not a secondary, purely administrative issue, but rather a matter of fundamental, substantive importance in relation to the production of knowledge. The quantity of scholarship will in every instance be directly correlated with the size of the scientific or scholarly community. In a reputation-driven institution of a craft type there cannot be a rationally administered and segmented division of labor; all scholars/scientists have an immediate stake in research activity. Every researcher is a direct producer of research results, an artisan so to speak, rather than an operative. There is a large-scale division of labor within scientific/scholarly disciplines which are subdivided into a relatively smaller cadre of researchers and a somewhat larger group of 'talking heads' – mostly secondary school teachers and popularizers, whose function is to teach and to publicize the achievements of the research cadre. The question of how big the research cadre should be within any given discipline is not itself a scientific question.[19] Nor is the relative allocation of resources among disciplines a question decided within autonomous disciplines.

Within the obviously political constraints imposed on the aggregate size of any research community there are further determinants in play in relation to the overall quantity of research produced. Since valid, potentially useful knowledge is what is wanted it might appear that a relatively small quantity of research ought to be published, and that this small quantity should consist exclusively of what is both good and original. In any concrete research community, however, things are never so simple that they can be regulated only by established disciplinary criteria – 'standards', 'rigor', 'falsifiability', or 'originality'. The history and sociology both of the natural and the human sciences suggest that original scholarship depends on a very large mass of routine, repetitive normal science. It is not by any means clear just how much normal science would have to be produced in order to facilitate the significant innovation that permits intellectual progress. Furthermore, innovation itself is not always recognizable as such within the scientific or scholarly community.

The advancement of a research program does not necessarily occur as a smooth sequence of incremental gains. On the contrary, important contributions are often eccentric and obscure when they first appear. Obviously then, it is contrary to the interests of any research community routinely to suppress and discourage bizarre and far-fetched proposals, or even ideas that are positively *outré* and irresponsible. Research unfolds in real, concrete history. The cogency of an emergent research program may not become apparent until various auxiliary disciplines and technical specialties have come into existence. As with communities generally then, scientific/ scholarly communities seem to require some margin of anomie if they are to function in accordance with their goal-values. Naturally, scientific and intellectual transgression may bring about a change in the interpretation of those institutional goal-values, or even their complete abandonment. The dialectic of research – that is the complex relations between the imperatives of paradigm stability and innovation – suggest not only that there is an irreducible level of conflict, tension, and anxiety in every functioning research community, but also that there must be a certain (perhaps quite large) quantity of boring science and even bad science produced in relation to every instance of significantly innovative research. On this view then the task of co-ordination of research activity cannot be understood as administrative control or policing within strictly disciplinary norms. It does, however, imply a significant role for theory, though not for theory of a substantive kind.[20] Theory here is not to be understood as the elaboration of a system of doctrinal imperatives. It is rather an epistemological protocol that serves to correlate the work of researchers and of research practices.

In a field organized by theoretical principles there will be variety, disagreement, and innovation along with the routine proliferation of 'normal science'. The emergence of contradictory results within such a field signals the onset of crisis, or the self-transformation of the theoretical paradigm. Such crisis solves the problem of accumulation by prompting the more or less complete abandonment of earlier stages of research. By contrast, a field that lacks even rudimentary epistemological controls cannot unfold in accordance with a pattern of contradiction, crisis, and self-transformation. Instead there is an explosive increase or 'runaway inflation' in the circulation of competing discourses. The problem is not quantity as such, but the impossibility of accurately charting disagreement. In this situation, dispersal and fragmentation are not the sign of crisis or of scientific revolution. On the contrary, they are symptoms of a legitimation crisis interminably postponed. At the present time, Shakespeare scholarship, like literary scholarship generally, is not a coherently organized knowledge-seeking institution or cultural science, though it does incorporate *some* practices characteristic of the repertoire of theoretically rigorous research programs. The deferral of crisis within this field, however, contributes to the stability of a hegemonic social order despite the avowedly emancipatory intentions implicit in these research agendas.

It is, I think, important to stipulate that the idea of a research program for Shakespeare scholarship in the American context has always been motivated by emancipatory possibilities sedimented within the material. These possibilities encourage the desire of Shakespeare scholars as a loose collectivity to be counted as separate from and oppositional towards the imperatives of the market, commodity exchange, and industrial discipline. Such oppositional orientation or distantiation from at least the cruder forms of the culture industry is shared by virtually all Shakespeare scholars, irrespective of ideological differences that may appear at other levels.[21] These sentiments are not of recent emergence, nor are they a monopoly of the political left. However, the meaning of such an emancipatory project is precisely what is contested by the various constituencies within Shakespeare scholarship. The issue is not whether or not reading Shakespeare is an emancipatory experience, but rather exactly what such reading is an emancipation from.

Neo-conservative culture critics within the community of Shakespeare scholars typically deplore the encroachment of vulgar popular or mass culture into the institutional reproduction of Shakespeare. The culture industry transforms the classical body of the authoritative text into something weak, flattering, and ultimately meretricious. Neo-conservative scholars would maintain that the study of Shakespeare liberates the individual both from vulgar common opinion and from various *pseudodoxia*, of which Marxism is generally held to be the most virulent. Shakespeare scholarship would then be part of a much broader elaboration of tradition supported primarily by philological research and highly resistant to more corrosive critical orientations. This view situates emancipatory practice 'inside' and 'above'; in other words its interest is identified with organized power as its patron against the social and aesthetic agendas of popular culture.

In the neo-conservative account affective loyalty to a uniform cultural code of 'western values' is imperative for a stable and functional hegemony. The liberal alternative to this cultural policy is usually legitimated under the rubric of pluralism. This is, of course, a differentiated hegemony of balanced or negotiated interests. Emancipatory interests in this construction of social relations take the form of a *quid pro quo*, or 'clarification' of competing legitimacy claims. It is an assumption within both these ideological formations that there is a stable core of value within Shakespeare that still eludes appropriation by the price system. In other words Shakespeare embodies an authentic tradition that may provide the basis for a stable and harmonious political culture, one that offers emancipatory possibilities *vis-à-vis* any programs of mass deception and social manipulation. The study of Shakespeare is thus a practice that could best be described not as a research program in any scientific sense, but rather as the administration of redemptive media. This practice can be understood only in relation to a careful analysis of the social significance of tradition.

Chapter two

TRADITION AS A SOCIAL AGENCY

Whether or not Shakespeare can be constituted as an object of knowledge-seeking or scientific inquiry may seem relatively unimportant in the light of another social and cultural imperative, namely the preservation and elaboration of tradition. And in fact in the United States at the present time this imperative is advanced with a sense of considerable urgency as an element in the neoconservative cultural policy agenda. In writings such as William Bennett's 'Lost Generation' and in Allan Bloom's *The Closing of the American Mind* the argument is made that a weakened and demoralized educational apparatus is no longer organized around a substantive curriculum that can forestall a general and pervasive breakdown of tradition.[1] Such breakdown in the sphere of culture, it is maintained, will lead to an even more widespread social anomie and possibly even radical social derangement. The exact political nature of this threat is left quite vaguely delineated, though it seems clear that the anticipated social and cultural changes that may result from the breakdown of tradition will be incompatible with the values of democracy and freedom.

Shakespeare scholarship, as a branch of literary studies and of research in the humanities, finds its primary institutional home within the university system, where its findings are disseminated not only to scholars and specialists, but also to a wider audience of undergraduates, many of whom are destined to become policymakers, or members of professional and administrative cadres. The normal function of the university, at least in the view of neoconservative culture critics, is to facilitate the integration of new personnel within the leadership strata, and at the same time to foster loyalty to a hegemonic social and cultural dispensation. Although the perceived threats to that system may take many forms, the

37

primary emphasis in this strain of culture criticism is on the antagonistic and critical role adopted by left-wing intellectuals.[2] Despite its ambivalent and sometimes openly hostile attitude to government, this cultural agenda does seem to require direct expressions of loyalty to the state. The role of the university in forming the political consciousness of students demands a positive emphasis on western achievements, especially in the field of social and economic organization, and even more so in the domain of those priceless values preserved in the traditional humanities curriculum.[3]

The popular rather than scholarly orientation of these interventions by no means diminishes their social and cultural importance. Arguments of this kind clearly attract a very wide readership among the larger intelligentsia. What makes these writings pertinent in the present context is that they use Shakespeare as the exemplary instance of a priceless cultural value, and there is virtually no likelihood that the example will elicit any challenge. Shakespeare is the one absolutely unassailable icon for a cultural tradition. In the neo-conservative cultural policy agenda it is not sufficient just to have students read Shakespeare. The plays must be read in the right way, that is, as the embodiment of our cultural heritage, of western values and above all of western achievements. This is, in some cases at least, utterly disingenuous. For Allan Bloom the breakdown of tradition argument is unmistakably linked to a reactionary sexual politics.[4] William Bennett makes it abundantly clear that for him the preservation of western values is indistinguishable from intensified cold war militancy and from the general ideological mobilization that will assure wider support for foreign policy decisions taken by the executive branch. But western values also means a more diffuse though equally substantive ensemble of doctrines and beliefs that are enshrined in Shakespeare's plays; the task of literary scholarship is, on the neo-conservative view, to elaborate and affirm those beliefs.

Although the partisan character of these arguments is perfectly self-evident, such writings nevertheless raise an important theoretical question, that is, 'What do we need new interpretations of Shakespeare for?' Once Shakespeare is repositioned within the institution of tradition, knowledge-seeking no longer has the meanings it has for scientific or critical research programs. Instead of trying to discover optimum social strategies for the production of knowledge, the question now becomes 'Why is there interpretation?' or 'What is commentary for?' This is an ethical or political question and it concerns the broader relationship of tradition to philosophical inquiry.

Any tradition, no matter how vitiated in its functioning, commands attention and affiliation on grounds both of its antiquity and of its derivation from an authoritative source or origin. But can we not identify tradition as simply *doxa* or common opinion, as the self-congratulatory reaffirmation of familiar and comfortable ideas that Heidegger characterized as inauthenticity, or as the unexamined life that Socrates claimed wasn't worth living? Obviously the tension between philosophically or scientifically motivated inquiry and tradition has been understood since antiquity. And from the standpoint of tradition the desire for knowledge, as opposed to simple affirmation, is understood to be an impiety, irrespective of the self-proclaimed good intentions of knowledge-seeking or knowledge-sharing philosophers.

Knowledge is a kind of transgression in so far as it departs from the received wisdom accumulated by a culture or community over time. Moreover, it breeds yet further transgression by encouraging irreverence among the youth. Within the university community, the disciplines of the humanities have been mandated both to seek knowledge and to preserve and elaborate tradition.[5] But the problem of integrating these two socio-cultural tasks, or even understanding their relationship, is extremely complex. Both knowledge-seeking and tradition are institutional modes that themselves contain internal equivocations or ambivalencies. There is also the troubling question of reconciling what appear to be mutually incompatible modes of social existence. Can there really be such a thing as a science of tradition? What would be the tasks of such a science; what would be the role in such a science of philological research and what else would be required to facilitate that science's research program? These questions are complicated in that the contemporary researcher no longer lives in any direct relationship with a traditional life-world and thus must gain access to tradition through the medium of literary and other documents. But, assuming that a tradition can be reconstructed from such archaeological detritus, what then? Is it not possible that at least some of our traditions would be better forgotten than recuperated? These questions suggest that a more detailed and complete theoretical analysis of tradition is needed in order properly to appraise the theme of cultural breakdown.[6]

RELIGIOUS TRADITION AND THE SOCIAL LIFE-WORLD

Despite the wide circulation of the common-sense understanding of tradition as the familiar, the tried and true, and so on, the concept of tradition is actually a difficult one. For one thing tradition can mean any contingent practice or fragmentary pattern of behavior. To speak of Dad carving the Thanksgiving turkey as a tradition is a perfectly legitimate usage, but the idea of a custom is not an important part of the range of meanings of the term to be considered here. Tradition can also mean a cultural/practical ensemble or totality, an aggregate of symbolic actions and of meanings; this can constitute a medium or environment in which a community can see its identity. Even in this sense, however, tradition is an equivocal term.

The notional meaning of tradition is usually given as a simplified idea of transmission – a handing down of cultural values from one generation to another. The idea of a social action, or process of transmission, seems to be easily confused with the notion of actual cultural goods that have been or ought to be transmitted. The confusion between the act of giving and the gift itself is complicated by a third sense of the term, namely the agencies by which a given body of cultural goods is transmitted. Finally, there is an etymological link between the notion of transmission and the idea of betrayal. If I hand something over or hand something down to you, there will be a moment at which I must let go of it. It is in this moment that the possibility of a cultural abyss or rupture opens up. Since that possibility is always present within what we call tradition, we can never understand this cultural phenomenon as a process of undisputed succession.

The conservative view tends to imply that tradition is a social process concerned with phenomena that do not change, with values that are stable over time, and which are unaffected by any historical process, not excluding the process of transmission itself. To traditionalists the changeless character of these values certifies their validity. The anti-traditionalism of a cultural movement such as the Enlightenment regards that same changeless character as evidence of nothing other than blind irrationality. But any serious account of tradition will recognize that change as well as stability are necessary features both of the process of transmission and of the values handed down.[7]

Marcel Mauss, in his classic study of *The Gift*, relates tradition to the complex pattern of giving and of reciprocal obligation that he finds operative in the exchange system of archaic societies. The Latin *traditio* is, in Mauss's account, a system of spiritual and affective bonds that comes into being as the result of distinct actions in which the exchange of a gift is central.[8] For the giver, the primary action is that of alienation; in other words the giver surrenders or separates himself from a valued object. The recipient performs the action known as *mancipatio*, in other words he takes the object into his hands. This taking, however, binds the recipient to the giver, who, in Mauss's account buys that recipient by means of his gift. In other words, the act of *traditio* is not a rational exchange of equivalents, as in bourgeois political economy, but is rather an asymmetrical and unequal hierarchization of the partners to the exchange. The inequalities created by the act of *traditio* are moral or ethical rather than economic; they are related to issues of prestige, authority, honor, and deference. The relationship of *traditio* can be expressed as the differentiation of magisterial from ministerial positions *vis-à-vis* the gift.

The idea of tradition as *mancipatio*, as opposed to *emancipatio*, is, of course, incompatible with the prevailing liberal and liberal-conservative account that has been in general circulation since the time of Matthew Arnold or even before. For humanist scholarship and teaching the rich heritage of our literary culture is affirmed for its liberating and liberatory capacities. The work of Harold Bloom could be cited as an important instance of a repudiation of the liberal-humanist idealization of tradition. Bloom refuses to view the great works of literary culture as simple values and still less as a reservoir of cultural treasures available for free circulation. These works are, in Bloom's account, only correctly understood as gifts in the archaic sense, that is as unasked for and perhaps unwanted obligations – great literature 'makes us an offer we cannot refuse'. The struggle of individual artists to escape from a ministerial relationship to their predecessors and to achieve a magisterial position in their own right constitutes the tragic dimension of tradition.

The inescapable character of tradition calls into question the comfortable idealizations of liberal and/or conservative humanism. But tradition as a social agency is scarcely operative in modern

41

societies. The full operation of tradition is evident only in pre-industrial and pre-capitalist communities, and to a certain extent within active religious dispensations with an extensive history. In its most radical form, tradition is institutionalized at the level of an entire community, which acts both as the recipient or beneficiary and as the agency of that tradition. A community in which the forms of social practice are fully given by tradition *and by nothing else* would fulfill that tradition in a wholly unselfconscious manner. In a wholly traditional community there is no self-consciousness because there is no self in the sense of a private ego. Instead, the individual subject lives up to and instantiates a role or set of narrative expectations already implicated in his given name. In a society organized along these lines, originating texts or narrative sources are likely to be preserved in an oral medium. The agency of traditional authority is personal and it is allocated in accordance with status – whether earned or inherited – rather than according to a specialized division of labor in permanently established administrative functions or offices.

It has often been suggested that various ancient peoples actually lived tradition in full and spontaneous immediacy. Whether the Jews of antiquity, or any other people, actually lived the 'life of myth' would be extremely difficult to establish as a matter of empirically confirmed historical fact. In any case it is clear that the situation within historical Judaism, that is, the Judaism of written scripture, is already very different. In this cultural setting the media of tradition are no longer confined to oral performance, individual memory, ritual form, and everyday practical life. These media continue to exist, but they are augmented by a textual authority which in fact takes precedence over those forms of tradition actualized physio-logically so to speak. A hierarchy among the redemptive media comes into existence and to this corresponds a system of institutional specializations that regulate life through socio-political functions and official positions, rather than through personalities. Tradition now has two bodies instead of one, since the collective body of the community now coexists with the more stable textual body animated by office-holders – scribes, editors and archivists, lawgivers, etc. Under these social conditions, tradition no longer speaks for itself through a physiological medium, a prophet, for example. The existence of a text encourages the formation of a new kind of institutional milieu in which interpretation is practiced. This interpretation or supplement to the textual embodiment of tradition is often perceived, however, as a kind of threat to the integrity of the tradition itself.[9] It is moreover, the very activity of interpretation, the effrontery of explicating a word already complete in itself, that arouses deep and pervasive suspicion.[10] To suggest, as interpretation must, that the tradition is not fully accessible through the text, and that even with the text in existence that there is still something more to say, is to admit either that interpretation is merely parasitic or, what is worse, that it constitutes a betrayal of tradition. And the more that interpretations proliferate the more vitiated tradition is likely to become.

In certain well-established and historically durable socio-religious communities a quite opposed judgement of proliferating interpretation prevails, encouraging a superabundance of commentary rather than any narrow channeling or constraint of interpretive practice. Such a system works from a core text outwards towards the humblest activities of everyday life. Jewish religious and social life is founded on the core text of the Torah in the narrow meaning of the term, that is, the pentateuch or five book of Moses.[11] This core of value and meaning is supplemented by two subordinate categories of scripture, the texts collected as 'the prophets', and 'the writings' – *Ecclesiastes, Psalms, The Book of Job*, etc. Surrounding this body of canonical texts is an even larger body of what might be called sub-canonical texts consisting of talmudic commentary and exegesis, fading into patristic analysis, popularizations, philosophical speculation, and so forth.[12] Beyond this is the even wider orbit of informal and interminable commentary in everyday life. The continual rehashing and instantiation of scripture, talmudic commentary, and Jewish literature takes place not only in the synagogue, but in informal institutional settings as well, since interpretation of scripture and everything attendant upon scripture spills over into and animates everyday life and material culture as well.

In terms of the self-understanding of observant Jews, the covenant extends into the tiniest details of everyday life, so that every moment of practical existence fulfills and instantiates – in other words, interprets the Torah. In sociological terms, the influence of an authoritative and canonical core text pervades the socio-historical life-world. In such a cultural setting supplementarity is by no means objectionable. On the contrary, this is definitely a situation in which the more interpretation there is, the richer and more fully actualized the communal life becomes. If a teaching is good, then it is good that it be repeated; the truth is not diminished by iteration. Furthermore, the core text has a being-in-the-world as well as a being-in-itself. Because the text must exist in history, tradition must be sufficiently complex to allow for social and interpretive creativity, if the teachings of the Torah are to be applied to novel situations that emerge through historical time.

The preceding account of Judaism as a historically self-sustaining community is intended to serve here as the model of that complex of socio-cultural relations known as tradition. In this example, the primary agency of tradition is the social life-world itself, rather than a formal, hierarchical institution such as a church or priesthood. In this community there is an interminable proliferation of interpretations flowing from a core text and its formal elaborations outwards into a historical life-world, which thus always signifies and instantiates that core text. This example should suggest that there is considerably more to tradition than either the notion of valuable cultural goods – that is a heritage or legacy of some kind – *or* the secondary notions of transmission, stewardship, and the fiduciary relations that the existence of such a heritage would entail. Tradition is in the first place an *Affektcomplex*. And central to any such *Affektcomplex* is a feeling of solidarity both with ancestors and with living community members. This solidarity is experienced in and through communal practice and it should be carefully distinguished from the abstract, sometimes ideologically sustained solidarities of the administrative state. In any case it is apparent that tradition has its primary meaning in the context of a sustained and sustaining concrete, practical life-world rather than in the sociologically cooler domains of legal imperatives, pedagogy, or substantive culture.

Tradition is both discursive and practical as it unfolds through lengthy historical intervals. In its long-term character, moreover, it takes on a complex structure. For any given community, tradition takes on a quasi-universalistic character by virtue of the ever-increasing scope of accumulated interpretive material. Enormous ranges of historically concrete experience come to be sedimented in the canonical, sub-canonical, and literary scriptures. Given a concrete orientation to the concerns of the social life-world, however, tradition is necessarily parochial in its interest as well as in its applications. The accumulated materials greatly exceed the capacity of any individual reader or commentator to absorb, but such a situation does not mandate the production of a synoptic overview or digest. Even the systematic organizing, indexing, and archival storage of the material is likely to seem pointless to members of the community. A tradition is not a research program. It is more like cultural improvisation combined with considerable recycling – let's call it conservatism – of cultural materials that nevertheless permit some margin of anomie, that is, both obvious innovation and innovation that appears in the guise of the familiar. The complex of core text, received interpretation, and the practical living of everyday life provide the guarantee of continuity in a traditional way of life.

The normative self-understanding of a tradition such as Judaism positions a hierarchically organized canonical and magisterial text at the center of things and makes provision for orderly administrative agencies objectified in the practice of rabbinical authority. On this view established law and custom take precedence over fresh inputs of authority through mystical or ecstatic inspiration.[13] The counter-normative view would be that authority of a rabbinical type is at best a vitiated, routine approximation of a truly vital tradition, and that the normative account enshrined in standard treatments of canonical and sub-canonical texts is a kind of cover story for an ancient usurpation of authority; it is a successful entrenchment of a bureaucratized priestly monopoly at the expense of authentic prophetic wisdom with its immediate physiological (as opposed to textual) embodiments and its unmediated relationship with a pre-textual origin. Such a counter-normative view will be associated with programmatic cultural agendas of a Renaissance type, in which much may be made of philological and curatorial achievements, the recovery of lost documents and the discovery of hidden master-codes that reveal the origin in its true shape, purified of priestly corruptions.[14] Oddly enough a similar story may be enshrined in the normative accounts themselves, where it seems to have the function of legitimating a Deuteronomic code by demonstrating that the apparent secondariness of that code is in actuality a recovery of a lost original.[15]

Historical Judaism illustrates the extreme complexity of tradition understood in the strong sense, its implication in the ethical dimension of everyday life, as well as the characteristic problems of authority that arise from issues of administration and succession. Christianity, which has always claimed to be the legitimate historical objectification of authentic tradition derived from a primary origin, in fact emerges as a counter-normative program or renaissance within Judaism. Over time counter-normative aspects of tradition drop away and the agency of tradition devolves upon the much disputed apostolic succession. This is itself a normative social agency functionally equivalent to rabbinical authority, though clearly morphologically distinct, especially in the institutional variant that nominates a single delegate as supreme pontiff. As far as canonical texts are concerned, Christianity has had to solve its own complex and extremely awkward Deuteronomic problems. These problems do not lend themselves to straightforward philological and curatorial solution, and this necessitates a complicated hermeneutics. In accomplishing these objectives, of course, Christianity becomes a normative tradition and this in turn has given rise to further counter-normative variants, including several powerfully disruptive schisms and reformations.

The institutionally sustained archive, the social form that Harold Innis has called a monopoly of knowledge, administers all other traditional forms in light of the pre-eminent authority of written canonical texts.[16] Monopolies of knowledge that derive authority from texts and their interpretation are often troubled by issues of security and of legitimation. Once texts actually exist in material form and are put into even very limited circulation, all sorts of complications arise. Foremost among these is the endless task of accommodating the text to the lived social practice it purports to regulate, and vice versa. In addition, texts make it difficult to forget things, but they make it very easy to compare alternative redactions and variant forms of the self-same text. Finally, there are practical questions of provenance, storage, accessibility, copying, everything connected with the physical and editorial management of textual materials, and these problems give rise to administrative/technical specializations with their own codifications and their own distinct claims to authority.

In a situation such as the one I have just described tradition takes on an essentially philological character. The experience of tradition in and through the forms of practical consciousness and the everyday practice of the social life-worlds do not by any means disappear, however, and this creates a situation with considerable potential for conflict. Conscientious philological and curatorial practices necessarily generate their own constellation of interests, and these are not always compatible with those of other sectors within the community. Differing narrative accounts of the propagation of authority and of the nature of local tradition may be in circulation at the same time, reflecting serious legitimation problems. It is under socio-cultural conditions of this kind that the issue of misinterpretation takes on substantive political importance. Opposing factions will generally agree that there is a tradition which requires loyalty to and affiliation with a specific origin. Typically, opponents of any given faction are denounced for the neglect or the falsification of tradition, which may be thematized as obscurantism and corruption, or as heresy and mischievous radicalism.

There is, however, a further equivocation in the idea of tradition that is not even hinted at in such an account. That equivocation stems from the extremely problematic relationship between what we might call the apparatus of transmission and the point of origin that such an apparatus claims to represent. The simple attitude of *pietas* supposes an absolute identification of the apparatus of transmission with the point of origin, and thus finds no difficulty in trusting the principle of legitimate or apostolic succession. But another attitude is also possible, one that finds the point of origin to be of infinitely greater worth and dignity than any self-ordained administrative apparatus. On this view unthinking loyalty to the authority of a social agency, no matter how venerable, is equivalent to an apostasy, a renunciation of any real faith in tradition, which is understood to be whatever was present at the point of origin. This view of tradition privileges a return to that origin or source, and in practical terms it means both a revival of interest in originating texts and documents themselves (as opposed to established interpretations of those documents) and a radical repudiation of the deadening mass of accumulated interpretation, which is seen as progressively more distant from the source, and increasingly degraded by accumulated historical debris. In addition, the social agency that has claimed the role of preserving tradition is seen in this counter-movement as increasingly venal in promoting the interests of an administrative cadre to the detriment of the primary relationship between the originating source and the faithful subject.

The idea of a radical return to the source provides an alternative meaning for the idea of tradition. A distinction is made between a priestly or rabbinical apparatus, and a mystical return to direct, unmediated contact with the originating source itself. This evidently revisionary project claims to restore the purity of the origin, to rescue it from the venality of priests, and to reveal its meaning undistorted by the historical accumulation of administratively sanctioned interpretation. In this view considerable emphasis is placed on notions of revision and re-interpretation; in place of such notions as apostolic succession, the mystical or *kabbalistic* sense of tradition privileges the singular prophetic insight as the authentic voice of tradition. Equally important here is the activity of patient philological research. The apparent swerves or heterodoxies produced in movements of this kind are interpreted by their proponents as evidence of authenticity. Naturally these revisionary – that is to say restored – interpretations seem like heresy, but only in relation to an institutionally corrupted *doxa*; what seems far-fetched in a mystical reading of the origin or of the founding text reveals just how far institutional interpretation has departed from original meaning. This is recognizably the spirit of the Protestant Reformation. And a suitably scaled-down version of this impulse has clear pertinence for understanding a number of types of business-as-usual literary scholarship, including both the New Critical dispensation that wants readers to return to something called the poem itself and traditional historicism that wants readers to understand a literary work in its own terms.

The tendency of tradition as a socio-cultural process to split into a social or rabbinical and a mystical or *kabbalistic* strain, each with its own claim to represent the origin, creates obvious difficulties both in analyzing the meaning of tradition and in actually experiencing it.[17] The question of interpretation and commentary complicates matters still further. Interpretation is the process of discharging the obligations of *mancipatio* implicated in the massive gift that we call a tradition. The textual *institutio* or foundation brings into existence a more mundane kind of institution whose function is the production of interpretive commentary. But interpretation is never seen as the discharging of an obligation; it purports to represent something else, whether this is an originating word, a singular individual who pronounces such a word, or an institutional beginning. All of this requires enormous creativity if the solidarity of a traditional community is to be maintained.

These large-scale examples suggest several things about tradition as a form of historical/cultural experience. First of all, the idea of tradition as the simple handing down of values – beliefs, practices, cultural goods, or whatever else – is entirely without cogency. Descriptions of the quasi-natural unfolding of tradition, and routine affirmation of cultural goods clearly belong to legitimation discourses but they serve no useful purpose within a critical history of tradition. Second, although there are normative movements *within* any given tradition, sociological and critical accounts cannot be normative. The reason for this is that no tradition is actually a stable form; the dynamic character and the potentially radical instability of tradition is an inherent feature of this socio-cultural phenomenon rather than some sort of contingent aberration or symptom of breakdown. Finally, tradition is concrete, and even sensuous in its vital manifestations. Tradition is above all *praxis*, it occupies the ethical dimension and the social life-world. Strictly speaking tradition is never an abstraction or an idealized value – certainly it should be distinguished from conventionalized ideological currency that circulates widely in the guise of tradition in the socio-cultural milieu of late capitalism. Tradition, finally, has at best an uncomfortable relationship with knowledge and knowledge-seeking.

The immorality of knowledge and of knowledge-seeking appears against a socio-cultural horizon in which morality is identified with customary forms of social behavior. The relationship of morality and custom, the idea that the ethical dimension is to be understood in light of well-established and durable concrete forms of social action is elaborated by Hegel, who evidently viewed tradition in this sense as a significant manifestation of the World Spirit.[18] But in Nietzsche's treatment of this topic the problem of belatedness is introduced, which is used to explain why the mere affirmation of tradition no longer supplies a satisfying moral feeling, and to suggest why the classical ideal of *pietas* is no longer viable as a primary form of consciousness.

The power of custom is astonishingly enfeebled and the moral sense so rarefied and lofty it may be described as having more or less evaporated. That is why the fundamental insights into the origin of morality are so difficult for us latecomers, and even when we have acquired them we find it impossible to enunciate them, because they sound so uncouth or because they seem to slander morality! This is, for example, already the case with the *chief proposition*: morality is nothing other (therefore *no more!*) than obedience to customs, of whatever kind they may be; customs, however, are the *traditional* ways of behaving and evaluating. In things in which no tradition commands there is no morality; and the less life is determined by tradition, the smaller the circle of morality.[19]

Nietzsche's primary sympathy in this discussion is with the individual whose life is a refusal of tradition, with such figures as Socrates who 'take a new path under the highest disapprobation of all advocates of morality of custom – they cut themselves off from the community as immoral men, and are in the profoundest sense evil'.[20]

But this is not simply a denunciation of conventional morals. What Nietzsche emphasizes in this discussion is that the fundamental principle of morality is communal solidarity, the reciprocal sense of responsibility of each for all and vice versa. As Nietzsche sees things, individual transgression is felt to be both grounds for exclusion from the collectivity and, at the same time, evidence of a collective guilt so that the punishment of the individual signifies in some obscure way the punishment of the whole community. Nietzsche suggests that the morality – or perhaps the ethicalness – of custom and tradition is in the end nothing other than superstitious dread of a higher authority, with the important consequence that 'originality of every kind has acquired a bad conscience'.[21]

The relationship between the customary and the ethical as it is presented by Nietzsche has considerable importance in a discussion of the pathos of modernity, a phenomenon widely interpreted as a failure or breakdown of tradition. Where conservative and neo-conservative culture critics see only a lamentable breakdown, Nietzsche describes an extremely complex historical situation that must be understood in the light of such issues as historically distant origins, cultural belatedness, transgression, and the persecution of originality. All of this has significant bearing on the reiterated claim that Shakespeare is a crucial element in our tradition and that this tradition is in imminent danger of collapse.

Is it really the case that Shakespeare objectifies or instantiates a tradition that scholarship can preserve and reaffirm? It should be perhaps apparent that the 'great Shakespeare' that we value today is one of the evil ones referred to by Nietzsche, a site of powerful originality or transgression. The very existence of a play by Shakespeare is an affront to tradition. To begin with, a theater is an institution with the capacity to create an alternative agential space, it fosters the 'right to be other'. Moreover, Shakespeare's characters reveal with great clarity how a histrionic calculus operates in their

50

actions. Finally, the plays represent social heterogeneity, dissonance, and contradiction. All of this is deeply troubling to the experience of social identity that helps to stabilize the traditional social life-world. Even though the plays may exhibit a nostalgia for that traditional life-world, they cannot be occasions for affirming reverence for tradition.

In our own culturally belated situation the Shakespearean evil or, in less inflammatory language, originality, has been transmuted entirely into cultural goodness. This positive cultural value circulates under the terms of our literary tradition or literary heritage. But, as I have tried to indicate in the preceding discussion, a tradition is something rather different from a heritage. In any case, neither term accurately describes the position of Shakespeare as a value within American culture. That position is better understood in terms of a transformation of the Shakespearean *oeuvre* into a reservoir of cultural capital.[22] In order to achieve such a conversion, it is necessary to remove or to disentangle Shakespearean meanings from their specifically European history. This massive transfer of cultural accounts is necessary if Shakespeare is to be appropriated for a specifically American cultural and social project.

CULTURAL CAPITAL AND THE REFUSAL OF TRADITION

In a sense America can be understood as a deliberate historical refusal of tradition, at least in its social forms. The earliest religious communities were in conscious flight from the degraded institutional life of religion as it was practiced in European society as they were also in flight from the traditional social practice of that same society. In these communities the counter-normative movement of tradition was experienced in its most radical possible form, and the early settlers did indeed act out a wish to be 'alone with God' quite literally.[23] Tradition in its alternative form, that is in the form of long-term cultural and social continuity has, by contrast, been much more problematic. Renewal and the return to origins are perennial themes of American cultural experience.

American society is, of course, traceable to revolutionary origins and specifically to the social and political projects of the Enlightenment. In this historical context reason is enshrined in the place of tradition, which is, as Gadamer suggests, historicized and made answerable to reason and to the tribunal of science.[24] Under these

51

conditions religious traditions are not abolished, but they are relativized and segregated within the private and domestic sphere. The freedom of religion articulated by the founding fathers really is a freedom *from* religion in the sense that scripture has neither the status of a magisterial source of authority, nor the capacity to saturate the social life-world. Such freedom from religion is not at all intended as an absence of religion from the social landscape, but inwardness and private religiosity are fostered as legitimate modes of religious experience. The visible church is inhibited in the exercise of secular authority.

Freedom from religion in this sense is also a freedom from tradition, or in other words it is a historical *emancipatio* in which authority is no longer derived from a magisterial *scriptural* source administered by a hieratic agency. Self-government as a social principle requires that the institutional ensemble of magisterial word, scripture, tradition give way to a public archive containing texts, among which are various charters of ancient liberty. Scripture is relativized, consigned to the general archive where it is to function as one among many other resources available for various knowledge-seeking projects of historical research and reconstruction. The repertoire of texts contained in this archive can be, roughly speaking, the functional equivalent of tradition, but only in the limited sphere of administration and publicity. It is precisely this process of secularization that makes it possible for profane works – including the works of Shakespeare – to be accommodated to the socio-cultural dispensation mandated by the revolutionary project in such charters as the US Constitution.

A detailed critical history of Shakespeare's position within American culture has not yet been written. There are, however, various synoptic and anecdotal accounts of American interest in Shakespeare since colonial times. Esther Cloudman Dunn's *Shakespeare in America* is not really a scholarly treatment of the problem, but many of her specific assertions have remained in circulation.[25] One of these assertions concerns the use made of quotations from Shakespeare by John Adams in his reflections on aspects of the US Constitution and on the organizing principles of the society of which he must be considered a founder. According to Dunn, Adams quotes the speech of Ulysses in *Troilus and Cressida*, 'Degree being vizarded/ The unworthiest shows as fairly in the mask' in support of an argument for establishing a system of 'degree' and of aristocratic privilege in American society. That John Adams should have cited this particular speech is itself a most intriguing historical fact, especially in light of the importance it has acquired after being singled out by E. M. W. Tillyard as a kind of centerpiece for his discussion of *The Elizabethan World Picture*.[26] Dunn is certainly accurate in identifying Adams's use of this particular quotation, but her description of the context and the function of this citation is very much at odds with the actual tendency of Adams's text. In fact, the *Discourses on Davila*, where this quote appears, takes an extremely dim view of the European aristocracy, characterizing it as irrational, nihilistic, and incorrigibly violent. This is part of a complex analysis of the problem of orderly differentiation, the derivation and allocation of sovereignty, and the separation of powers. Since Adams does indeed make strategic use of quotations from Shakespeare, it is quite useful to look at this text in more detail. As the following analysis will show, however, the real point of Adams's analysis is a critique of tradition as a principle of social organization. In that context Adams clearly has in mind an appropriation of Shakespeare for the interests of the Enlightenment as he understood it.

In a diary entry of April, 1786, Adams described a journey he made in the company of Thomas Jefferson to Shakespeare's birthplace. Their itinerary included Worcester, where Adams admonished some of the citizens for their ignorance of the historical importance of their own locale: 'And do Englishmen so soon forget the ground where liberty was fought for? Tell your neighbors and your children that this is holy ground; much holier than that on which your churches stand.'[27] Adams expresses a similar sense that the English fail to display proper reverence and care for their own traditions when he visits Shakespeare's birthplace at Stratford-upon-Avon. He makes mention of a number of tourist attractions that are made available to visitors, including an old chair in which Shakespeare allegedly sat. He and Jefferson cut off a chip, 'according to custom'. But apart from these trivial and mean expressions of historical interest, there seems to be little real appreciation for Shakespeare's cultural and historical significance.

There is nothing preserved of this great genius which is worth knowing; nothing which might inform us what education, what company, what accident turned his mind to letters and the drama. His name is not even on his gravestone. An ill-sculptured head is set up by his wife, by the side of his grave in the church. But paintings and sculpture would be thrown away upon his fame. His wit, his fancy, his taste and judgment, his knowledge of nature, of life and character, are immortal.

(Adams, 1971a 394)

The entire excursion produces in Adams what can only be described as a melancholy effect. Shrines and monuments commemorate the wrong things, while truly significant historical struggles are forgotten, neglected, or trivialized. The treatment of Shakespeare, a figure of much more than parochial interest, is particularly depressing. The entry records an encounter between a vitiated, parochial sense of tradition and a deliberate return to origins. Tradition as the quasi-natural continuity of meaning preserves nothing of value. Only in the more arduous and self-reflective return to origins is that value fully recuperable. For Adams, Shakespeare's universal character is identified with 'knowledge of nature' and it is this knowledge that makes his work appropriate for inclusion in the general archive of the new society.

A more exact account of the position Shakespeare might occupy within this archive is suggested in Adam's *Discourses on Davila*. This text is subtitled 'A series of papers on political history, by an American citizen'. It is in fact a kind of annex, or lengthy postscript to an even longer text by Adams, his *Defense of the American Constitution*. The *Discourses*, though ostensibly a commentary on Davila's *History of the Franks*, is at once an oblique discussion of the French Revolution and a series of second thoughts about American government and social institutions in the light of events in France under Napoleon I. Adams struggles in this text to keep faith with his understanding of the Constitution as *emancipatio*, that is a collective historical refusal of tradition, metaphysical irrationalism, and routine institutional life of unrelieved social inequality and despotism. The refusal of tradition is not, however, an end in itself, since the historical actualization of this *emancipatio* demands some sort of critical social theory to define the subject's relationship with the archive of texts and charters that are to provide a new experience of collective life. Central to that critical social theory is the view that rational social organization demands a coherent account of the individual subject. Since society is constituted in and through the manifold decisions of individual agents, it is clear that some understanding of individual motivation is necessary to any found-

54

ational social project of the sort to which Adams was committed.

The methodological individualism of the *Discourses* is an interesting variant on the classical political economy worked out in Adam Smith's *Wealth of Nations*. For Adams, the individual is not a rational economic agent engaged in a primarily hedonistic calculation, but rather a mimetic figure dominated by primarily imaginary desires.[28] Adams's point of departure is the observation that although men are undoubtedly gregarious, they are nevertheless driven by a 'passion for distinction'.[29] Human sociability is natural and therefore rational. Distinction, by contrast, is neither natural nor rational, but it is nevertheless grounded in an ineradicable will to self-differentiation. On this view, people are both rational and irrational, equally impelled towards association, collective life and the public interest and towards differentiation, individuality, and private well-being. The impulse to seek distinction is, moreover, oriented towards imaginary goals and purposes, and achieved through mimetic and specular activity. The strictly economic calculations of the individual subject of classic political economy are replaced in this theory by a primarily histrionic subject animated by mimetic desire rather than by strategic calculations of profit and loss.[30]

Adams's analysis of distinction is elaborated through a typology of separate, well-defined drives or desires that animate both rational (or virtuous) and irrational conduct. The primary motive of ethical, socially rational action is emulation, which Adams characterizes both as the search for truth and as the wish to practice virtue. Emulation is thus other-regarding rather than self-regarding and it leads towards a reconciliation of the rational impulse towards sociability and the irrational passion for distinction. '*Spectemur agendo* expresses the great principle of acting for the good of others' (*Adams* 1971b: 234). Actions that are seen, or in short, publicity, elaborate and extend the field of ethical conduct and guarantee solidarity. The desire or need to be well-regarded by others, to achieve a position of public notice, is satisfied mimetically, that is, through an imitation or copy of ethical conduct as it appears in others. Emulation is thus a double principle, in that it entails both seeing and being seen; it provides for Adams a definition of citizen as someone fully engaged in and identified with the public sphere. But emulation is an extremely complex impulse in that it imitates both in the sense of 'equalling' and in the sense of 'rivalling' others. The citizen is thus one who acts according to a dialectic of likeness and unlikeness, the desire to resemble others and the desire to individuate and to separate from others. In political terms then there are two incompatible principles of social organization: relations of equality and relations of inequality or hierarchy. The chronic friction created between ideas of domination (*Herrschaft*) and ideas of solidarity or comradeship (*Genossenschaft*) create a kind of split political consciousness not easily reconciled either by informal social institutions or by structures of governance. This split in consciousness can work to promote sociability if there is available a reservoir of powerful examples of virtuous conduct; imitation would thus channel the need for self-differentiation back towards the collective interest.

Emulation, for Adams, is a fundamental social energy, despite its complex, contradictory, and largely irrational character. Indeed, emulation would be fundamental both to democracy as a form of social/political practice and to the republic as the social/political structure or *mise-en-scène* for such a practice. But Adams understands perfectly well that the passion for distinction is not only irrational but radically unstable in its orientation and purpose. The drive towards individuation, that is mimetic identification and mimetic rivalry, are by no means confined to patterns of virtuous conduct and acting for the good of others. On the contrary, the passion for distinction is a generative source for a wide range of self-interested and socially destructive goal-values. On this view the idea of democracy, and in fact the notion of sociability is already compromised at its origin, since the motivational calculus that gives rise to emulation is also the source of ambition, jealousy, and greed, which are not merely private vices but public incivilities that radically derange the patterns of reciprocity and other-regarding social actions.

If, as Esther Dunn maintains, Adams is elaborating a defence of degree and difference, it would appear that those principles cannot be derived from distinctions of family, lineage, and aristocratic privilege. On the contrary, Adams's reflections on aristocracy are unequivocally critical, and even derisory. The various principles of degree are in fact forms of parochial social interest.

A death bed, it is said, shows the emptiness of titles. That may be, but does it not equally show the futility of riches, power, liberty, and all earthly things? 'The cloud-capt towers, the gorgeous palaces, the solemn temples, the great globe itself' appear the 'baseless fabric of a vision' and life itself, 'a tale told by an idiot, full of sound and fury, signifying nothing'.   (Adams 1971b: 242)

Adams appropriates Shakespeare's words to sum up and to validate this series of reflections on the vanity of human wishes. But his use, both of the traditional *topos* and of Shakespeare's poetry, is intended as more than a conventional treatment of private vice and folly. The discussion of individual motivation, and in particular of the most universal of all passions, is part of a larger argument about the nature of associated man.

The general *telos* of both the *Defense of the Constitution* and *Discourses on Davila* is that 'real merit should govern the world' (Adams 1971b: 249). The problem of achieving this result is the task of historical agents, men actively engaged in the construction of their own social situation. It is clear that Adams does not regard universal suffrage or the revolutionary leveling of social differences as very promising means for bringing this about. But the system of European society, in which honor is annexed to land, offices, and families has been a depressing and interminable failure, a 'thousand years of barons' wars . . . [and] aristocratic anarchy' (Adams 1971b: 251)

It is at this point in his argument, immediately after a long discussion of the utter failure of the European nobility either to achieve anything that could reasonably be called a socio-political *order* or even, for that matter, to 'maintain their own population', (Adams 1971b: 256) that Adams again turns to Shakespeare for the authoritative text to confirm his argument. Shakespeare is named only as the 'Great Master of Nature'; Ulysses' speech on degree is then quoted at length (Adams 1971b: 264–6). Adams states explicitly that the passage is to be understood as an 'inference . . . upon these dispositions to imitation, emulation, and rivalry'. The emphasis is not on the desirability of order so much as it is on the difficulty of achieving it. And even though there may well be a chain of being in the order of nature as a whole, it is precisely in the imitation of that order of vertical differentiation that social disorder, dissension, and conflict is created. The pattern of 'Associated Man' cannot simply be read off from the hierarchy of created things. But a complacent interpretation of social order as derived from the conventional *topoi* of cosmic order could hardly be what Adams would have had in mind, since a good part of his life was devoted to a project which began with the permanent and decisive abolition of

57

monarchical order. It was Adams himself who untuned *that* string in favor of a radical new beginning based on rationalization of the discord in emulation, that most ambiguous passion for distinction.

Adams does not give a normative reading of Ulysses' speech of the kind that was in circulation during the 1940s and 1950s. But what exactly is his reading of Shakespeare and how does that reading function in his own socio-cultural context of the post-revolutionary period? Shakespeare is a kind of trans-cultural authority, an author who represents more comprehensively than any other the nature of that generic Enlightenment subject known as Man. However, to judge from the quotations selected and their specific application within *Discourses on Davila*, it would appear that Adams favored a dark reading of Shakespeare as the orientation that most truthfully discloses the perdurable character of Man as he appears in changing historical contexts. Adams interprets Shakespeare tragically, that is, as a 'master of nature' who reveals what is most disorderly and destructive in Man, who is something other than what he appears to be in the affirmative Enlightenment myth of the generic human subject. Adams invokes Shakespeare to authorize his own refusal of myth as the basis for his constitutional project, the arduous task of making social institutions as opposed to simply affirming either what has been received or what has been newly instituted. Shakespeare clearly functions as part of *praxis*, that is, political action informed by theoretical reflection as well as by strategic deliberation.

Despite the deep reservations expressed about the French Revolution and its aftermath, or possibly because of them, Adams continued to affirm his belief in the moral and political validity of the American Revolution as the founding of a new kind of society. For Adams the negation of European origins, the abolition of European social forms, and the instituting of a balanced constitution *in written form* are decisive and necessarily interrelated actions. The newly constituted American government and social system is a genuine historical emergence, an action in the strong, negative sense of energetic social initiative not bound over to traditional form. The sense of initiative and new beginning cannot be separated from what we might call Adams's Europophobia, his deep conviction that neither the socio-political structures nor the traditional life-world of Europe offers anything positive to the American project. Even in the context of such a Europophobia, however, Adams obviously feels that Shakespeare can be invoked as a valid and dependable authority.

In *Discourses on Davila* Adams detaches the work of Shakespeare from its specifically European context, so as to make it available for a new socio-cultural dispensation. That new dispensation is the regime of bourgeois political economy.[31] In the historical environment of Europe this liberal regime was in more or less constant collision with the massive inertia of feudal and pre-bourgeois social forms. However, in the American context the autonomous individual and the general rule of the exchange of equivalents becomes hypostatized as a description of an eternal human nature. The result of this is that these concepts no longer have strategic force, but become instead dogmatically entrenched first principles. Within such a dispensation tradition as a system of gifts, affective bonds, and personal obligations that bind generations together can no longer subsist. The ethical imperatives of tradition are subordinated in this dispensation to the ethical imperatives of an exchange economy.

TRADITION, BREAKDOWN, AND THE MANAGEMENT OF CULTURAL CAPITAL

In the post-Enlightenment culture of our own historical moment, tradition no longer has any quasi-natural and homely immediacy. It is replaced by a system of institutions that conserve and administer a massive fund of intellectual capital. The values sedimented in art and literature become a type of wealth 'without qualities', free of archaic entailments and available for accumulation. Such accumulation does not, however, guarantee a smooth and quasi-natural unfolding of ethical consensus or provide the basis for communal life.

By making cultural goods subject to the dispensation of the price system, accumulation of artistic and intellectual capital takes the place of tradition as a source of authority. Neo-conservative culture criticism nevertheless maintains that the ethical and political authority of tradition is in decline for other reasons. This breakdown or loss has been variously attributed to such factors as narcissism, misguided educational reform, rising consumer expectations, and pointedly to divisive foreign ideologies such as Marxism or feminism. To offset the effect of breakdown, various programs of education are suggested, and prominent among these programs has been the recruitment of literature as the alternative to the traditional redemptive media.[32]

The idea that an established curriculum based on a substantive *literary* culture can become a functional equivalent for religion raises some interesting questions. To begin with, it is not immediately obvious why any sane and reasonably well-educated person would entertain such an obviously fantastical idea, or imagine its implementation as a serious cultural policy. But advocates of traditional humanistic education evidently regard belief systems as primary social elements, so that a secular and literary substantive culture can indeed seem a plausible substitute for a religion. At least, the argument goes, a uniform curriculum – one that must include Shakespeare – will provide all the members of a society with a common fund of experience. The problem with this idea is not so much in the election of literature, or even something more general like cultural literacy or western values as the medium of tradition, but in the notion of breakdown itself and the misreading of the social nature of tradition that this entails.

Traditions do not break down because of ignorance, forgetfulness, or misguided educational reform. Nor do they break down because people are encouraged or enabled to satisfy their desires. Traditions do not break down for these reasons because *traditions do not break down.* Tradition sustains collective life through relations of unequal exchange that bind generations together in solidarity. But this is finally incompatible with the rational exchange of equivalents that constitutes the dispensation of bourgeois political economy. Within this dispensation there are neither gifts nor obligations, but only the general audit that leads to a final settling of accounts. Under the combined pressures of industrialization and the growth of the state apparatus, the traditional social life-world is destroyed, more often than not in abrupt, radical, and violent ways.

The claim that a substantive culture, nurtured and propagated by humanistic scholarship, can compensate for the loss of tradition, let alone conserve or restore it, is simply untrue. The programs of substantive culture, the revanchist but essentially non-secular humanism of Alan Bloom, E.D. Hirsch, or William Bennett can only function as the agency for a carefully administered circulation of reified cultural values. This instrumentally defined cultural legacy or heritage thematizes various legitimation discourses in and through a fund of carefully preserved literary artifacts.[33] This has not come about, however, simply because it is in the interests of the power structure.

It is true that interest in Shakespeare has increased at a pace roughly comparable to the growth of a corporate/governmental power structure, and that this interest has been actualized in the form of valuable real estate, collections of rare books, and other expensive physical resources. That Shakespeare serves the interests of class domination is not, however, the whole story. It might make just as much sense to say that the concrete elaborations of Shakespeare have softened the impact of the hegemonic order, or even helped to reveal its contradictions, as to claim that it has served the interests of class domination. In fact the hegemonization of Shakespeare has come about as the result of complex historical factors, some of quite long standing. Within the infrastructure of these institutions radical potentiality is still held in reserve. In the construction of Shakespeare as a complex of institutions and practices, critical and oppositional potentialities have been incorporated into various archaeological strata. This is true in part because the hegemonic institutions are themselves built on contradictions, so that a self-defeating element is in a sense built into the structure of those institutions. But, in addition, institutions are actually peopled by social agents who themselves may have agendas that differ substantially from those initially mandated. The release of those potentialities would presumably be the over-arching interest of a critically motivated research program. Those interests cannot, however, be actualized by a novel re-staging of the counter-normative script, nor simply by saying forbidden things about Shakespeare.

Chapter three

THE FUNCTION OF THE ARCHIVE

The library as an institutional type is of fundamental importance to any consideration of professional literary scholarship, since it objectifies an extremely complicated set of working conditions or relations of production within the community of scholar-practitioners. These social relations of production can predetermine which questions can be effectively posed, as well as what kinds of evidence can be discovered and brought to bear on those questions. Libraries, however, embody two radically contradictory types of social experience. First, libraries are unusual among the institutions of modern industrial society or monopoly capitalism in that they are organized according to collectivist principles. All libraries reflect this co-operative and collective ideal – the general pooling of intellectual resources and the democratic allocation of those resources for the purpose of scholarly inquiry.

Libraries, by definition, imply not only the conservation of intellectual capital, but provision of access to that capital. Access is never completely unrestricted, of course, and in the case of the research library access is usually limited to individual with the proper formal credentials. The limited access to the resources or intellectual capital reflects the second, conflicting aspect of the libraries' institutional form. Libraries come into existence as the expression of large monopolistic accumulations of wealth and power; in the case of research libraries these concentrations of authority are likely to represent either national interests as these are embodied in the state apparatus, or private interests transformed into public institutional reality. Libraries cannot, of course, be thought of except as manifestations of a conservation function, and they are thus connected with the idea of stable cultural and social relations. In light of the costly physical requirements for establishing and maintaining library buildings and collections, the culturally conservative function is often inseparable from a politically conservative function and from the social experience of privilege. No library facility, however, can be kept secure from the activities of critically motivated researchers. Despite their objectively conservative structure, libraries remain as one of the primary conditions of possibility for the creation of radical, action-orienting research programs.

The history of libraries goes back to ancient Hebrew, Sumerian, and Greek civilizations, and indeed the discursive practice and even the very experience that we know as 'history' necessarily coincides with the existence of the library. The emergence of new types of library foundation in the period of the Enlightenment is related to political events, and in general corresponds to the emergence into historical self-awareness of newly forming social classes.[1] In the United States the public library is conceived as a project of broad popular education, related to similar projects such as the general encyclopedia. [2] Public libraries in combination with wide access to literacy constituted a 'people's university' and this made it possible to break the educational monopolies of entrenched social and economic privilege. Initially these projects were voluntaristic and syndical in character. Towards the end of the nineteenth century, the Carnegie Foundation provided funds for towns to finance their own public libraries, so that the library as a people's university was repositioned within the structures of government and private capital.

In the United States there is also a distinct type of research library, the private, free-standing foundation that houses a significant collection of manuscripts and early printed books. Unlike the public libraries with their popular and populist orientation, specialized research libraries reflect the converging interests of wealthy private collectors and of professional cadres of scholars. Libraries like the Folger, the Huntington, and the Newberry as well as the Horace Howard Furness collection at the University of Pennsylvania, have particular importance for the study of Shakespeare. In the case of the Folger and the Furness collections, Shakespeare is the reason for the very existence of the institution. In studying the history of these foundations it is possible to discover some of the social and political forces that have helped to shape and to direct the activities of Shakespeare scholars.

Institutions like the Folger Shakespeare Memorial Library are not just concentrations of intellectual capital. Academic research in the humanities has been organized as a guild of more or less autonomous craft workers functioning without direction from any centralized agency that sets the agenda for research. The agenda-setting function has, to some extent, however, been fulfilled by the research libraries and the role of the Folger library in this respect has been a most important one. From the time of their establishment, research libraries like the Folger and Huntington have functioned as intellectual clearing-houses, more or less permanent and ongoing academic conferences. It appears, moreover, that this function is, at the present time, an expanding one. The Folger Library is now the home for the Folger Institute, a consortium of universities that sponsors advanced research and that offers formal seminars in the area of Renaissance studies. In light of such initiatives, a more detailed account of the historical development of the specialized, private research libraries is of particular importance for understanding the orientation of Shakespeare studies in the United States.

HORACE HOWARD FURNESS AND HIS COLLECTION

One of the more curious facts that emerges from an investigation of specialized research facilities like the Furness collection or the Folger Library is the way a professional, academic research program evolves out of the amateur pursuits and interests of men like Folger, Huntington, and Horace Howard Furness. Furness, for example, was an attorney by training rather than a scholar.[3] During his undergraduate career at Harvard, no formal training in English literary scholarship would have been available to him, although he would certainly have had the opportunity to engage in serious discussion of certain literary works, undoubtedly including the plays of Shakespeare.[4] Reading and discussion of Shakespeare's plays was a social activity rather than a specialized academic *métier*. Furness helped to create the idea of Shakespeare scholarship as a profession, though he never himself earned a degree in literature.

Furness's career as a man of letters began when he joined the Shakespeare Society of Philadelphia sometime in the fall of 1860. The Shakespeare Society of Philadelphia is the earliest formally established organization devoted to the study of Shakespeare's plays, older even than the *Deutsche Shakespeare Gesellschaft*.[5] Furness was active in this association, which met on a monthly basis to read and discuss selected plays. The avocational and leisure class orientation of this organization can be gauged from its exclusive character, and from the elaborate banquets that were a feature of the monthly meetings. Since the meetings were held at the law offices of one of the members, the discussion had a vigorously forensic and argumentative character.[6] These occasions were *symposia* in the original classical meaning of this expression, feasts of both intellect and of body. The exact nature of the issues raised at these discussions is not easy to reconstruct. It appears, however, that the selection of topics and of 'research problems' would have been *ad hoc*, idiosyncratic, and extremely fluid even by today's standards. As practicing attorneys, the members were primarily interested in the 'mooting' of various cruces and contradictions in the text.[7] This forensic orientation also extended into consideration of character and motivation.

Furness and his associates in the Philadelphia Shakespeare Society were primarily interested in the discussion of individual characters and in the analysis of particular speeches. For this reason, the Society worked from the *Variorum Edition* of 1821, and supplemented this text with a small reference library of commentary, together with editions of Shakespeare that provided numerous textual variants and emendations. Evidently the handling of all this reference material was something of an inconvenience and in order to eliminate this cumbersome physical apparatus Furness conceived the idea of a new Variorum edition to facilitate the Society's discussions.[8] The *New Variorum* edition of *Romeo and Juliet* was ready for publication in 1871. Just before the official publication date Evans Rogers, H.H. Furness's father-in-law, died, leaving a very large estate to his daughter, Kate Rogers Furness. As a result of this turn of events Furness was no longer obliged to practice law as a livelihood, and was thus able to transform his avocational interest in Shakespeare into a full-time career as a professional man of letters. That career is marked by two extremely significant, closely interrelated achievements: the Furness collection and the *New Variorum* itself.

It is important to stress that Furness was somewhat atypical as a collector, in that his objectives had substantive intellectual content. The Shakespeare collection he had in mind was to be a working library, rather than an accumulation of rare objects. The material collected could not, of course, determine in any direct way a specific ideological tendency for the interpretation of Shakespeare's text. However, the existence of this material could clearly have a decisive impact on what might count as a legitimate research problem.

The highest priority for the collection was to acquire as complete as possible a set of early editions of Shakespeare's plays, together with a comprehensive collection of all known later editions. Other libraries, notably the Folger, have far more extensive holdings in early Quartos and Folios, but the Furness collection does contain a virtually complete history of the Shakespeare editions; certainly there is no influential version of the text that cannot be consulted there. These editions are supplemented by three ancillary categories. First, there are commentaries and interpretations of Shakespeare. Second, there are extensive holdings in other writers of the sixteenth and early seventeenth century, primarily in English. Finally, since Furness was extremely interested in the details of theatrical productions of Shakespeare's plays, there are extensive holdings of important theater records, such as promptbooks, and related memorabilia.

The interests that helped to shape the Furness collection are certainly connected with Furness's position within the larger intelligentsia and with the privileged social position he enjoyed. However, these relations are extremely complex. Furness's training in the law, and his early association with the attorneys who belonged to the Philadelphia Shakespeare Society suggest that there may be some sort of residual connection between a group of lawyers 'mooting' the interpretation of literary characters, and the professional, academic discourse that emerges in the early twentieth century with its similar preoccupation with such singular cases as Hamlet or Othello. The evidence suggests, however, that Furness did not see the study of Shakespeare primarily as an extension of legal forensics. Both the Furness collection itself, and the research program that collection implies, are the expression of a particular structure of feeling in which class interests and political power are powerfully mediated. It is this ensemble of affective concerns which was put into circulation by Furness and his associates, rather than any form of consciousness specific to his original *métier*.

Furness and his associates formed a cadre of intellectuals that was cosmopolitan in scope. These individuals were editors, private scholars, in some cases wealthy and cultivated amateurs. At first very few of his correspondents were English professors, since departments of English scarcely existed before the end of the nineteenth century. The circulation of Shakespeare scholarship was not primarily through formal educational channels, certainly not through the curriculum of university English departments. Shakespeare was the concern of well-educated individuals with sufficient wealth and leisure to devote to such a highly specialized ensemble of secular interests. Bernard Quaritch, a bookseller with whom Furness was to have extensive dealings, characterized this as a society of gentlemen:

> I have extended my business very much with American *gentlemen* (not the trade) and I am determined to extend my relations with American scholars, collectors, and librarians. My staff of assistants is especially drilled to execute American orders with accuracy. Middlemen are not any longer required between myself and the better kind of American buyers.[9]

Quaritch identifies scholars, librarians, and collectors as gentlemen and differentiates these groups from 'the trade' or in other words from American book dealers. The remark about the elimination of middlemen is particularly interesting however. It indicates that Quaritch recognized that there was now a class of 'better . . . American buyers' who were fully qualified to deal directly with British sources. Even if this observation is motivated only by commercial considerations it suggests an emerging 'community of interests' between English and American gentlemen scholars. It also points to a freer circulation of physical and material resources among an international – or at least an Anglo-American – intellectual community.

Furness's social status was important in facilitating the acquisition of scholarly materials. It was useful in another way for the dissemination of a complex experience of interpretation and response to Shakespeare's plays. Woodrow Wilson, in a letter to Furness dated 2 October 1902, extends the following invitation.

> I write to ask if it will not be possible for you to give us the treat sometime during the winter of having one of your delightful readings from Shakespeare? We have too seldom had an opportunity of profiting by your extraordinary acquaintance with the Poet, and of feeling the power with which you interpret him.[10]

The *mise-en-scène* for this interpretation or dramatic reading was social rather than strictly professional. The occasion was evidently more an intimate family gathering or *soirée* rather than anything resembling an academic conference. Furthermore, it seems that the purpose of the experience was the sharing among friends of a sensory and affective experience, rather than the exchange of rigorously conceived intellectual arguments. Considering the influential and powerful positions that Furness and Wilson would eventually occupy in the educational and political life of the nation, however, it seems likely that the pattern of feeling generated by social occasions of this type would enter into the emerging professional discourse on Shakespeare and on cultural history generally.

The impact of Furness's work as a private scholar and of the structure of feeling that motivated him on the academic community can be traced more directly in his correspondence with professional scholars. One of the more interesting examples of such correspondence is a letter from that quintessentially *English* man of letters, Sir Walter Raleigh. The letter begins with a curious acknowledgement of American priority in the project of British Shakespeare scholarship, at least on the level of particular individuals. 'The debt is all from me to you,' Raleigh writes; 'I think that my first significant introduction to Shakespeare was reading your Variorum *Romeo and Juliet*.'[11] Raleigh goes on to say that it was this experience that first made him aware not only of Shakespeare's 'greatness' as a poet, but also of the possibility that a life's work could be organized around the monumentalization of that greatness. There is, however, a certain melancholy connected with this project. This is apparent in Raleigh's sense that Shakespeare belongs to a historically remote cultural and spiritual horizon.

> I did not altogether like the business of writing a short work on Shakespeare. His stuff is so alive – how to keep it clear of the immense deposit on it? Especially when that deposit is so valuable? It occurred to me the other day that Samuel Johnson was nearer to Shakespeare in time than a man of fifty now is to Johnson. And perhaps Johnson's England was more like Shakespearës than ours is like Johnson's. We are drifting (or steaming) very fast, and losing the old marks. So the commentators deserve a kind of Encomium which is seldom given them. . . . As to Shakespeare I admit we know hardly anything about him. The men of the Renaissance are curiously far from us. Marlowe? Spenser? who has really gotten alongside of their green vein of sensuality.[12]

This letter represents in some detail the pattern of shared feeling in circulation among private scholars and professional academics at this time. Since it is the pattern of feeling, rather than any overt political agenda, that is actualized in concrete, institutional form by Furness and his associates, it is useful to analyze the letter closely.

The melancholy aspect of studying Shakespeare is in the intensified sense of drift or, even worse deliberate and purposeful movement, away from the 'old marks'. This is an instance of the historicist nostalgia that informs the professional discourse on Shakespeare well into the second half of the twentieth century. The loss of the old marks, expresses, though most obscurely, Raleigh's sense that the cultural and social conditions of modern life are inimical to an expressive fullness and coherent order in collective experience.[13] But Raleigh shows no interest in taking up those specific resources of modern consciousness that would provide a critical understanding of the alarming 'drift' or movement away from stability and reconciled wholeness. Scholarship is not an action-orienting program of inquiry, it is instead a 'remembrance of things past'. Raleigh's sense of belatedness, his gloomy foreboding about the direction of historical change, entails a yearning for two distinct kinds of experience. The suspicion that even Samuel Johnson, to say nothing of Shakespeare, lived in a very different kind of England is the expression of a desire for a stable and harmonious social order marked by clear differentiation, deference and *noblesse oblige*. But the remarks on Spenser and Marlowe, with their nostalgic reference to a 'green vein of sensuality' indicate a contrasting desire for immediate, full, and vital sensory/affective sensation that can be enjoyed in a kind of innocence. Shakespeare offers both the experience of order and the *frisson* of innocent spontaneity, but this experience can be had only at the cost of knowing that such things can exist only in the private, contemplative sphere.

Furness's own psychic investment in Shakespeare was similar in kind to Raleigh's, although it seems that the affective and sensory aspects were of considerably greater importance for him than the idea of stable social order. He was powerfully motivated by his sustained affection for Shakespeare's characters and by a passionate identification with the emotional rhythms of the plays. Tragedy was far less congenial as an emotional experience, however, than comedy and he evidently found *Othello* almost unbearable to read, let alone edit.[14] Clearly the institutions he created were mandated by this commitment to Shakespeare as the privileged site of affective and expressive fullness. The spiritual and imaginative range, intensity, and even excess of the Shakespeare experience is, however, constrained, not so much by codes of civility and decorum as by the imperatives of a strictly contemplative orientation to the dramatic material.

Horace Howard Furness is an extremely interesting figure in light of the important role he played in the modernization of a great university. In addition to making the Furness collection itself, he was instrumental in the comprehensive re-organizing of the general library collections, and in the establishing of a department of English at the University of Pennsylvania. These changes helped to accelerate the social processes of transformation that would eventually limit the role of the private scholar and gentlemanly amateur in literary and historical scholarship. The interests of those gentlemen scholars, in the form of a generalized structure of feeling were, however, successfully interposed within the professionalized cadres that have emerged since these changes were first instituted. These interests give rise to English departments and to the profession of literature as an academic discipline. However, the institutionalization of literary study is not a fully self-contained and autonomous historical development. Research libraries and departments of English are situated within a much larger ensemble of institutional relations.[15] The story of the Folger Shakespeare Library reveals, in a more direct way than the study of any university-based collection, how academic research may be co-ordinated with larger national interests and cultural policy.

THE FOLGER LIBRARY AND THE NATIONAL INTEREST

Henry Clay Folger was born in 1857, the descendant of an old New England family. The dignity of this lineage – one of his family connections was Benjamin Franklin – did not bring with it any inherited wealth, and in a very real sense Folger's biography is an exemplary American success story. Ralph Waldo Emerson is said to have first stimulated Folger's interest in Shakespeare. While in his final year at Amherst Folger certainly attended a lecture that Emerson gave; this performance was evidently so impressive that Folger began an extensive reading of Emerson's writing and this led him in due course to Shakespeare.[16] Emerson's influence on modern

Shakespeare studies has been far more influential than most Shakespeare scholars realize, but discussion of Emerson's role in the elaboration of a discourse on Shakespeare will have to be deferred until a later section of this book. His impact on the formation of specific institutions is clear through his influence on the activities of Folger.

Emerson may have been responsible for initially triggering Henry Clay Folger's lifelong fascination with Shakespeare, but it would be a mistake to overlook other influences that reinforced this initial focus. Folger's wife Emily Clara Jordan had studied English literature at Vassar College and had written her Master's thesis on Shakespeare. The slow and painstaking task of building the Folger collection was done by the two of them working together. This project occupied considerable time and energy in the couple's life despite what must have been fairly heavy demands on Folger in his capacity as an executive and eventually as president of Standard Oil. The Folger collection did not, of course, take shape in isolation. Both the Folgers were part of a lively and cosmopolitan community of book-collectors, scholars, and devotees of Shakespeare both in his text and in performance. The Folger collection would eventually become exceptional in its size and scope, but it could never be regarded as a purely idiosyncratic preoccupation of two individuals.

Among the influences helping to encourage and to shape the Folgers' project, the work of Horace Howard Furness must rank as an important one. Folger certainly took note of Furness's work on the *Variorum* Shakespeare, which he appreciated, though with the critical scrutiny that any colleague applies to his peer/competitors. Furness preceded Folger as a collector of Shakespeariana and it was Furness who was first recognized as an important authority in the field. But although Folger's collection was destined to surpass that of Furness, he none the less acknowledged Furness's prior authority. 'The Keen pleasure which the writer continuously enjoys from his use of your Variorum edition of Shakespeare is his excuse for sending you this note. . . .'[17] This note contains a tactfully worded correction of one of Furness's assertions as to the source for *The Merchant of Venice*. Folger at this time had copies of Percy's *Reliques*, and also of the Italian novella which was the source both of *The Merchant of Venice* and one of the ballads. The point of his letter is to dispute *one* of Furness's annotations which Folger considers erroneous, based on his possession of rare early editions. Folger uses the occasion of this letter to express his appreciation for Shakespeare's superior gifts as an artist. He is able to compare Shakespeare's 'spirited description of *the whetted blade*,' with a corresponding passage in the prose narrative which 'coldly says, "the Jew had prepared a razor, etc."'[18] As with Furness, Folger's interest in Shakespeare is focussed on particular detail, and especially on poetic or aesthetic detail rather than on systematic interpretation. Aesthetic sensation and the accumulation of individual detail about texts and their performance were more congenial to Folger than intellectual speculation on larger issues or even attempts to describe the structure of an entire play.

Although Folger's concern with Shakespeare was not of a systematic academic kind, he was nevertheless motivated by something considerably more than private aesthetic sensation. In the latter part of his life, as his collection increased in size and importance, Folger's purpose became increasingly political. His aims and objectives were expressed primarily in his actions rather than in manifestoes, critical writings, or even private correspondence, but these actions were themselves sufficiently striking to indicate the general outlines of a cultural policy. In general Folger wanted to make his library a public trust, an objective more or less fully achieved by the time of his death.

As one of the leading importers of intellectual capital, Folger helped to make the United States a leading center of cultural authority. He did this first of all by acquiring private collections mostly held by wealthy British families. What Folger accomplished at the same time was the democratization of privately held intellectual and cultural capital. Of course the Folger Library was never conceived as a 'people's university' along the lines suggested in the Carnegie Foundation projects. It does, however, represent a concentration and rationalization of resources that is in general characteristic of all capitalist enterprise. By 'liberating' these rare books from the vagaries and eccentricities of residual proprietary holdings, Folger also freed American Shakespeare scholars from their dependency on England and on the *noblesse oblige* of owners of 'great houses'. Social qualifications thus became less important than professional credentials in achieving access to the material.

It is easy to sketch out what Folger did; it is not so easy to give an account of his reasons. The social transformation of scholarship that is implied in the Folger Library is, of course, only a democratization relative to the situation that existed earlier. Folger's actions could hardly be construed as those of an intellectual populist and still less as a cultural radical. As in so many other instances, however, the impact of capital is felt in the way it accelerates the disintegration and break-up of a residual feudal or proprietary cultural and economic dispensation. Folger's *motives*, as distinct from his actions, lean more toward nationalistic sentiments rather than to any distinctly articulated wish to make scholarship more democratic. In the end he wanted to have his library situated in an American city and made available for the cultural and spiritual improvement of the American people. The idea of simply reproducing the aristocratic, privately-held collection on a more grandiose scale does not seem to have been in his mind, although the Folgers were often accused of 'hoarding' books while plans to build their library were being developed.

Folger's will stipulates that except for certain bequests to family members the bulk of his estate is to be held in trust for the purpose of establishing and maintaining the Folger Library. The trustees of Amherst College are named as Trustees of the new foundation, and this particular provision suggests something of Folger's ideological alignments. According to Samuel Cadman, the pastor of Folger's congregation,

> Mr Folger had a passion for the spiritual culture of life. When he was a boy, evangelical religion was crashing down in ruins through sheer stupidity . . . it was therefore, a great boon for him when on New England's fragrant hills, nurtured by his Alma Mater, Amherst, which he regarded with reverent affection, he found what he had previously desired and longed for from the time of his boyhood, the guiding light that does not fail.[19]

Folger was certainly a loyal alumnus of Amherst College, and he was also a regular and faithful member of Cadman's Brooklyn congregation. The exact nature of his religious convictions is probably much more complex than the description Cadman presented in his funeral oration. At the time Folger was in attendance, Amherst had shifted its orientation considerably from its earlier commitment to restoring and preserving the faith of the original Puritans. Nevertheless, there was more emphasis on the development of character than on the pursuit of knowledge for its own sake. The intellectual life of the campus community was a kind of compromise between new philosophical orientations strongly influenced by German idealism with the old evangelical stress on personal salvation. The ideal was to promote the liberation of men through a synthesis of Calvinism, capitalism and political democracy. This perfect liberty would be a perfect obedience to a perfect law.[20] It was in this kind of atmosphere that Folger, together with such figures as Calvin Coolidge and Harlan Fiske Stone received his 'education for life'.

Folger is an exemplary instance of private wealth devoted to public good, but his project for appropriating European cultural capital for the benefit of the American people was carried out very discreetly and without benefit of justificatory publicity. His ideological statements took the form of real-estate transactions, and even those were carried out by agents and representatives. Folger only revealed the scope of his plans when the Library Committee of the House of Representatives announced plans to acquire certain parcels of land for the purpose of expanding the Library of Congress. These new buildings were to occupy the land intended as the site of the Shakespeare Library. On 19 January 1928 Folger wrote to Dr Herbert Putnam, Librarian of Congress outlining his plans.

> Recently there was a brief mention in the *Washington Post* of a movement for Congress to make it possible for the Library to secure the two squares directly to the East across 2nd Street. I would like to now confide to you that after working on it for some eight or nine years I have acquired the Grant Row property on East Capitol Street, which, you will recall, is directly East of the Library, owning the entire front on East Capitol Street between 2nd and 3rd Streets, going back to the alleyway in the middle of that square. Upon this I had hoped to build a structure which would harmonize with the Library and would be the home of my collection of Shakespeariana at least for some time in the future. This newspaper mention raises in my mind the question as to whether it would be safe to do this. I know I can tell you in confidence, which I am sure you will not misunderstand nor mis-use, that I have been able to collect a library of Shakespeariana finer than anything that has ever been acquired. This is better known in England than here, and considerable pressure has been put upon me at different times to give it a permanent home at Stratford-on-Avon, in England. But my ambition has been to help make the United States a center for literary study and progress.[21]

It seems extraordinary that Folger was able to keep his intentions so confidential and so closely guarded when the real estate he was in the process of acquiring was literally across the street from the Library of Congress. The choice of site was no less extraordinary, especially in light of Folger's rejection of Stratford-on-Avon as the location for his library. Before considering the symbolic geography of the Folger building, however, it is helpful to look at Herbert Putnam's response to the letter disclosing Folger's plans.

Putnam may have been unaware of Folger's plans for the location of the library, but he certainly understood the significance of the collection itself. He literally dropped everything on receiving the letter of 19 January, which he characterized in a telegram to Folger as having 'extraordinary interest and supreme importance'. In a follow-up to this telegram Putnam elaborated his response as follows:

> Your letter of yesterday opens a prospect more thrilling (I am frank to say) not merely for the National Capital [sic], but for the cultural interests of this country, than anything that has happened for Washington since the establishment of the Freer Gallery.
>
> And any governmental project involving the two squares to the rear of the Library would assuredly be subordinated to yours (for the utilization of the northern strip which you control). With your intention made definite, the governmental undertaking (as respects the remainder of the area) would then become complementary and auxiliary to yours. Indeed, were your structure in existence, the government should acquire the remainder of the area (to Pennsylvania Avenue) in order to assure it a dignified background.[22]

The alacrity of Putnam's response and the absolute sense of conviction that the Folger collection is in the national interest are reflected in the subsequent negotiations with Congressman Robert Luce of Massachusetts, then chairman of the House Committee on the Library. The bill for the acquisition of the squares east of 2nd Street was amended, leaving the Grant Row properties in Folger's possession, but acquiring the balance of the land for annexes to the Library of Congress. In a letter to Folger of 19 April 1928 Luce reported that he anticipated no opposition from any of his colleagues, and in due course the amended bill was passed. Luce's letter confirms the opinion expressed by Putnam of the cultural importance of the Folger Library for the nation:

> You may be glad to know that the announcement of your project has

been received here with the heartiest expressions of gratification. Congress is particularly proud and jealous of its library and in all matters either directly or indirectly relating thereto shows a sympathy both admirable and surprising. Such a structure as you contemplate and such a gift to the scholarship of the nation make all of us who have any share in their acknowledgment grateful for the opportunity. Furthermore, we are particularly pleased because your project promises still further adornment of the surroundings of the Capitol and betokens impetus to the progress towards creating here what in time will be the most beautiful Capital [*sic*] in the world.[23]

The Folger building, which is situated in close proximity to the Supreme Court and to the Library of Congress, is certainly very much in keeping with the architectural dignity of its surroundings. The geographical positioning of the building, moreover, symbolizes a certain cultural structuration, and helps to explicate the claim that Folger's Shakespeare collection promotes the nation's interest.

The symbolism of the Folger's position was pointed out and explained by William Slade, the first director of the library, in the speech he gave at Folger's funeral. He began by quoting Ashley Thorndike's observation that 'Washington, Lincoln, Shakespeare . . . are the three whom Americans universally worship'. Slade then explained exactly how this trinity was positioned physically and spiritually in America.

[A] line drawn from the site of the Folger Shakespeare Memorial through the Capital building and extended onward, will all but touch the monument to Washington and the memorial to Lincoln – the two Americans whose light also spreads across the world. The amount of deviation of the extended line will, in fact, be only great enough to indicate the alteration from the older order which finds its summation in the name of Washington, for more than half his lifetime an English subject, albeit an English colonial, and which again finds its summation in the name of Lincoln.[24]

The idea that Shakespeare constitutes a crucial link or point of mediation within what is now conceived as a historically unified Anglo-American culture is an important element in circulation within the discourse of Shakespeare criticism since about the time of the First World War. The positioning of the Folger Shakespeare Memorial, in Slade's view, objectified the social/cultural continuity

76

and shared tradition between the two societies. The revolutionary break between England and America was so diminished in significance here that the military leader of that revolution could be described as an 'English colonial'. In Slade's account the Declaration of Independence 'registered the solemn and momentous fact of the dissolution of political bands, not those of culture and civilization. Indubitably Shakespeare continues to belong to America as he does to England or to Australia.'[25]

This sense of belonging or cultural continuity was thematized by Slade in the identification of Shakespeare with the great Elizabethan explorers, who represented an entrepreneurial spirit and with Hooker, who represented the 'rule of law'. The obvious Shakespeare text for all of this is, of course, *The Tempest*, a play that Slade read as expressive of the two great American ideals of union or reconciliation and freedom.[26]

In much of this text Slade sounds more like a spokesmen and a publicist for the Folgers than like a scholar or cultural historian attempting to situate Shakespeare within American culture. His remarks were made in the context of a funeral oration, and so due allowance must be made for the setting and the audience. Nevertheless, these observations do articulate a set of assumptions that are at least implicit in Folger's plans and which have been operative in the administration of the library since the time of its founding. Foremost among these assumptions is the idea that America is a successor-culture to England and in a sense the fulfillment of political liberties already immanent in the English scheme of things though imperfectly realized there. Given that assumption the idea of making Shakespeare a 'naturalized American' makes a good deal of sense. Folger was responsible for creating the foundations of an institutional infrastructure for such a grandiose cultural project.

The idea that Shakespeare belongs to America is forcefully suggested by Emerson in *Representative Men*, a text that Folger undoubtedly knew. Folger understood that in order to naturalize Shakespeare and to Americanize the institutional setting for the dissemination of his work it would be necessary both to acquire extensive material resources and to democratize access to those resources. Since at the time of his death the library was still unfinished it is not possible to know exactly how he would have attempted to implement these aims. It took many years for the

Folger Shakespeare Memorial to evolve into its present form as an academically oriented research library; in order to understand this evolution it is necessary to look at the cultural policy assumptions, and the administrative practice of two of its early directors, J. Q. Adams, and Louis B. Wright.

THE MANAGEMENT OF INTELLECTUAL CAPITAL

Joseph Quincy Adams was born in 1881 in South Carolina, the son of a Baptist minister who preached in a number of small towns throughout the state. Despite the suggestive middle name, this Adams is not descended from the New England family of presidents and statesmen. Adams was educated at Wake Forest, and received his doctorate in literature from Harvard in 1903. From 1919 until 1931 he was Professor of English literature at Cornell University. In 1931 he was invited by the trustees of the Folger Shakespeare Memorial Trust to take up the post of Director of Research at the new library. Adams was well qualified for such an appointment. He was widely recognized as a leading scholar of Elizabethan drama through his achievements as an editor and stage historian. Perhaps equally important was his role in developing the Cornell Library and in assembling a distinguished collection of materials in the field of Renaissance literature. Adams was nominally the subordinate of William Slade, director of the library. However, the lines of authority and the division of responsibilities were at first vaguely articulated, and for the first year of operations the library administration functioned poorly.[27] After intervention by Stanley King, president of Amherst College and chairman of the Folger Trust, Slade resigned and Adams was appointed director with full responsibility for all operations.[28] King had a very high opinion of Adams's administrative and professional qualifications and he later played a significant role in an extremely important purchase recommended by the director.

In addition to his unquestioned professional qualifications, Adams brought to his work as director of the Folger Library a clearly articulated sense of the political mission to which the institution would be oriented. This cultural policy is given very forthright expression in Adams's inaugural statement at the opening of the Folger Library in 1932.

[About] the time the forces of immigration became a menace to the preservation of our long-established English civilization, there was initiated throughout the country a system of free and compulsory education for youth. In a spirit of efficiency, that education was made stereotyped in form; and in a spirit of democracy, every child was forced by law to submit to its discipline. . . . In our fixed plan of elementary schooling, [Shakespeare] was made the cornerstone of cultural discipline. . . . Not Homer, nor Dante, nor Goethe, nor Chaucer, nor Spenser, nor even Milton, but Shakespeare was made the chief object of their study and veneration. [29]

The characterization of immigrants as cultural other and as a 'menace to civilization' does not, of course, originate with Adams. Ideas of Anglo-Saxon (or Anglo-Norman) superiority and of the proprietary claims of English descent had been in circulation within the multi-ethnic American population for decades. In fact these ideas were already enshrined as official policy in the racially and ethnically restrictive immigration acts of 1905 and 1924. It is a bit surprising to find a scholar advancing this national and racial chauvinism as the *raison-d'être* for a national curriculum and for the research foundation that constitutes one of the centers for the elaboration and perfection of that curriculum. There have always been *some* scholars who regarded scholarship and learning as cosmopolitan and essentially stateless activities. But at the time there was nothing in the least eccentric or controversial about Adams's views, which were widely shared both within the professional cadres of scholars and educators and within the larger intelligentsia.

Shakespeare, though naturalized in America, was still definitely English, which meant that he was also definitely white. The study of Shakespeare was one of the means to guarantee the security of a quite specific form of white civility and social conduct and everything that this entails. There is no *overt* racism in Adams's cultural policy, although 'our English civilization' hardly seems to include Afro-American culture within the range of its meanings. What is absolutely explicit, however, is the idea of a uniform cultural discipline based on exclusively English and English-derived models. The 'menace of immigration' is in the broad threat to the integrity of these standards and to the erosion of 'civilized' canons of language, of gesture, and of the body, to say nothing of the threat to 'civilized'

79

sexual politics and the 'English' tradition of the rule of law. Behind all this, of course is the unexpressed hope that Shakespeare can somehow help to ward off the threat of foreign ideologies. The idea that a bolshevik-inspired revolution of the working class could somehow be prevented by making people read Shakespeare seems entirely implausible when it is starkly put.

There is no doubt that J. Q. Adams, like a great many other scholars and educators, regarded Shakespeare as a fundamental element in cultural discipline, and moreover regarded such cultural discipline as a good thing. Although this was intended as a serious cultural policy statement, there is no reason to believe that Adams had actually thought through all the practical implications of such a policy, or that he was consciously advocating a racist or politically reactionary ideology. It is clear, however, that the idea of cultural discipline formed the enabling and justificatory framework for his understanding of research. Adams saw the clientele of the Folger as an elite cadre whose access to the collection would be severely limited. In his first annual report to the Trustees Adams suggested that much of the research undertaken at the Folger would take the form of written replies prepared by the resident staff in response to written inquiries by scholars.[30] This view reflected the not unreasonable belief that the expense and inconvenience of travel to and from Washington DC would make visits to the Folger prohibitively difficult. In line with this view Adams made no effort during his administration to install a standardized cataloguing system, thus more or less guaranteeing the fulfillment of his prophecy that the Folger would have only a very small resident clientele.

Two observations need to be made about Adams's policy on the accessibility of the Folger collection. First, the idea that research can be conducted through a kind of mail-order reference service suggests a very narrow, positivistic definition of research as the compilation of determinate facts that require no interpretation by the primary researcher. It further implies a closed research agenda. Second, the restriction of access and the very close regulation of the research agenda reveals something of a dilemma built into the notion of cultural discipline. Restricted access is a powerful strategy for achieving disciplinary control and surveillance. This can help in achieving the aim of uniformity, but it definitely impedes the speed and efficiency of dissemination. Wider and more egalitarian access, together with a standardized research apparatus makes it possible to develop a larger cadre for the circulation of the disciplinary imperative, but only at the sacrifice of the steering and gatekeeper functions. In passing it is worth pointing out that the interminable laments about the decline of standards in schools, in colleges, and in university faculties are editorial comments on various attempts to resolve precisely this dilemma. Both the decline of standards and the democratization of access are aspects of this contradiction, which is built into the disciplinary project itself.

The difficulties of achieving a desired political/cultural structuration through the activities of an elite cadre are highly resistant to definitive solution, and thus it is not surprising that J. Q. Adams had so much difficulty with developing reasonable policies for access and public services. Adams's main contribution to the evolution of the Folger Library was, however, in another area. The collection of Shakespeariana assembled by Henry Clay and Emily Jordan Folger was without doubt a significant accumulation of intellectual/cultural capital. The Folgers' collection of early editions of the plays, especially the numerous copies of the First Folio, guaranteed that it would become a major center for specialized Shakespeare study. The expansion of the library's holdings during Adams's tenure as director, however, enabled him to widen the scope of the collection.

In 1937 Adams learned that the collection of Sir Leicester Harmdsworth was about to come into the market. This was then the largest privately held collection of early English printed books in the world, and Adams recommended to the Folger Trustees that an offer to purchase the collection be submitted to the Harmdsworth estate. The financial negotiations were conducted by Stanley King, who was helped in his efforts by the family's pressing need for cash. Although the Folger bid was relatively low, they were in a position to close very quickly and this assured the success of the project. The acquisition of the Harmdsworth collection is more or less typical of the pattern of American purchase of rare books, paintings, and other cultural capital from declining European estates. This purchase, however, was fundamental in transforming the Folger from a valuable but highly specialized collection into a world-class research library. The Harmdsworth purchase was the most spectacular of J. Q. Adams's feats of library acquisition, but it was not the only one, and during his tenure the collection continued to expand.

The Folger Shakespeare Library now contains a comprehensive

range of books and other printed materials from the early modern period, representing not only England, but all the European countries that participated in the cultural movements of the Renaissance and the Enlightenment. The collection now greatly exceeds the original parameters, and it is this very excess that tends to subvert at least one important sense of disciplinarity. The traditional disciplinary boundaries, the 'cartelization' of intellectual activity, is initially encouraged by a specialized research facility like the Folger. As the collection expands, however, and the possibilities for using the materials multiply, alternative modes of contextualization are developed. The original disciplinary center, in this case Shakespeare, can begin to take on new guises. Feminist scholarship is only one example of the transgressive or revisionist modes of research now possible, and indeed it is precisely this mode that makes the sex-gender system immanent in the Shakespeare text visible for the first time. It is extremely doubtful that J. Q. Adams intended to assemble a body of evidence for a feminist research program that still lay in the future. Nevertheless, this has indeed been one of the consequences of an aggressive and expansionist acquisitions policy initially mandated by Adams's deep convictions about Shakespeare as the site of a uniform cultural discipline.

At this point it might be helpful to suggest that private collectors like Horace Howard Furness, or Sir Leicester Harmdsworth, represent something like the stage of primitive accumulation in the sphere of cultural and intellectual capital, and that the Folgers and J. Q. Adams represent a later stage of concentration of that capital. In these terms then the administration of the Folger Library's second full time director, Louis B. Wright, would represent the stage of administrative rationalization that makes active and rapid deployment of capital resources feasible.

Like Adams, Wright was originally from South Carolina, and in fact it would be interesting to explore the 'South Carolina connection' and for that matter the 'Scots-Irish connection' in relation to Shakespeare studies in the United States. Wright's *Middle Class Culture in Elizabethan England* was virtually an instant classic of literary and historical scholarship and it is still frequently cited more than fifty years after its first appearance. He was an amazingly prolific scholar who wrote on a wide range of topics.[31] In both his scholarship and his career as an administrator, first at the Huntington Library and then for more than fifteen years at the

Folger, he was guided by a very specific cultural/political agenda, one that is already clear in the study of the Elizabethan middle class. It is not really necessary to infer from Wright's scholarship what his cultural policy views were, since he committed those views to print for a variety of audiences. Before considering those documents, however, it is useful to summarize a few of his practical achievements as director of the Folger Library.

In his extensive memoirs written after his retirement as director Wright identified two technical innovations that he considered of paramount importance in the development of the Folger Library as a research facility.[32] One of his first decisions on taking over the directorship was the appointment of a professional cataloguer and the installation of the Library of Congress system as the basis for the Library's storage and retrieval systems. Wright grasped the need for standardization as a fundamental requirement for the Folger's mission as a research facility. In addition he understood that the value and the utility of the Folger collection of early printed books was closely linked to the availability of an extensive reference collection. The project of assembling reference books and appropriate contemporary studies tended to accentuate the clash of interests between book collectors and academics.[33] According to Wright, Henry Huntington thought very little of those scholars who could be so easily satisfied with a 'flood of cheap books', but then Huntington evidently had trouble understanding that it was the intellectual content of a book that interested scholars and not its material properties or its provenance.[34] Wright saw the mediation of this difference between book-collectors and scholars, between the owners of intellectual capital and the potential users of that capital, as a primary element in his position as director. He certainly did not underestimate the difficulty of this task, which he understood as a chronic divergence of interests rather than as occasional lapses or misunderstandings. Before turning to Wright's understanding of his role as cultural mediator, however, one other practical decision of his administration should be noted.

Wright considered the installation of a standardized cataloguing system one of his main achievements as director. The other – in his view equally important – was the decision to install an air-conditioning system in the reading room and the other public areas of the library. The vaults containing the rare books were already air-conditioned in order to preserve fragile materials. J. Q. Adams saw the summer weather in Washington as a natural fact that would limit the size of the Folger clientele; he certainly made no effort to expand that clientele, concentrating instead on expanding the collection. The more expansive Wright saw heat and humidity as problems that would have to be overcome if the Folger library was to achieve its full potential as a public facility. Wright had a much better sense than Adams of research as a dynamic *activity* rather than as the compilation of determinate facts. He also appreciated the elements of *Sitzfleisch* and of seeing things with your own eyes in research practice. In a sense the air-conditioning might even have been more important socially and politically than the LC cataloguing system, though it is difficult to imagine the Folger operating at its current levels without having both these improvements in its physical resources.

Wright's position as the mediator between professional scholars and the Folger's clientele among a wider intelligentsia had a complex relationship with his role in the formation of scholarly research agendas. In an important article published in *Shakespeare Survey* for 1963 Wright attempted to summarize the contradictions and the difficulties of his own institutional position. He describes himself as a broker of information, thus linking himself and the activities of the Folger Library to the financial system. Commercial and economic ideas also govern Wright's discussion of scholarly production. The quantity of Shakespeare scholarship in 1963 was no less disturbing than it is at the present time, but Wright refused to join in the lamentation over this fact.

> As an individualist and an advocate of free enterprise, I would think it
> both unwise and impracticable to try to curtail or regiment the activities
> of Shakespearean scholars. They ought to be free to follow their own
> inclinations and to write as wisely or as foolishly as their capacities and
> judgements permit.[35]

Free enterprise here does not, however, mean anarchy of production, because Wright also envisioned a regulatory agency made up of the 'wise men in the profession' who would appraise and evaluate the various contributions. The elite cadre of 'first class minds', now disembodied and genderless, would, of course, be engaged in the allocation of reputation and of other professional rewards. In other words they would be determining the research agenda for other scholars. Wright was clearly unable to recognize in this informal and unstructured regulatory institution any curtailment or regimentation of scholarly research. The obvious questions of who gets to be one of the wise men and how such a position is achieved are left unanswered. To judge from his praise of the work of Muriel Bradbrook, Wright evidently was prepared to admit some women as honorary wise men, provided they had other, unspecified qualifications. There is at least one hint as to the appropriate criteria in Wright's distress over the 'substitution of controversy for truth' and the subsequent 'deterioration of good manners' among younger historians. Here the implication that truth has a special relationship with canons of civility and with consensus has both a political and an epistemic thrust. To put it crudely, scholars shouldn't make waves, either within the disciplinary community or for that matter in the wider world. Again, this requirement will just as surely affect the shape and direction of research agendas as overt censorship and ideological control.

The shaping of the disciplinary research agenda through discrete and primarily extra-disciplinary means is related to Wright's understanding of the scholar's obligation to the public. That obligation is understood in accordance with a venerable humanistic ideology that positions professional intellectuals in a close but subordinate relationship to leadership cadres.

> Several years ago, the then American Ambassador to the United Kingdom telephoned me from New York with a request that I recommend a book about Shakespeare. He was flying back to London the next day and he had to make a speech at Stratford almost immediately on his arrival. He wanted a single volume that would explain to him the amazing appeal that Shakespeare retains for the mid-twentieth century and the significance that Shakespeare has for our generation. Perhaps it was my own ignorance, but not even the resources of the Folger Library enabled me to recommend a single book that would fully answer the Ambassador's needs. Since he was a trustee of my own institution, I felt doubly embarrassed. Ever since then I have been wondering why, with all the energy we have devoted to Shakespeare, somebody has not attempted that sort of book in language that an Ambassador of cultivation and intelligence would comprehend.[36]

This is in many ways an amazing little text and it might possibly be an example of very subtle irony. Certainly if Wright had used the phrase 'a book in language that *even* an Ambassador . . . could

85

comprehend' it would underscore the trivial and callous nature of the original request. Wright must have understood, at some level of consciousness, that the demand for a single volume that would explain Shakespeare's appeal was both stupid and insulting. But Wright claims to be embarrassed, not for the ambassador, but for himself. Here no less a figure than the director of the Folger Shakespeare Memorial Library is forced to play the role of Charlie the Tuna. The ambassador clearly hasn't the time for good taste, he wants tuna that tastes good and Wright is forced to admit that this is a need he cannot satisfy, even with the resources of the Folger Library at his disposal.

It would be wrong to make too much of this singular anecdote, but it would be naïve to ignore its implications completely. There is no doubt that without some solid basis of ideological sympathy and shared interests with individuals and groups within the leadership cadres, Wright simply would not have been able to function as director of a facility like the Folger Library. Despite obvious difficulties it is possible to manage and administer such an organization even when an important constituency for that organization stands outside the discourse and the professional sanctions of the institution.[37] However, bizarre contradictions are likely to be manifested on a more or less regular basis. In order to function well in these circumstances, it is extremely helpful to have a strong and well-developed ideological outlook. Louis B. Wright's ideology is abundantly clear in his voluminous scholarly output.

One of the many small ironies of contemporary intellectual history is the way *Middle Class Culture in Elizabethan England* is so frequently cited in contemporary Marxist criticism. It is unlikely that Wright really wanted to advance the interests of Marxist scholarship, but there is a reason for this odd convergence. Marxists have frequently described the age in which Shakespeare lived as the moment of the heroic emergence of the bourgeoisie. At that moment of emergence bourgeois practical consciousness still had a primarily emancipatory thrust, and it represented the most progressive sector within the population. Wright's work, in *Middle Class Culture in Elizabethan England*, and in his other historical writing, provides both documentation and elaboration of this hypothesis. The greatness of Elizabethan literature is, moreover, ascribed to precisely this historical energy. Unlike the Marxist literary scholars who were his contemporaries, however, Wright made an analysis of this historical phenomenon that is uniformly affirmative. Furthermore, as far as

Wright is concerned the heroic emergence of the bourgeoisie is still going on, and he is himself a participant in that emergence. His elaboration of themes like the entrepreneurial spirit, the conquest of the frontier, and the rule of law, reveal that Wright has fully embraced a hegemonic ideology in all its contradictoriness. It is this ideology that enables him and the institution that he represents to share a common ground with a wider ensemble of hegemonic interests.

In a sense the Folger and the Furness libraries are exactly what their founders might have claimed, that is, enduring monuments to their love for Shakespeare, a love they intended to share with others. Since this love and generosity are offered without any obvious expectation of return, it has every appearance of being both innocent and disinterested in the very best sense. It is undoubtedly churlish to take up a critical attitude to this, but at this point some sort of provisional conclusions about the effect of an institution of this kind on the actual practice of scholarship are in order. It should be clear that such humanist notions as the erotics of reading, the ethos of preservation, and devotion to the public welfare that are the primary themes in the self-understanding of the founders cannot provide an adequate account of the actual practice of the institution. These notions are 'true' in the sense that they are the expression of genuinely felt impulses and desires. But they are also idealizations that mask other aspects of the social order instantiated by the institutions in question.

Libraries can lock their doors, or they can restrict access to their resources, but libraries as organized collections of books and other artifacts cannot directly control what their clients will produce. Professional librarians are by training and inclination 'content neutral' with respect to the research interests of individual scholars. In general, academic freedom is fully respected within the immediate life-world of librarians and their clientele. A library like the Folger Shakespeare Memorial can serve a variety of interests, but this does not imply that as an institution it is innocent of ideological investment. As it is presently constituted the Folger has a differentiated constituency, an ensemble of publics unified by the feeling that Shakespeare is central to the cultural identity of the United States. Under the direction of O. B. Hardison the Folger Library became more worldly and less parochial in its public orientation. During this most recent period of its development the library has been very closely integrated both with important government agencies, with a consortium of universities, and with private industry and finance.[38] It is this constellation of interests, this differentiated system of publics that constitutes Shakespeare's America. The library effects an interpretation of Shakespeare's America not by determining what scholarship will say, but by predetermining what there is to talk about.

Specialized research libraries exert a shaping influence on scholarly research through policies that decide not only what is worth collecting but also what constitutes a complete and coherent body of materials. In these terms Shakespeare defines a cultural plenitude. He becomes both center and origin for the activity of research. For scholars, the lavishness of collections like the Folger Shakespeare Memorial Library is seductive. Research in such an environment becomes identified with personal responsiveness to the wealth of materials collected. Such responsiveness is best expressed in accordance with a humane, liberal ideology oriented to research projects that unify the disparate items in the archive. Projects like editing texts, theater history, historicist accounts of sixteenth- and seventeenth-century world-consciousness, and genre-oriented literary studies all fulfill in different ways the requirement of synoptic unity. By the same token these research problems respect the autonomy and affirm the completeness of the object studied, whether text, performance, or historical period. Shakespeare's America takes shape as a successor culture to Shakespeare's England. That cultural identity is confirmed by the prevailing historicist orientation prompted by the organization of the Folger collection.

The Folger collection is not just a carefully housed, passive collection of intellectual objects, but a complex social agency that facilitates a particular set of tasks. Obviously one kind of task that is made much easier to conceive and to carry out is the project of editing the Shakespeare text. Although ostensibly the resources exist to serve the needs of editors, at times it seems as if the activity of doing editions, and indeed the need to edit itself, is mandated by the existence of these rich resources. The range and heterogeneity of the early editions, and their centralized location in the Folger collection defines the task of editing as a problem in the determination of origins. The text becomes a way to unify at least one source of authority.

The rare book library has perhaps a more subtle kind of impact on the practice of historical scholarship. The Folger collection is selected in accordance with two related theoretical models for cultural history. First and most obvious is the notion of 'The Man and His Works'. This notion entails the tacit incorporation of the practice of individualized artistic production as an ethical norm applicable both to Shakespeare and to research about him. Second, by assembling materials on Shakespeare and his immediate contemporaries, collections of this kind incorporate a distinctly historicist bias in the way the archive defines an orientation to the problems of history. Researchers are prompted to conceive historical periods as self-contained and self-defined periods, epochs, or moments. As a methodology this requires that research select and privilege those elements in a culture that are specific to that culture understood as a synchronic unit. But of course there is never an historical ensemble of social and cultural relations that consists only of elements specific to its own chronological moment.

Historicism in both its older traditional form and in its new, improved variant, is best understood as a method or even as a hermeneutic based on the idea of development.[39] Objects and states of affairs are explained by their position in an historical sequence defined by currently existing conditions. On this view the meaning of the past can be understood in its own terms, because each synchronic period is finished and complete as a stage in a unified pattern of development. This organic view of change may be inflected either as an optimistic or as a sentimental interpretation of history. In both of these orientations, however, the concept of development privileges notions of the organically unified individual and of the organically unified nation. What is missing from these accounts is not the possibility of individual resistance or contestatory social agencies, but rather the idea that history is still going on, so that its meaning is therefore necessarily provisional and strategic.

Libraries like the Folger, the Huntington, and the Furness collection are 'objectively conservative' in that the acquisition, organization, and format of the materials reflects the social and affective interests of the founders, trustees, and directors of the facilities. Nevertheless, such collections contain texts and other kinds of potentialities that are oppositional and contestatory vis-à-vis the dominant social groups of which these individuals are representative. It is important to realize that the interests of the people who created these facilities are complex, not easily summarized, and that their motivations cannot satisfactorily be reduced to the desire to enhance their own social and cultural power. Quite apart from the specific intentions of the institution-makers, however, radical and critical potentialities are built into the institution's founding impulse, which is to accumulate a very large reservoir of intellectual capital on a comprehensive plan. This capital is then obviously available for appropriation by interests other than the 'objectively conservative' ones referred to above. It is also clear that these institutions not only *contain* history in the sense of providing physical storage for historical documents, but also participate in history in the sense that policy-makers, and therefore cultural policy itself, is subject to revision and even radical alteration. The cultural inertia sedimented in these institutions is very powerful; the direction in which these forces move is not predetermined. Despite the tranquil atmosphere and the urbanity of those who work in these centers of scholarly research, there is at present a very real and in some ways acrimonious struggle taking place within the institutional space. This is primarily discursive struggle, and it is by no means recent in its inception. Even purely discursive struggle, however, has real political import-ance and can ensue in real political action – or inaction.

Chapter four

EDITING THE TEXT: THE DEUTERONOMIC RECONSTRUCTION OF AUTHORITY

The status of Shakespeare as a canonical author is well established and has not been in doubt for a considerable period of time. Although that status is the result of self-replicating institutional structures and of strategic deliberation within those structures, the discourse on Shakespeare does not reflect the political and administrative concerns that determine his cultural positioning.[1] Shakespeare's status is treated as a natural fact; the institutional elaboration of his work is then implicitly described as a natural consequence of intrinsic qualities that exert an irresistible force on later generations. This idealization of the literary material sanctions a 'return to the text' as the decisive ethical move, conceding authority to Shakespeare and then moving directly to the question of what the great author has to say. The idea of a return to the text is an axiological assumption within the discourse on Shakespeare, but such an idea has immediate sociological consequences within the institutional practices that concern themselves with his writing.[2]

The history of the text is closely tied to the hermeneutic problem itself and to the emergence of new definitions of editorial principles in both an ethical and a methodological sense. But no matter how the hermeneutic problem is resolved, the idea of a return to the text assigns very considerable secular authority to editors and philological researchers. A number of specialized research facilities appear to have been organized so as to facilitate this task. Within the hierarchy of professional activities editing continues to be assigned a high rank. Nothing confirms a professional reputation more securely than 'doing an edition' and nothing is more likely to be controversial.[3]

91

THE FIRST FOLIO AS A DEUTERONOMIC PROGRAM

In writing the history of textual editing as an institution, the publication of the First Folio must be recorded as the decisive founding event. The broad, implicit claims of the First Folio have not been, indeed could never have been questioned, at least not within the practical domains of pedagogy and philological research, or within the social domain of elite culture. To begin with, the First Folio established the principle of legitimate succession, although not necessarily the identity of the legitimate successors. This legitimate succession is, moreover, to be embodied in a text that will provide the exclusive channel or medium of transmission.

> We pray you do not Envie his Friends, the office of their care and paine, to have collected and published them; and so to have published them, as where (before) you were abused with diverse stolne and surreptitious copies, maimed and deformed by the frauds and stealthes of iniurious imposters, that exposed them, even those, are now offered to your view cur'd and perfect of their limbes (sig. A3).

The primary claim here is made against rival editors, whose 'stolne and surreptitious' texts are stigmatized as unauthorized and deformed. But there is a further, implicit claim here as well. Alternative media of tradition, that is, other institutional vehicles such as oral preservation in a theater company, are also excluded from the line of legitimate succession and for all intents and purposes abolished as primary sources of authority.

Interpretation within new or different social and historical contexts will be dominated by the ethical imperatives of preservation, restoration, and the return to lost origins. In addition, the First Folio establishes the principle of closure and indeed offers the guarantee that it will put an end to the sporadic appearance of more plays by Shakespeare. The declared aim of the editors of the First Folio is to provide a faithful and accurate scribal transcription of various works by Shakespeare which have reached the public through unauthorized channels and in degraded form. In a sense, however, they are not merely the founders of a program of inquiry into the correct textual form of an origin, but the inventors of that origin. Heminge and Condell, like Peter and Paul, create the foundations of the Shakespeare institution itself, by turning Shakespeare into a properly formatted and presentable literary author.[4]

The achievements of these founding editors were imperfect, to be sure, and the First Folio is certainly not regarded as definitive or even particularly reliable as copy-text for Shakespeare's editors. The canon of writings as specified by the First Folio contains a fairly large number of anomalies, exceptional cases, and atypical examples – 'early plays', 'problem comedies', collaborations, corruptions, and typographical errors. In addition, many canonical text are intractably problematic from an editorial point of view, derived from heterogeneous and not always reliable textual sources with differing relationships with what is assumed to be the author's original composition. Nevertheless, the First Folio is a decisive event in the foundation of the Shakespeare institution and in the definition of a canon of his works in that it establishes its own Deuteronomic program as the basis for defining Shakespeare's authority.

To speak of a 'Deuteronomic program' in relation to the works of Shakespeare is to emphasize the element of secondariness and of retrospective constitution of the definitive form of those works. This should not be construed as a suggestion that this material was really or originally written by some other person. The Deuteronomic program, however, applies to various unfinished original writings by Shakespeare a specific and historically limited model of literary authorship, specifically the model of individualized artistic production. The compilers of the First Folio thus seem to have followed or imitated the practice, eccentric and innovative at the time, of Ben Jonson, in presenting theatrical scripts to the public in a finished literary format as if they were classical (that is, ancient) texts. Jonson was at some pains to nominate himself an *author* (rather than a playwright), and, in his encomium for his colleague, he recruits Shakespeare to the same *métier*. What this amounts to is not a case of 'the death of the author' but rather the posthumous coming-into-being of an author. Shakespeare's dramatic works, as published in the First Folio, are Deuteronomic in respect of earlier modes of textual production. These were characteristic of a quite different set of working conditions and a radically different allocation of authority and division of labor from that implied in the proto-industrial reproduction of collected literary works.[5]

Shakespeare's authority thus enters into our cultural history via this particular pathway of dissemination; this entails the creation of a specific 'monopoly of knowledge' the function of which is to administer certain redemptive media by regulating the material form in which the authority is mediated for a public. This has obvious social and political implications in that the administrative regulation of a textual corpus obviously takes precedence over the practical, day-to-day exegesis of any part of that corpus. Determination of what is to constitute substantive culture is perhaps even more decisive than the administrative policies that determine access to that substantive culture. In any case the Deuteronomic program is one that follows the practice of assigning responsibility for its own work in producing both substantive culture and modes of consciousness defined by that culture to a nominal authority who is at once removed from direct accountability, and at the same time firmly in the control of the administrative institution that functions in his name. The First Folio is a fascinating example of the type of cultural event known as a renaissance in the way it promises an archaeological rescue operation, or Deuteronomic reconstruction, of an originating authority who is historically absent.

Deuteronomy is taken from Greek *deutero* or second and *nomos* or law, but this is only a rough translation of the Hebrew term sometimes rendered as 'the law of Moses' and sometimes as 'repeated law'. It is now widely believed that this is the only one of the books of the Pentateuch that was actually written by Moses, though strict traditionalists still adhere to the position that the five books of Moses are a single, unified scripture.[6] The story of the accidental discovery of a copy of what we now call Deuteronomy is related in 2 Kings: 22. This discovery leads Josiah, then King of Israel, to rend his garments as he begins to understand that 'our fathers have not hearkened unto the words of this book, to do according unto all that which is written concerning us'. The passage suggests a chronic tension between alternative redemptive media and between competing institutional agencies for the administration of political/religious authority.[7] It also suggests the idea of a 'restored text' as a resolution of that tension. In any case it is clear that a 'second law' can supplant an apparently earlier institutional dispensation. In the structure of the Pentateuch, the book of Deuteronomy is last, not because it is 'later' but because it repeats and sums up the various historical narratives and legal codes that are set forth in the preceding books. The 'second law' is actually a restored form of an original law, and therefore it can claim ethical priority over its predecessor. The business-as-usual dispensation that precedes the restoration is an institutional milieu that compromises the purity of the origin.

In the case of Shakespeare the 'first law' or original institutional medium would have to be defined in terms of a vernacular protocol of speech, by a popular theater defining the sociology of reception, and by relations of production characteristic of the atelier or guild milieu in which Shakespeare worked. Within this ensemble of relations a text is always unfinished and in a sense ephemeral. The second law or Deuteronomic program is constituted in accordance with notions of a literary language, by elite canons of reception, and by the practice of individualized artistic production.[8] Textual scholarship is in fact implicated in something considerably more complex than simply guaranteeing accuracy of transmission. The very idea of a specifically *textual* accuracy already pre-supposes notions of property rights and rights of succession in respect of that property. In the case of Shakespeare this idea of property rights is understood from the outset to be an indivisible unity.

The publication of the First Folio should be seen as an early and a decisive victory for the Deuteronomic program in which a full and unified conception of 'The Man and His Works' virtually abolishes all other local, fragmentary versions of Shakespeare. This event gives precedence to a written text in final form over all manifestations of prophetic or charismatic authority, and in particular over the forms of anomie and of illicit authority characteristic of the theater.[9] The existence of such a text is, in fact, an expression of a profound anti-theatricalism in the cultural institutions of early modern Europe and in the successor cultures of North America as well.[10] The superior force of written or printed textuality favor the formation of a complex monopoly of knowledge that has the capacity to disseminate a uniform version of a particular canon over a wide geographical and social space.[11] This superiority of force gives rise to a distinctive ideological formation connected with all canon-formation, namely the ethos of preservation. This outlook assumes that it is definitely better for the Shakespeare canon to exist than for it not to exist. It assumes further that the canon should be both large *and* exclusive. The more of Shakespeare we have, the better for us, provided only that no spurious or wrongfully attributed material is smuggled in. The First Folio then does rather more than merely preserve the text of plays that might otherwise have been lost. It also provides the basis for a full and elaborate classification and hierarchization of Shakespeare's *oeuvre*.

The aim of the First Folio was to round up all the genuine Shakespeare plays and to put them inside the safe confines of a single volume where they could be easily distinguished from plays by anyone not Shakespeare. The First Folio accounts for the preservation of roughly half the plays we know to be Shakespeare's. In other words, without the efforts of Heminge and Condell the list of plays would very much smaller and we would not have any knowledge that texts such as *Coriolanus* ever existed. The existence of a larger rather than a smaller canon of plays makes it possible to extend the domain of application of the concept of the Shakespearean without confusing the boundary between the genuine and the spurious. It also establishes the basis for a critical meta-narrative of development and expressive unity. In that meta-narrative considerable importance is given to the idea of a Last Play, one that provides a synoptic resolution of contradictions present throughout the development of the Shakespearean *oeuvre*. The apparently neutral efforts of philological research and reconstruction of the text are clearly motivated by some such idea of synoptic resolution.

Viewed from a certain distance the canon of plays appears stable and quiescent. But from another perspective the entire project may appear quite ready to come unravelled. In addition to the two mutually exclusive categories of plays (Shakespeare's, not Shakespeare's) there are several others which can give rise to particularly uneasy feelings. In addition to such minor anomalies as 'early plays' and incidental corruptions which do not materially threaten the ideal form of the finished and complete *oeuvre* there are also canonical plays, parts of which were not written by Shakespeare. There are *pseudepigrapha*, plays wrongfully attributed to Shakespeare, although some of these were published in later editions of the Folio text, for example, *Locrine*, and *The Merry Devil of Edmonton*. Finally there is at least one play, *The Two Noble Kinsmen*, that is apocryphal in the complex sense of something hidden or held in reserve, supplementary to the canon but excluded from full and equal membership.[12]

The First Folio thus accomplishes several purposes at once. It establishes priority for the conception of 'The Man and His Works' as a unified totality. It effectively claims cultural authority and power for the printed text as the 'legitimate' institutional medium of transmission and diminishes the theater to the status of a subaltern, the dutiful agent of superior cultural authority. It substitutes the ethos of preservation for radical or prophetic revisionism, and emphatically opposes the legitimacy of the anomie and social effervescence most characteristic of the Elizabethan popular theaters. Finally, it sets the pattern for the practice of Deuteronomic reconstruction as such, a practice which is thematized as a restoration or return to origin, in other words the salvaging of values for an authentically reconstructed tradition from the decay and degeneracy of an illegitimate institutional succession. The First Folio, then, even with its many imperfections, objectifies the very principle of legitimate authority as restored by patient philological erudition; Heminge and Condell in this respect emulate the humanist scholars of the Renaissance whose work was devoted to the restoration of classical rather than vernacular writings. The Shakespeare institution is thus founded within the larger humanist project of philological research and editorial scholarship, although hints of a shady institutional past persist both in the text and in the history of its reception.

The historical success of textuality and of the powerful institutional apparatus that supports it coincides with the virtual collapse of theater as a strong, independent center of cultural authority. In the case of the canonical, that is to say, the Deuteronomic Shakespeare, the power of the text has been used against the theater, disabling its capacity as the site of cultural and social institution-making, and cancelling its function in the creation of an alternative agential space. This is, I take it, the real meaning of the incessant border disputes, skirmishes, and raids carried out between advocates of performance-oriented interpretation and the practitioners of more strictly literary and textually based hermeneutic procedures. The text versus performance debate, like so many other professional disputes, is in fact a quarrel over precedence and the allocation of authority. One reason for the largely trivial character of this debate is that the question of authority is never openly addressed, nor is there any sense among advocates of the autonomy of performance where their own authority might come from.

Canon formation is never an entirely self-evident process. The unity and coherence of the conception of 'The Man and His Works' is of course itself open to question. But the idea of a canon is in any case not identical with the existence of 'great work'; recognition of canonical status is a social event that necessarily occurs after the fact. The specific case of Shakespeare is one with peculiar philological difficulties. Although the social event of canonization has undoubtedly taken place some time ago, it is now accepted by some textual scholars that access to Shakespeare's original compositions may not be possible in principle. More radically, it has been suggested that the plays' first form of existence was as a series of more or less ephemeral 'versions', and even that no *finished* originals of any kind ever existed. The situation is complicated by the existence of a number of case-by-case preservations, some of which have been traditionally designated as 'bad', which is to say contaminated by the presence of writing or other modifications not by Shakespeare. Despite this there is a very broad consensus that there are some thirty-seven plays, possibly thirty-eight, which count as members of a Shakespeare canon, even though the actual creation of that canon and not merely the fact of canonization happened in retrospect.

Notwithstanding the historical peculiarities connected with the preservation and the transmission of these texts there is now a full Deuteronomic compilation. This *oeuvre* has been elaborated and 'perfected' over time by a powerful constellation of institutions whose task has been to preserve and to represent, through a process of complex philological reconstruction, the lost original documents. In fact these editions, beginning with the First Folio, should probably be thought of as representing in the sense of 'standing in for' or acting as a kind of delegate or textual fiduciary for the lost originals. This substitution might appear to weaken the claim of the Deuteronomic project to authoritative status, but in fact the force of this project is actually enhanced and strengthened by the effacement of the originals, which can be nuanced and reconstructed in ways that favor the continuity of certain institutional forms, and the discontinuity of others. One reason for this enhanced authority is, of course the incremental value that the textual objects have acquired by virtue of their threatened loss and subsequent recuperation. This is further enhanced by the retrospective character of all Deuteronomic projects, which carry the implicit guarantee that everything merely ephemeral has been excluded from what is otherwise a finished totality. There is an additional guarantee of course, namely that this is the last word of the author in question, and that there is therefore nothing more to be added at a future date. Finally, the editors or compilers of a Deuteronomic project do not write or compose in their own name, but in the name of an authority who is already absent, receding from contingent social reality. The authority of a Deuteronomic project is thus from the outset 'traditional' even though it ultimately purports to derived from an individual authorial source.

Gerald Bruns has suggested that the idea of a canon is a political rather than a literary category. What is at stake in the definition of a canon, that is the listing and classification of a body of canonical texts, is nothing less than a struggle for secular power, in particular the power to invoke the force of collective tradition and to specify its content. This is in effect a religious power, the power to administer and control the redemptive media. Such control is not limited to purely textual or interpretive issues, however, but is also clearly related to secular functions connected with the allocation of social status.[13] In the light of the importance of editing to the social/political positioning of Shakespeare in American culture, a fuller analysis of the history of this practice is in order.

SCIENTIFIC BIBLIOGRAPHY AND THE IDEAL TEXT

The first American editions of Shakespeare's work appeared on the market early in the nineteenth century, but these were essentially reprints of British editions. The first significant editorial scholarship to be done by an American is generally considered to be Horace Howard Furness's *New Variorum*, which first began to appear in 1871. However, even before that, an important *theoretical* discussion of the problem of text and authorship had been developed by Ralph Waldo Emerson. Although he was not by any means a textual scholar, Emerson's view of authorship, especially as this is related to Shakespeare, certainly had its impact on the work of Furness and his many successors.

Emerson's view of authorship derives primarily from a romantic ideology of expressive individuality. His views were, however, conditioned by the achievements of the 'higher criticism' that radically altered his sense of the 'authority of scripture'.[14] The philosophically complex view of the autonomous subject elaborated by Emerson is deepened and reinforced in his historical account of the sociology of literary production operative in Shakespeare's time. Emerson clearly realizes that proprietary notions of the literary work, individualized artistic production, and such auxiliary phenomena as copyright law are institutional forms of relatively recent historical appearance.

Shakespeare's atelier, his working conditions, are those of a theater not yet organized to favor the interests of proprietary authorship, and certainly not yet subordinated to the modalities of the printed text.

> At the time [Shakespeare] left Stratford and went up to London, a great body of stage-plays existed and were in turn produced on the boards. . . . All the mass has been treated with more or less skill, by every playwright, and the prompter has the soiled and tattered manuscripts. It is now no longer possible to say who wrote them first. They have been the property of the theatre so long, and so many rising geniuses have enlarged or altered them, inserting a speech or a whole scene, or adding a song, that no man can any longer claim copyright in this work of numbers. . . . Shakespeare, in common with his comrades, esteemed the mass of old plays waste stock, in which any experiment could be freely tried.[15]

Emerson's view entails both an idealization of authorship as sovereign and magisterial originality *and* a diametrically opposed sociological view of authorship as a collective practice ultimately dispersed back into the most diffuse sphere of social utterance. This position thus contains two entirely different ways of understanding the dialectic that exists in the relationship between a magisterial originating word and the ministerial reproduction, dissemination, and exegesis of that originating word. From these alternatives, two entirely different editorial philosophies can be derived. One of these is the project of Deuteronomic reconstruction, which has already been described. Emerson's privileging of 'originality' certainly authorizes such a project. It is that orientation, rather than the alternative view of authorship as the recycling of 'waste stock', that has been predominant in all subsequent editorial practice.

Horace Howard Furness's *New Variorum* edition has already been mentioned in the context of Furness's other institution-making activities. It is probably only a coincidence that Furness would eventually apply his considerable editorial experience to the project of a new translation of the Bible, but the connection is certainly suggestive.[16] In any case, the *New Variorum* has a distinctive importance in its own right as a contribution to textual scholarship. Furness's edition did not discover any novel editorial principles, nor did it derive from new evidence or even fresh research into old

100

evidence. Although he appreciated the need to return to the oldest versions and especially to the First Folio, the immediate basis of his *New Variorum* was the Old Cambridge Edition edited by William Aldis Wright. This edition was considered by many the most careful and most nearly definitive of the critical or eclectic editions of Shakespeare.

Furness adopted the format used in the Old Cambridge Edition, together with many substantive readings, but this was augmented by an extensive apparatus that provided readers with an exhaustive account of innumerable textual variants. The Cambridge Edition had been eclectic in that variantswere chosen on a more or less *ad hoc* basis, sometimes on philological grounds, sometimes on sheer editorial preference. The objective was to produce a single 'best' text and to exclude undesirable variants at the same time. Furness was not able to go beyond the theoretical horizons of the eclectic text; however, in his apparatus he aimed not at excluding undesirable variants, but rather at making those variants available for comparison. One of the distinctive features of the *New Variorum* is in Furness's judicious presentation of the claims of alternative readings. The *New Variorum* was thus valuable as a concise textual history, quite apart from its perhaps questionable standing as a reliable text of Shakespeare's plays.

The original aims of the *New Variorum* are a manifest impossibility, and in fact the project is still unfinished. Despite the Quixotic ambitions of Furness and his successors, however, the idea of a comprehensive overview of all existing variants has had real importance in the overall development of research agendas in respect of Shakespeare. The idea of rationalizing the history and the dispersal of the text through a complete archive of its variants has real cogency. However, it seems evident that such an archive cannot itself take the form of a printed edition, since any determinate edition instantiates the very problem the archive is supposed to overcome, that is, the concretization of a historically determinate set of editorial decisions. Even the most comprehensive variorum would be subject to the same historical obsolescence it was designed to rationalize. Nevertheless, Furness's more or less democratic and ecumenical attitude to the text's multiple historical identities has had durable importance in the subsequent history of textual research, even though the *New Variorum* as a unified project seems destined to remain forever unfinished. Furness's was not the first variorum edition to be published, but its impact on textual and bibliographical scholarship was unprecedented. Although it was at first based on the Old Cambridge Edition, the *New Variorum* eventually encouraged the formation of scholarly techniques that would in turn bring about the complete elimination of the eclectic text as the horizon of editorial practice.

The idea of an archive of historical variants is, of course, best realized in the spatial form of a library and in this respect Henry Clay Folger's contribution to textual scholarship should be counted as extremely significant, even though he was not himself an editor or scholar. The Folger Library contains 79 copies of The First Folio, a fact that is no mere feat of acquisitiveness but that has real bibliographical and editorial significance. The various copies are not in fact identical, and reveal changes of many kinds within the Folio text itself. Obviously inspection of these differences can be done with much greater efficiency once they have been brought together in one place. An even higher level of technical efficiency can be achieved through techniques of mechanization. Charlton Hinman's pioneering work in this regard eventually led him to become a textual agnostic.[17] But the idea of minute and exhaustive inspection of all known variants has encouraged other textual scholars to pursue a more definitive and final goal, namely the achievement of an established text that would bring to an end the process of interminable editorial labor and interminable textual obsolescence.

The most militant and for a time at least the most influential of the advocates of an established text over the past fifty years has been Fredson Bowers.[18] Bowers's hopes were predicated on the principles of scientific bibliography first elaborated by W. W. Greg, R. B. McKerrow and A. W. Pollard.[19] These scholars had developed a research program that was designed to advance textual scholarship beyond the unsystematic and *ad hoc* selectivity of the eclectic editors like W. A. Wright, or the random and whimsical philological conjectures of C. M. Ingleby. Bowers is particularly critical of the misplaced and naïve literary judgement that guided so many of the editorial decisions in the Old Cambridge Edition. According to Bowers the editors of that text had no rational method for distinguishing the original from its piracies. Instead, editors like W. A. Wright exhibited

a humanistic faith in the ability of literary taste to recover by successive refinement a substantially exact text for an author like Shakespeare. Any doubts could be traced to the fear that the extraordinary history of corruption of the Shakespearean texts at the hands of players and venal printers might . . . defeat critical taste.[20]

Bowers regards the eclectic editors as dupes or patsies; the real villains are the players and venal printers. But even though eclectic editors are exonerated from deliberate and willful malfeasance, their decision-making protocol is denounced as unprincipled. The irrationality of the eclectic reliance on literary taste is apparent once the aim of editing has been defined as the restoration of an original – as opposed to its improvement. Bowers's own irrationality will become evident at a later point in the argument; in his own self-understanding, of course, the desirability of adopting 'scientific bibliography' lay in its ability to place editorial scholarship on a rational basis.

The eventual purpose of scientific bibliography is to achieve an established text that represents, as nearly as possible, the 'ideal text' as it existed before the fall into materiality and corruption.[21] The aim of re-pristination of the text must, of course, be qualified in light of irreparable damage or loss, but it nevertheless constitutes for Bowers and for many of his associates a genuine horizon of possibility. On this view the objective of reaching the established text is not an end in itself, but the means for a more reliable and authoritative exegesis. A 'critical text', in Bowers's lexicon, is a text that critics and exegetes can work with without having to engage in textual researches on their own.[22] This assumes, of course, that textual scholars and exegetes understand each other's real interests and that there is a background consensus that permits orderly control of the redemptive media. This is manifestly a project that exceeds textual scholarship as such, one that incorporates both a hermeneutics of reconstitution *and* a specific sociology of reception. For Bowers these larger principles are self-evident. His energy is devoted to advocacy of particular techniques for achieving these ends.

The methods of scientific bibliography demand the minutest physical scrutiny of material evidence with the aim of reconstructing the actual process of textual production. For reasons that he does not provide, Bowers incorporated into this project of reconstruction the doctrine of an ideal text and a lost original. These two categories are themselves somewhat equivocal, since at times Bowers appears to regard the terms as synonymous, while at other times they are definitely two historically distinct states of affairs. Although there is nothing in the method of scientific bibliography that requires such a doctrine of an ideal text and a lost original, or even suggests it, this model of textual origins nevertheless held compelling sway over Bowers's thinking.

> Once we temper the too violent reaction to the faulty conventions on which early editors based their eclecticism, and do not confuse bad practice with good principle, we may view the cult of the single, most authoritative original document with clearer eyes. And viewing this equally faulty counter-reaction at its true value, we may grant that the problem of the 'most authoritative words' cannot be solved by facsimile or facsimile-style reprints which in their conservatism provide no more than textual raw material to the critic. The eclectic effort to recover from the transmitted documents the exact wording of the author's lost original does not constitute unnecessary editorial interposition, we may continue to grant, so long as its principles are critically, linguistically, and bibliographically sound.[23]

On this view, the purely mechanical reproduction of the *earliest* printed texts would only perpetuate errors and degradations connected with the faulty practice of the early editors and compositors. Bowers is committed to a higher aim in his own project, which is precisely to remove, so far as possible, the residual errors that hinder access to the author's original.

The idea of a 'lost original' in the very restricted sense of a single working copy that the various compositors used to guide their work is not unreasonable. Nor is it unreasonable to suppose that the copy provided to the printers was just that, a copy of some other document which is 'closer' to the author, or at least in some different relationship to the author than the printing-house copy. Even in a situation where the various sections of a text were worked on by several different compositors or even in different locations, both the concept of the 'job' as a unified task and some notion of the administrative co-ordination of the various workers must have been in operation. The problem is, of course, in determining exactly what relation the printing-house copy had to work produced by the *individual* author. Here a variety of hypotheses come into play, though the technical alternatives – author's foul papers, playhouse foul papers or prompt copy, various fair copies of differing accuracy and trustworthiness, piracies, and so on will not be discussed here. The technical questions as to how a text is 'transmitted' presuppose a set of interrelated axiological or normative assumptions and various sociological hypotheses about texts, authorship, the printing industry, and the way these social relations of production are related to the specific institutional setting of the theater.[24] It is clear that as far as Bowers is concerned the various types of 'textual raw material' have differing social status and that the social differentiation is construed hierarchically. The highest position in that hierarchy is occupied by the author, a singular figure who enjoys full discursive sovereignty over an 'ideal text'. The historical life of that 'ideal text' is then read in the light of an irresistible communications entropy; the text can only suffer degradation, distortion, in short, insult and injury. Nothing in the historical life of that text can augment its existence, its worth or social status, at least not in relation to the originating ideal text. Bowers certainly understands that editors can and do emend texts and thus improve them, but the improvement is judged in relation to the accumulated prior degradation and is not meant to bear comparison with the 'lost original'.[25] The author, projected in an ideal text, is by definition that which cannot be improved.

Although Bowers's commitment to the ideal text was absolutely militant, he recognized that a historical individual such as Shakespeare or Dekker may have had considerable difficulty in actualizing such an ideal text. Further, Bowers is clear in stipulating that the ideal text does not necessarily exist in any historically specific time or place. In other words imperfectly actualized holograph versions of the ideal text may be transferred or transmitted into imperfect or inaccurate printshop copy without ever passing through the state in which the ideal text is embodied in material form. The ideal text is a normative concept rather than a practical or historical one. For Bowers and other like-minded critical editors the ideal text is simply the preferred form in which to locate a magisterial authority. In a sense then all material forms of transmission are diminished to a ministerial status. If this logic is followed through rigorously then the physical act of writing down the ideal text is itself a diminution of a prior, magisterial authority. Writing something down already introduces a corruption into writing as such. This is without doubt a logocentric orientation, but somehow it seems pointless to discover that Fredson Bowers is guilty of logocentricity. Bowers in this sense clearly has nothing to hide, it would never have occurred to him that there was anything wrong with a logocentric bias. And indeed much of his writing about problems of the text and its transmission develop legitimations of this position.

It is certainly clear from everything he has written that Fredson Bowers regards the 'ideal text' as something that really exists even though there is no material object that actually corresponds to such an existent. The point of the axiological assumption of an ideal text is that it provides the ethical basis for an important social/sociological distinction. For Fredson Bowers the crucial moment, the 'fall into materiality' and the consequent 'fall into textual corruption' happens at the moment the ideal text is transferred to the workplace. The crucial boundary line is the one that separates the life of the mind from the sphere of manual labor. In its broad outlines the distinction between mental work and manual work is an ancient one. Bowers is working with a more recent version of this binary opposition, one in which the distinction is made between the 'priceless values' associated with the ideal text and the corrupted world of 'players and venal printers', a world characterized not only by the predominance of market relations and a preference for the meretricious over the authentic, but also by a further degradation in the form of an ignorant and depraved working class.

Despite his stress on sovereign, individual expressivity, it would be difficult to convict Bowers of an over-investment in a romantic ideology of genius and of genial authorship. Bowers certainly assumes a sovereign and magisterial authority flowing from an author and presumably sedimented in the 'lost original' that forms the basis for the transmission of a text. However, his views of that authority are more those of a latter-day Augustan than of a romantic. For Bowers the magisterial authority of an author stems not from expressive autonomy, wholeness, and freedom, but from the social status achieved by the individuals who create literary texts.

The dream of achieving the 'final establishment of Shakespeare's text' now seems, in light of the volume of critical argumentation arrayed against it, pathetic and perhaps downright ludicrous. But what could have motivated Bowers to cling to this ideal so tenaciously? Bowers's unexamined belief in the existence of an ideal text and his faith in the methods of scientific bibliography are the primary visible elements in this longing for a state of achieved finality. Less apparent is the socio-political motivation for these beliefs. The idea of the singular and definitive resolution of the text is never separate, in Bowers's mind, from the problem of the practical exegesis of that text.

> A text suitable for a critic must, inevitably, be an established text. Hence an edition is critical in the . . . sense that critical principles have been applied to the textual raw material of the authoritative preserved documents in order to approach as nearly as may be to the ideal of the authorial fair copy.[26]

The existence of 'textual raw material' suggests to Bowers that there must be a singular origin in the form of an authorial fair copy. In order to understand exactly what this imperative *means* however, it is necessary to consider Bowers's view of exegesis itself.

> [it] is still a current oddity that many a literary critic has investigated the past ownership and mechanical condition of his second-hand automobile, or the pedigree and training of his dog, more thoroughly than he has looked into the qualifications of the text on which his critical theories rest.[27]

Bowers is advancing the altogether reasonable view that it makes a difference whether or not an interpretation of a text is based on a typographical error in the transmission of that text. In addition, however, there is the implication that all exegesis must have a common referent. Exegetical unanimity can hardly be expected in a situation where there is no philological unanimity, or in other words when there is no 'established text' to which disagreement can be referred. And exegetical unanimity, or at least an ample background consensus is required as a social imperative. Without such broad consensus both as to the identity of the scriptural text and as to its exegesis, chronic fragmentation of tradition into various antagonistic cults and schisms is inevitable. But although established texts, exegetical unanimity, and social consensus are binding imperatives, the fall into routine institutional life is unacceptable. The project of establishing a text should not give rise to any form of priestly monopoly, or vitiated and worldly 'popish' institutional structure. Given these contradictory imperatives, Bowers and his followers could hardly be expected to dispense with the 'ideal text', simply because the ideal text is the only form of existent that could legitimate the project of the established text. Editorial and exegetical unanimity that rested on secular authority and institutional power and on nothing else would simply be a sanctioned form of cultural violence. For Bowers and for his many associates within the humanist dispensation, the idea of unanimity must be sanctioned by an idealized communicative situation, in which the task of both the editor and of the critical exegete is to remove barriers between the ideal text or the mind that produced it, and the individual reader.

In Bowers's conception of the ideal communicative situation and of the deplorable actuality of communicative entropy, there are two primary impediments in the relationship between Shakespeare and his readers. The first is the printing house, where the low educational and cultural levels of the workers, compounded by the 'venality' of their employers, leads to a rapid degradation of the pristine, originating form of the plays. The second is the theater. Even though Shakespeare was himself an actor, and a primary shareholder in a theatrical enterprise, Bowers continues to operate with a strongly anti-theatrical bias in his attempt to account for the transmission of the text. That anti-theatrical bias, oddly, is already present in the introduction to the First Folio, and it persists, especially in romantic aesthetics, certainly throughout much of the nineteenth century and well into the twentieth. Bowers, in common with many of Shakespeare's editors, is continually alert to the presence of transgressive improvisation on the part of the players. These improvisatory or vulgar interpolations belong not to the ideal text but to the history of its degradation. Bowers was too good an editor and student of Shakespeare to proscribe all traces of 'vulgarity' or to flatten the aesthetics of Shakespearean drama according to bland neo-classical canons. But like the majority of editors he did wish to separate the incremental impertinence of mere players from the authentic and authorized literary material. This naturally assumes an answer to the question 'What is literature?'. Bowers's answer is to indicate in a variety of ways those things that are *not* literature, and here the ephemeral transgressions that arise in actual performance are of paramount importance. Literature, on this view, is private, impassive, transcendent. It is a category of existents that excludes contingent social interaction, 'crude contact', to say nothing of purely local forms of aggression and impudence.

In reading Bowers there is rarely any sense that 'doing Shakespeare' could involve any kind of fun, or any experience of the unpredicted or unpredictable. Shakespeare on this view is appropriate for 'high culture' and moreover he is appropriated without remainder to the interests represented by high culture. One of the tasks of editors then becomes that of policing theatrical performances by coming to the theater equipped with a copy of the play and a tiny flashlight. But the surveillance of theater and the policing of its impertinencies is a paradoxical institutional role for any editor who is by definition situated in a ministerial relationship with Shakespeare's authority. If Shakespeare's plays are understood to be play texts, then it can be argued that the primary form of actualization is not in a printed edition at all but precisely in a physiologically embodied, but ephemeral performance. On this view the idea of an 'established text' stands in direct contradiction with the 'original's' existence as theatrical performance.

TEXTUAL REVISIONISM

Given the present state of knowledge of Elizabethan theater practice, the hypothesis of an ideal text and a 'lost original' now seems untenable. Such a hypothesis posits the existence of ethereal entities (ideal texts, lost originals) for which evidentiary support is conspicuously absent. G. E. Bentley has shown that the Elizabethan playwright typically did not have any property rights or proprietary interest in the play-texts prepared for theatrical companies.[28] And furthermore, such play-texts were not treated as finished literary productions. The example of Ben Jonson is now thought to be quite atypical of Elizabethan and Jacobean playwrights, and in any case it seems clear that Jonson's painstaking efforts to 'establish' his own text happened after the fact of theatrical production.[29] It is certainly apparent that the re-composition of play-texts into the format of literature reflects Jonson's disaffection with the institutional setting of the popular theater. Shakespeare, by contrast, seems to have worked with an older ethos of writing in which playwrights engaged in the revision of their own plays as well as in the more or less extensive rewriting and adaptation of plays originally composed by others. Given these facts, editors and bibliographers have all but abandoned the concept of the ideal text as the source of magisterial authority in favor of the principle that Shakespeare himself revised his own texts.

Michel Foucault's much cited essay 'What is an author?' has

encouraged a much-needed reconsideration of the historical and institutional nature of authorship. In the field of textual scholarship, Foucault's essay has been reinforced by Stephen Orgel's important article, 'What is a text?'[30] These essays demand a rejection of romantic and reified notions of 'The Man and His Work' as historically invariant realities in favor of the view that both authorship and work are socially constructed within historically changing institutional settings. This position is summed up in a recent article by A. M. Hjort.

> It should . . . be recognized that the terms 'author' and 'work' are the product of human praxis and that they belong to a specific cultural and historical period. Human action and creativity do not, in any obvious way, invite us to think of the acts of the individual intentionality in terms of sovereign and autonomous undertakings. Thus, if the terms 'author' and 'work' carry a particular weight within our culture, it must be because this culture directs its human energies and capacities in a certain way. It is because agents of meaning have constructed intentional objects called 'author' and 'work'. These objects are intentional because an author cannot be reduced to a biological individuality and because a work is different from the sum of its material features.[31]

The privileging of the category of the author in the standard hypothesis is, Hjort maintains, governed by a constellation of interests or goal values; in this the idealized picture of the artist as an autonomous private ego legitimizes while at the same time hides the editorial interest in its own curatorial or ministerial and exclusionary functioning. Hjort argues that the 'ideal text' is an axiological requirement in a humanistic theory of exegesis that attributes value to the autonomous creativity of an exceptional subject while denying the presence of comparable value in socially diffuse or collaborative production of cultural goods. And this idealization of the exceptional subject masks other, proximate interests, and in particular the proprietary interests of those designated as trustees of the values in question.

The historical life or being-in-the-world of the play can be construed not as a story of violation and fallen virtue, but rather as a story of vital adaptation and development. This is the view taken by advocates of the hypothesis of revision, a view that has been elaborated in the controversy over the text of *King Lear*. The hypothesis of Shakespeare's revision of his own text was first presented in an important paper by Michael J. Warren, 'Quarto and Folio *King Lear* and the interpretation of Albany and Edgar'. Warren begins by pointing out the element of wishful thinking and irrationality in the prevailing editorial assumptions of a 'missing copy' of an ideal text and of changes attributable to corrupting influences.

> The concept of the 'ideal *King Lear*' is problematic because its existence cannot be known, and second because in the absence of such knowledge it is nevertheless further assumed that all alterations of any nature from that imaginary text are by hands other than Shakespeare's. Such an assumption is based on no evidence . . . . Of course, it is conceivable that this standard hypothesis may indeed be true, but the confidence with which it is assumed is unwarranted.[32]

Warren's own position, it should be pointed out, is not based on any new discoveries, or on physical evidence not available to advocates of the standard hypothesis. This does not, however, diminish the force of his argument. The Warren hypothesis simply explains all the evidence there is. On the other hand, the standard hypothesis maintains that the textual scholar must explain both evidence that definitely exists and evidence that definitely doesn't exist, on the grounds that the non-existent documents are required by an a-historical and doctrinaire conception of literary creativity. Moreover, in the standard hypothesis, the non-existent material, since it is considered more perfect than anything provided by the existing material evidence, is assigned the dual function of the goal of bibliographical research and the general criterion or norm for the evaluation of that research. The manifest irrationality of such a position and its reliance on sheer wishful thinking makes it appear all the more remarkable that it could have been so profoundly entrenched for so long. Warren does not devote any attention to the cultural or social factors that might account for the tenacity of a hypothesis that is neither supported by the material evidence nor logically required by the methods developed within textual scholarship. Indeed, the strongest part of his own argument is the negative element, that is, the brief and incisive repudiation of the notion of an 'ideal text'. The supporting arguments in favor of his own hypothesis of revision rely on the somewhat tenuous strategy of using interpretation of minor characters to support the claim that the two different texts have different but equivalent authority.

The hypothesis that Shakespeare revised at least some of his own plays seems extremely plausible in a prima-facie way, especially as the explanation for the existence of two or more versions of many plays in folio and in quarto formats. The only thing puzzling about this hypothesis once it is fully articulated is that the theory of revision has only become visible in the last few years, and only after so much laborious editorial effort to reconstruct the 'lost original'. The 'late emergence' of the revision hypothesis suggests quite forcefully the durable appeal of notions like 'the ideal text' and the dream of its definitive and final reconstruction. That appeal, as I have suggested, rests on social and ethical imperatives that are not themselves intrinsic to the practice of editorial scholarship.

The revision hypothesis is a renunciation of the quest for the established text, but it is at the same time a product of research methods initially devised to pursue that quest. The revisionists are an interesting group in that they have used the methods of scientific bibliography to undermine certain of the axiological categories that seemed initially constitutive of the very project of 'scientific' or 'principled' editorial scholarship. In the discussion of revision neither the extremely low probability of recovering the lost originals, nor the fantastical inutility of basing empirical research on such absent presences is given as the primary objection to the hypothesis of the ideal text. Scholars who adopt this position may declare flatly that 'finished originals never existed'. This statement means that the plays were never composed within the institutional horizons defined by private readership and finished literary formats, but were routinely adapted and rewritten against a horizon of ephemeral theatrical performances. The theorists of textual revision do not, of course, deny that compositors were working with some sort of document or that it was their task to reproduce that document. Revision certainly does not imply anything like absolute free play in the composition of dramatic texts. The notion of revision actually implies both conscious strategic deliberation and the careful preparation not of a single text, but of a sequence of texts that exist as the orderly structuration of a historically 'living' textual identity. The 'revisionist' position is a rejection of the Bowers notion of an 'ideal text' as a trans-historical and perfect existent from which magisterial authority is derived. Scholars like Michael Warren and Steven Urkowitz challenge the doctrine of an ideal text by asking *when* such an ideal text can be said to exist. In this view the text is repositioned within historical time, and specifically within the theater as a concrete, historical institution. Notions of theatrically significant time enter into the problem of the text. The phenomena of 'long runs' and 'return engagements' suggest the possibility of textual changes mandated by the original author.

Steven Urkowitz has argued that Shakespeare's brilliance was manifested primarily in a theatrical setting rather than a literary one, and that the revisions of *King Lear* constitute a primary and compelling instance of that brilliance. This still preserves the primary differentiation of masters and servants in the reproduction or the actualization of Shakespeare's durable 'capacity to strike us dumb with amazement'.[33] And it still preserves the element of social distinction between mental and manual work, in that the 'brilliance' still comes from Shakespeare. If there are now two *King Lear*s where before there was only one, that is because both *King Lear*s have been authorized by Shakespeare. The expanded range and complexity of magisterial authority now gives rise to expanded scope for the ministerial activity of editors, not by the discovery of new evidence or of better research methods, but by redefining the task of editorial scholarship itself.

The revisionist position is less radical than it appears. To begin with the social structure of magisterial and ministerial authority is retained and magisterial authority is still derived from a historically individualized author, although this category is no longer treated by advocates of the revision hypothesis as a self-evident normative concept. Revisionist handling of the problem of authorship could be characterized as a shift from a canon of authorship based on a sovereign and autonomous private ego to one based on an opportunistic and reflective social agent, though here the notion of opportunism has the mainly positive sense of tactical and strategic alertness rather than mere self-interest. The author is no longer characterized as the alpha point at which an ideal text is produced in finished form, but rather as an open, flexible, and responsive site of continual modification. In place of notions of authoritative, singular authorship or genial creativity, revisionism inserts the idea of a socially interactive authorial consciousness. Steven Urkowitz uses the idea of an adaptive and socially engaged author as grounds for the recuperation of ministerial authority for theater artists, and in particular for directors, whose interests can be said to reflect those of the original, magisterial source. Unlike conventionally trained and

113

basically conservative editors, directors are in a position to appreciate the theater as a place of instabilities, transgression, surprisals, and contingent social responsiveness. On this view the text is not an existent whose form can be 'established', but is rather something related more closely to the process of scientific discovery or 'openness to the future'.

One problem with the position developed by advocates of the revision hypothesis is that authority begins to proliferate at its very source, with a consequent dispersal and disintegration of stable meanings. If there can be more than one version of a play, why stop with only two? The doctrine of revision implies a veritable abundance of 'authored' Shakespeare texts. Stephen Orgel, for example, has suggested that the complexity of the 'text' of *Hamlet* may reflect the fact that it is a kind of 'anthology of performances'. This view implies first that any number of different permutations and combinations of scenes contained in the text of *Hamlet* may have been performed and that each one of these variants was in a sense authored by Shakespeare. It further implies that improvisatory contributions to 'the text' by one or more of the players might not have the status of a contamination but would have instead some kind of authorized position within the textual complex as a whole.[34] This position seems to have alarming implications, especially for more conservative-minded scholars, who see in suggestions of this kind both unacceptable notions of 'authorship by committee' and also a 'slippery slope' leading to the radical decomposition of the text as a stable and self-identical entity.

The view that a play has a historically unfolding existence need not entail disastrous or destructive consequences, though it should lead to historical investigation of the 'social relations of production' within the Elizabethan theatre, and of the *Wirkungsgeschichte* of the plays in specific cultural settings. The relatively modest claims put forward by the advocates of the revision hypothesis have been interpreted by some scholars and critics in the light of post-structuralist and post-modern ideas that cluster mainly around the slogan 'the death of the author'. This is not the appropriate place for a review of this protracted and extremely contentious argument. However, it is necessary at this stage of the discussion to analyze the consequences of a rejection of notions of the 'ideal text' in relation to competing notions of an 'unstable text' and textual free play. The argument put forward by advocates of Shakespeare's revision of his own text demands a rethinking of the historical *practice* of authorship within the larger ensemble of social relations in Elizabethan England. This does not entail any sort of metaphysically overwrought conception of the death or disappearance of the author; ironically, one of the concrete achievements of post-structuralist criticism was to demonstrate that 'the author' was itself already a pathetic and overwrought metaphysical category, a discovery that should have revealed the pointlessness of proclaiming the 'death of authorship'. In any case, as I will argue, the implications of the revision hypothesis point in a very much more mundane direction.

The post-structuralist view suggests that the collapse of a notion of singular, autonomous, and finished literary artifacts discloses the reality of an 'unstable text'. It is not entirely clear exactly what is meant by 'unstable' in this argument, or how the idea of revising a text is to be equated with such instability. Certainly there is no indication that the text is to be regarded as unstable in any material sense. The fact that texts reveal evidence both of deliberate alteration of their verbal content and of a communicative entropy in their physical actualization cannot be construed as 'instability' unless instability is being used in so loose a sense as to be virtually meaningless. Evidence of change is just that, evidence of change, and it suggests only that a text has a historically contingent life.

Advocates of a post-structuralist understanding of the recent developments in textual criticism view the evidence of revision as negating all proprietary claims to 'own' the text or to 'administer' its meanings.

> As textual properties, Shakespearean texts are produced by a multitude of determinations that exceed criticism bent on controlling the text or assigning it determinate meanings or structures. . . . No one can own the text. No one can clean it up. . . . Every text of a Shakespeare play exists in relationship to scripts we will never have, to a series of revisions and collaborations that start as soon as there is a Shakespearean text.[35]

This textual and authorial atheism is, in my opinion, of fundamental importance as a working methodological principle, but mainly in relation to metaphysical conceptions of the author prevalent in humanist scholarship. The author-god of traditional humanism doesn't exist and Goldberg is correct in his insistence on this point. It does not follow from this determination, however, that a more

115

mundane kind of author as a specific social agent in a specific ensemble of production did not exist. Furthermore, the existence of a 'multitude of determinations' is not the same thing as an infinite universe of free play and Derridean *differance*.

Goldberg links his own de-idealizing and anti-humanistic position to the much vaguer and in some ways incompatible conception of a destabilizing criticism. 'The destabilizing, de-idealizing criticism that coincides with modern textual criticism must recognize the historicity of textuality and the textuality of historicity.'[36] Goldberg's rhetoric implies a perfect equivalency between historicity and textuality, but these phenomena, though linked, are not interchangeable. The textuality of history does not follow logically from a determination of the historicity of texts. Historical events are certainly mediated by texts, and may even have text-like properties. But it cannot follow from this that the events, as opposed to their records, can be reduced without remainder to the status of contingent fictions, unless one is prepared to maintain that the affirmation *and* the denial that specific events have occurred have equivalent epistemological status.

Goldberg is on much stronger grounds in arguing the historicity of the text, since it is certainly true that no one can own the text, at least not in perpetuity. In conceding this, however, I assume that 'no one can own the text' has a normative rather than a descriptive force, since it is quite obvious that control of texts and other redemptive media amounting to virtual ownership is precisely what has been achieved in certain social settings. Nevertheless, the presence of indeterminate elements in the text sets a limit to the possibilities of such reification. The indeterminacies reveal that an indefinitely large number of concretizations could be actualized in real social time and space. However, it does not follow that a critical doctrine must be espoused that would accord equivalent ontological importance to those concretizations that could have existed or that might exist some day with those that have actually existed.

Whatever the merits of a de-idealizing and de-stabilizing criticism, and it should be noted that these two categories do not necessarily go together, it has only the most tenuous relationship with the new textual criticism. To begin with it does not appear to be the aim of the new textual criticism to abolish the category of a historically determinate text, but only to redefine the social nature of that text and its modes of production and reproduction. Second, although the results of the new textual criticism lead away from certain axiological assumptions of the standard position, the new bibliographers are really very conventional as to their methods and their epistemology. In fact the new textual criticism takes over more or less wholesale the empirical *technique* of the scientific bibliographical method initially worked out by W.W. Greg, A. W. Pollard, and developed in the second wave represented by Charlton Hinman and Fredson Bowers. Nor is there any element of epistemological novelty in the revisionist hypothesis, which still rests on close physical scrutiny of textual material. This is de-idealizing but emphatically not destabilizing, and in fact the new bibliographers are pretty much the old bibliographers subjecting their hypotheses to much more rigorous logical scrutiny in the light of existing evidentiary support.

Critics with a post-structuralist orientation may well be able to make common cause with the new textual scholarship, because these are two groups who wish to make a united front against a common enemy, namely the advocates of a humanist ethos of the exceptional subject and of curatorial preservation of priceless artistic values. Over a period of many years that common enemy has exercised an autocratic control over many aspects of scholarly research, and it is understandable that people might want to adopt the slogans of 'free play' and 'undecidability' as battle cries of a cultural resistance. But there are important negative consequences to this. The first is that if 'all is permitted' then there are no grounds for maintaining that the overthrow of the humanistic dispensation constitutes any kind of progress, social, intellectual or otherwise. Further, if everyone can 'do his own text' so to speak, then what are the reasons for excluding a conflated text that claims to represent a 'lost original'?

The doctrine of textual free play is an obvious and crude negation of the autocratic and doctrinaire claims of the militant standard bibliographers. In so far as this negation entails a commitment to a more or less vacuous conception of expressive autonomy, however, it seems very unsatisfactory. The alternatives of a rigid policing of the redemptive media and of a complete freedom that has no substantive social content seems in the end an absolutely futile and pointless dilemma. And indeed, hidden within these choices is the same tyranny of the exceptional private subject, construed either as a sovereign, princely ego or as an equally sovereign principle of free expressivity. Both the doctrine of the ideal text/lost original and the doctrine of textual free play are regressive in that they reinstate the argument from authority, though in quite different ways.

I want to conclude this discussion of textual scholarship by considering the implications of Shakespearean authorship by committee. This expression is, of course, a shibboleth of neo-conservative culture criticism, where it serves primarily to separate the idea of significant achievement from any notion of the collective. In standard neo-conservative usage, 'authorship by committee' has an obviously derisory function. This usage implies that cultural goods have value only on the condition that they are produced by autonomous individuals acting more or less in isolation from routine social/institutional life. To characterize all forms of collective practice as 'authorship by committee' reveals just how impoverished the neo-conservative conception of the social really is. Neo-conservatives generally vacillate between extremely repressive commitment to social control over individual desire and an equally extreme commitment to untrammelled individual initiative. What is more or less consistent in this position, however, is the notion that collective action, syndical initiative, or to put it crudely, socialism, cannot produce any of the priceless values we know as art. The idea that the antithesis of art is socialism, rather than, let's say, science, or mere vulgar bad taste, is in its own way an interesting concept, one with some degree of objective cogency. Certainly socialism can be regarded as antithetical to bourgeois idealization of its own art, or for that matter bourgeois ambivalence towards that same art. In any case, this militant individualization of the work of art makes it extremely difficult to pursue the hypothesis that Shakespeare's works develop out of a collective and collaborative mode of cultural labor of the kind described by Emerson.

Authorship by committee, or in less inflammatory language, the idea of collaborative authorship, is not a particularly recent idea. However, it is now becoming a much more acceptable hypothesis, due in large part to the work of Stephen Orgel. Orgel's recent article, 'The authentic Shakespeare' sums up much of his own thinking on this problem over the past several years. In general the argument is made that a play is actualized in a specific social event, namely a theatrical performance of the play-text, and that this kind of social realization is always and inherently collaborative. The 'lost original' that textual scholars desired was never a written document or even an ideal existing in a poet's mind, but a practical collaboration between a playwright and other parties to the performance.

> What is it that is being realized in the production of . . . a text? To ask this question is not merely to ask what is being added to the written text by actors and directors, elements like tone, stage action, interpretation. The point is that the acting text of a play always was different from the written text. . . . It also means that this was the situation obtaining in Shakespeare's own company, of which he was a part owner and director – it was a situation he understood, expected, and helped to perpetuate.[37]

Orgel's argument clearly points to a more diffuse, collective allocation of authority at the point of origin than is usual in the more exclusively individualistic conceptions of authorship that have constituted the discourse of editorial scholarship. But Orgel takes the collaborative argument even further, by showing, through a discussion of several different performance versions of a scene from *Macbeth*, that Shakespeare must be understood as collaborating with other theater artists operating in historically distant contexts. This is finally a quite radical notion of creative partnership or co-operation among equals in a concrete theatrical setting. Orgel rejects the conventional humanist wisdom that judges performance as a purely ministerial service to a finished original. Instead, Orgel insists that dramatic literature has no existence except in historically concrete social practice, which must find its moment of truth in its own immediate political surroundings. This sounds suspiciously like the Brechtian dictum that 'the theater must learn to speak up for the interests of its own time' (Brecht 1964: 201). Orgel's argument is slightly more cautious; he does not attempt to go beyond the already given institutional and economic realities in which theatrical performance has actually been situated. Shakespeare's authority is divided, but in the complex structuration described by Orgel it is an authority still confined to the domain of the aesthetic. The 'interests of our own time' are the interests of sensibility rather than of substantive change, and therefore Shakespeare cannot exceed the horizons of the presently existing culture industry. Whether those limits can be exceeded at the present time remains highly questionable. Orgel's essay is important, however, in its insistence on recognizing the symbolic contributions of agents other than the idealized author to cultural practice.

Part 2

AMERICANIZING SHAKESPEARE
CRITICAL DISCOURSE AND IDEOLOGY

Chapter five

SHAKESPEARE IN THE AMERICAN CULTURAL IMAGINATION

The relationship between American society and its European cultural past has never been easy to define. Although America is a new society, it is also a successor culture to Western Europe. Shakespeare certainly has the important and necessary function of providing an otherwise lacking depth of cultural tradition and at least some sense of durable continuity for American culture in relation to the European *longue durée*. At times it may seem that the study of Shakespeare permits American culture to take itself more seriously by virtue of its appropriation of this unquestioned cultural treasure. In general the hypothesis adopted here is that Shakespeare has been recruited not only as a compact and convenient functional equivalent for tradition in the broad sense, but also as a screen memory used to rationalize a chronic ambivalence towards both the practice of democracy and archaic forms of authority and the absolutist state.[1] 'Shakespeare' and 'America' are elective affinities, linked in a return to origins that promises both an alternative to and a compensation for the failures of tradition in its vitiated European manifestation.[2]

RALPH WALDO EMERSON: SHAKESPEARE AS REPRESENTATIVE MAN

Shakespeare's originality is closely tied to the primary affirmative theme of much American, and also British, criticism: the analysis and celebration of individuality and of the values of expressive autonomy as these are revealed both in various characters and in the poetic textures of the plays. The great theorist of Shakespeare's originality is Ralph Waldo Emerson, who provides a fully elaborated account of 'the poet' in his essay in *Representative Men*. Like Adams,

123

Emerson takes note of the poor state of preservation of knowledge of Shakespeare as creative source and origin.

> The Shakespeare Society have inquired in all directions, advertised the missing facts, offered money for any information that will lead to proof . . . they have gleaned a few facts touching the property, and dealings in regard to property, of the poet. . . . But whatever scraps of information concerning his conditions these researches may have rescued, they can shed no light upon that infinite invention which is the concealed magnet of his attraction for us. (*Emerson 1968:*, 204)

This situation stems in part from the general failure of Shakespeare's own contemporaries fully to appreciate his importance. Although Shakespeare was the 'founder of a dynasty', and 'the horizon beyond which, at present we do not see', the collective genius of the Elizabethan age 'failed to find out the best head in the universe' (Emerson 1968: 202–3).

Shakespeare's originality, his status as a representative man, is a kind of cultural secret, something held in reserve over time until the appropriate conditions for full critical reception emerge historically.

> It took a century to make [Shakespeare's greatness] suspected; and not until two centuries had passed, after his death, did any criticism which we think adequate begin to appear. It was not possible to write the history of Shakespeare till now. . . . Now literature, philosophy and thought are Shakespearized. (Emerson 1968: 204)

Emerson's description of this process is in some ways extremely puzzling. Before considering his conception of 'originality' therefore, it is useful to analyze more fully this notion of belated emergence and recognition.

Emerson seems to argue that society cannot appropriate Shakespeare until society has in some sense been appropriated by Shakespeare, that is 'Shakespearized'. This notion appears paradoxical. How can a society become Shakespearized when Shakespeare's own society failed to suspect the secret of his importance? Whatever social or cultural processes might be at work here, it is clear the 'great Shakespeare' *does emerge* even though such an emergence cannot result from the operation of tradition in the sense of cultural *pietas*. Shakespeare 'takes hold' in socio-linguistic contexts quite alien to his own native environment. Emerson nominates Shakespeare as the 'father of German literature', in and through the translations by Wieland and Schlegel, and the critical interventions on his works by Lessing and Goethe. Presumably Emerson considers himself in the same mediating relationship to American culture in the nineteenth century.

Emerson does not contemplate anything like a smooth and quasi-natural continuity with the Shakespearean context of production. Shakespeare's originality can become apparent only after the passage of sufficient time makes it possible for his 'otherness' to be more powerfully felt. 'It is the essence of poetry to spring . . . from the invisible, to abolish the past and refuse all history' (Emerson 1968: 206). In this sense originality is a power specific to individual agents with a capacity to appropriate and wholly to subsume the past. An origin appears to negate tradition, although, as Emerson shows at some length, such apparent negation is a kind of historical illusion. But the sense held by Emerson and his contemporaries that Shakespeare founds and constitutes modern experience is not a self-deluding appropriation of the past by the present; it is rather an action in the present of a powerful cultural agency that appears only after a lengthy historical gestation.

Emerson takes the view that Shakespeare's originality is specific to modern socio-cultural and subjective experience. The 'wisdom of life' discovered by Shakespeare has 'universality of application', but for Emerson the Shakespearization of consciousness is most fully and most unreflectively felt under the conditions of modernity.

> He [Shakespeare] wrote the text of modern life; the text of manners: he drew the man of England and Europe; the father of the man in America; he drew the man, and described the day, and what is done in it: he read the hearts of men and women, their probity, and their second thoughts and wiles; . . . he knew the laws of repression which make the police of nature. (Emerson 1968: 211)

Shakespeare's extraordinary transumptive power, his ability to appropriate everything that precedes him, creates an appearance of striking and sudden emergence. At the same time Shakespeare's work is possessed of an extraordinary proleptic and anticipatory power, so that his work has an absolutely convincing but altogether precocious modernity. These are effects of Shakespeare's originality. They do not provide any explanation of what originality actually is, nor any account of the coming-into-being of that originality. Emerson does, however, present a very concrete and detailed description both of originality as such and of the actual context of production in which Shakespeare's originality was achieved, and it is to these issues that this discussion now turns.

Emerson begins his discussion of Shakespeare's greatness and originality by specifically denying that either of these qualities entails anything like creation *ex nihilo*. This notion is discredited by the use of such traditional *topoi* as spiders spinning webs 'from their own bowels' or the builder 'finding clay and making bricks and building the house' (Emerson 1968: 189). In this sense of the word, great men are not original. Nor is originality connected with mere idiosyncracy, eccentricity, or freedom from cultural indebtedness. On the contrary, valuable originality is identified with those individuals most fully saturated with 'influence' and most fully identified with the interests of their own time. On this view originality cannot be identified with the unique private experience of an isolated individual, but rather with a representative power, the ability to speak for large and diffuse collectivities. 'It is easy to see that what is best written or done by genius in the world, was no man's work, but came by wide social labor, when a thousand wrought like one, sharing the same impulse' (Emerson 1968: 199). The greatest and most durable of cultural works are created by anonymous collective agencies. Two examples of great works produced collectively are the English Bible and the English Common Law. In making this comparison, Emerson implies that literature is not an ahistorical aggregate of singularities and beautiful objects, but a social institution in which collective understanding and practical consciousness are sedimented.

Shakespeare's originality is of this kind, and furthermore the social institution that originates in his work is that of individual subjectivity or consciousness itself. 'In the composition of such works the time thinks, the market thinks, the mason, the carpenter, the merchant, the farmer, the fop, all think for us' (Emerson 1968: 201). Latent meanings held in reserve within literature become visible in successor cultures in ways unforeseen and unforeseeable by the author and his contemporaries. Works characterized by great originality are not only works created over a long period of time, they are also works that come to have a long history.[3] This latter-day coming-into-being then will have the character of novelty, precocity, unexpectedness, or – in Emerson's terms – originality. In both philosophical and in sociological terms then, Emerson denies that originality in its common notional meaning has any importance, or even any existence. The power of great creative genius is not an originating power in the vulgar sense, but a receptive power in which the mind is fully open to influence or to the 'spirit of the hour'.

What Emerson has done in this essay is to redefine originality by abolishing the concept of absolute beginning. This further entails a redefinition of authority in both its sociological and its moral-existential sense. Authority is never unprecedented, it is a diffuse literary energy, always 'coming-into-being' and ephemeral. Shakespeare's authority, the claim his writing has on the attention of Emerson's contemporaries, is the result of an ability to reanimate prior meaning, to reinvest lost or discarded language with renewed life.

If authority is a transumptive and in a sense redistributive socio-cultural power, a paradoxical relationship evolves between whoever has held such power and those who follow after.[4] This paradox is expressed socially in the tension between scribal and prophetic forms of institutional authority, a tension later codified by Weber in his distinction between prophetic charisma and its routinization in bureaucratic cadres.[5] Emerson was evidently interested in working out the relationship between authority in its living, social manifestations and its enshrinement in written documents and printed texts. He expressed interest both in the 'higher criticism' of *New Testament* writings and in the speculations of Delia Bacon as to the 'real authorship' of Shakespeare's writings.[6] The dilemma here is that the very existence of a great work pre-empts and expropriates the creative faculty, it disempowers contemporaneity in its impulse to generate fresh originality. But the abolition or destruction of books and libraries would hardly be the solution to such a problem, since it is through great or representative men that Man (or spirit) gradually realizes itself.

The figure of Shakespeare moves through all of Emerson's writing, and yet throughout all these reflections there is hardly any specific commentary on individual plays. *Hamlet* is admired and appreciated in the nineteenth century because its culture finds its own speculative genius reflected in Hamlet's character and situation. But apart from scattered observations of this kind Emerson shows no inclination whatever to interpret anything Shakespeare actually wrote. In fact he expresses a certain disappointment over the disparity between Shakespeare's power of expressivity and the primarily trivial uses to which he applied his genius. But Shakespeare is not important for anything he actually 'said' and that is why there is no real use for a hermeneutics, nothing on the agenda of scholarship really worth pursuing. It is expressivity 'as such' rather than any determinate thought expressed that Shakespeare as 'Man the Poet' represents.

American thinkers like Adams and like Emerson are able to embrace Shakespeare without the slightest fear or diffidence, without any sense that obsolete parochial modes of consciousness might compromise the free individualities that constitute the new society. The reason for this ease of access is that Shakespeare is understood to stand in direct relationship to Man as such rather than to any contingent historical men and women, or to specific forms of material life and culture. Adams posed the problem of 'associated man' in terms of a motivational calculus based on the category of emulation. For Emerson, the category of 'associated man' hardly exists at all. It is true, he concedes, that we cannot and must not deny the substantial existence of other people, but this does not imply any natural gregariousness that would override a fundamental solitariness and isolation. Interiority and self-reliance are the strong forms; social life, though it offers valuable amenities, is distinctly epiphenomenal. On this view Man is a localization of powers rather than an aggregate of desires. The relationship of self to others then is never mimetic; it is rather reflexive and appropriative.

> I can do that by another which I cannot do alone. I can say to you what I cannot first say to myself. Other men are lenses through which we read our own minds. Each man seeks those of different quality from his own, and such as are good of their kind; that is he seeks other men, and the *otherest*. The stronger the nature, the more it is reactive.
>
> (Emerson 1968: 5)

In political terms this is a concept of individual autonomy understood as social agency. Although Emerson's focus is predominantly on the individual self, I would argue that his is not a philosophy of privatism, but rather an action-oriented world view in which individuals achieve self-realization through a process of differentiation from others. 'Great men . . . clear our eyes from egotism and enable us to see other people and their works' (Emerson 1968: 25). It is this ability that prevents both the fragmentation of social life into endless rivalry and competitive strife and the agglutination or assimilation of society in 'complaisances which threaten to turn the world into a lump'. Emerson's notion of radical individual autonomy is neither an exclusively economic idea of material self-interest, whether predatory or enlightened, nor the expressivist antithesis enshrined in a slogan like 'do your own thing'.[7] He takes the ideas of democracy and of self-government absolutely literally, so that the political life he proposes is in the end an absolutely radical form. And although Emerson does not specifically envision the 'withering of the state', he does contemplate the eventual abolition of all coercive state power or, to use Marx's terminology 'civil society'. This will come about only when self-interest and self-reliance are fully understood and fully experienced in relation to the 'otherest', that is as self-transcendence.

Autonomy and independence depend crucially on knowledge, which is a movement of self-exteriorization. Without education, individualism can only produce weak and oppressive forms of social and political life. Great men educate, that is, they lead the individual out of privatism, out of inauthentic and uncritical affiliation with tradition or with mass culture. Education in this sense is not an instrumental function within a state apparatus, but the substance of a political life-world no longer dominated by the commodity form. This is certainly a politically radical idea, but nowhere does Emerson propose either a critical diagnosis of the existing social structure, or for that matter any programmatic agenda for political change. Instead, Emerson proposes a 'science of the mind', specifically derived from Shakespeare, as the most promising agency for the actualization of his vision.

Both Emerson and Adams believed that Shakespeare revealed Man as animated by the moral sense or 'moral sentiment', a natural impulse towards higher forms of emulation or of self-interest. For this reason Shakespeare and America are well suited to each other, for it is in America, presumably, that the moral sentiment is to be most fully realized. It does not seem to have occurred to either of these writers that the Shakespearization of America might entail a concurrent Europeanization of America, a recapture of the emergent social project of American democracy and self-government by supposedly abandoned modes of traditional privilege and domination. Emerson had advised his audience at Harvard in 1837 that the strength of American intellectual life lay in the bold appropriation of past, present, and future for the creation of a nation of fully autonomous men. The American scholar is to renounce all deference for European culture. The implication that Americans can nevertheless appropriate Shakespeare without any fear of contamination by any European social pathology must be based on an Americanization of Shakespeare as complete as the complementary Shakespearization of America.

GEORGE LYMAN KITTREDGE:
SHAKESPEARE AND EXPRESSIVE AUTONOMY

Emerson's impact on the cultural work achieved by Horace Howard Furness and Henry Clay Folger has already been discussed; his ideas are sedimented in such concrete institutional realities as research libraries and textual studies. The effect of Emerson's ideas on the professional academic discourse is mediated through these infrastructural foundations, but there is also a direct line of succession through the influence of George Lyman Kittredge, a powerfully charismatic figure who taught several generations of Shakespeare scholars during his long career at Harvard.[8] Kittredge's most significant medium of cultural influence was his pedagogy, since it is through his many students that his ideas have been most widely disseminated. That influence was amplified through the very wide circulation of his selected edition of Shakespeare's plays. As a teacher Kittredge used the contrast between the heavily bowdlerized edition of W. J. Rolfe and his own more accurate editorial practice as a primary pedagogical tactic in the classroom. It is hard to imagine a practice that would more effectively foster such notions as a 'return to the original' as the central experience of scholarly research. The aesthetic and cultural agenda that generated this practice was given explicit articulation in Kittredge's lecture of 1916, commemorating the birth of Shakespeare.

Kittredge's lecture on 'Shakspere' [sic] was given at the request of the president and fellows of Harvard College, but this address reached a much wider audience through the frequently reprinted and widely circulated text.[9] Emerson's conceptual vocabulary, and even something of his rhetorical style, resonates throughout this performance. The primary theme here is the sovereign expressive power embodied in the plays, an expressivity that pre-empts every conceivable attempt at explication.

Of Shakspere's life we know a good deal, but nothing that explains him. Nor should we be better off in this regard if we had his pedigree to the twentieth generation, with a record of everything that his forbears did and said and thought and imagined and dreamed. God is great, and from time to time his prophets come into the world. 'The wind bloweth where it listeth and thou hearest the sound therof, but canst not tell whence it cometh and whither it goeth. So is everyone that is born of the spirit.'

Still, I can analyze Shakspere roughly, though I cannot account for him. He had the ability to put himself in your place, and then – to speak. Sympathetic knowledge of human nature we call it, and the gift of expression. Rarely, very rarely, do they hunt in couples.

(Kittredge 1916: 9)

Ultimately there is no accounting for a cultural phenomenon like Shakespeare, since the fullness of expressive power sedimented in his work is a moment of prophecy, the sudden disclosure of the workings of absolute spirit or the Logos. For Kittredge these notions are not merely figures of speech, but ontologically privileged, though fundamentally inaccessible, categories of existence. The manifold formal properties and the 'infinitely' meaningful contents of that prophetic utterance cannot be analyzed by the strategies of a knowledge-seeking 'science' no matter how comprehensive its repertoire of techniques. But understanding of a certain kind is possible, though only through the medium of individual subjectivity.

For Kittredge the idea of an 'objectifying' knowledge, or of a politically motivated research program is inadmissible. The only ethically permissible 'knowing' is an inter-personal knowing, based on principles of empathy and respect for the integrity of both self and other. On this view character is not simply one of several possible analytic categories within a strategic ensemble of interpretive resources, nor is the idea of character 'privileged' within some hierarchy of structural articulations. Shakespeare's characters are genuine existents, no less real than the individuals we encounter in real life, though occupying a separate ontological 'dimension'. Because these characters are 'fellow creatures' they must be grasped in their totality, even though such wholeness is profoundly elusive. Understanding of a 'fellow creature' is, however, the only thing that can really matter in Kittredge's view, and therefore no possible value can be assigned either to the dissolution of 'character' into linguistic

131

or psychological elements, or to the opposing vector of dissolution into the ensemble of social relations. Given these assumptions, the private act of interpretation remains as an irreducible fact of social differentiation.

> Each of us must read the riddle of motive and personality for himself. There will be as many Hamlets or Macbeths or Othellos as there are readers or spectators. For the impressions are not made, or meant to be made, on one uniformly registering and mechanically accurate instrument, but on an infinite variety of capriciously sensitive and unaccountable individualities – on *us*, in short, who see as we can, and understand as we are. Your Hamlet is not my Hamlet, for your ego is not my ego. Yet both your Hamlet and mine are really existent; and mine is as much to my life as yours to yours – and both are justifiable, if your personality and mine have any claim to exist. (Kittredge 1916: 12)

This is as much a social doctrine based on the idea of closed and finished individuality as it is a theory of literature. Private subjectivity defines what can be known, because there is nothing else to be known. This does not lead, in Kittredge's argument, to radical notions of mutually unintelligible difference and dispersal, however. Given the full entitlement of private acts of reading and interpretation, the claim that Shakespeare's 'Hamlet' has a 'solid existence' seems more a matter of wishful thinking than a well-founded element in a coherent philosophical position. The positing of this 'solid fact' of Shakespeare's characters as genuine existents is, however, a requirement of Kittredge's ethical agenda. This is an attempt to delineate a politics derived exclusively from the interaction of autonomous private subjects. 'Each of us has a prescriptive right to his own Hamlet; but none of us has a charter to impose it either upon his neighbor or upon himself as the poet's intent' (Kittredge 1916: 13). It is extremely difficult to see, given the right of individual interpretation, how a determinate reconstruction of 'Shakspere's Hamlet' would be possible. The right to a private interpretation is absolute, but it is a strictly *individual* right that provides no entitlement to annoy or to interfere with the neighbors. This is a common liberal view, of course, but the oddity of such a view is not often remarked. The idea that a cultural meaning might be appropriated because of its social importance is extremely difficult to envision. But the classic liberal doctrine enshrined here does not acknowledge anything like collective endeavor.

Kittredge's emphasis on private subjectivity and expressive autonomy does not encourage the formation of a critical social theory. There is, however, a very sketchy consideration of the sociological issue of authority and its allocation. In general Kittredge understands social relations in terms of masters and servants. This can be illustrated by his comments on the porter scene in *Macbeth*. Kittredge wants to argue that the scene has a dramatic function in the complex aesthetic totality of the play, providing strategically necessary comic relief from the horrors identified with the murder of Duncan. The humor in the scene is explained as the spectacle of a drunken porter philosophizing when he should be opening the door (Kittredge 1916: 24). Kittredge uses this functional interpretation against the idea that the scene is an actor's unauthorized interpolation or a vulgar concession to 'the mob'. Kittredge's analysis saves the text along with the low comedy, and at the same time saves Shakespeare's social position with persons of taste and judgement by deriving the laughter from normative satire of a servant who does not know his place.

In identifying the porter's failure to carry out his assigned duties promptly as the primary occasion for laughter in this scene, Kittredge reveals quite unequivocally his own attitude to servants. The sovereign subject celebrated in Kittredge's doctrine of expressive autonomy does not inhabit a social universe made up exclusively of equally sovereign and autonomous individuals. There is, in fact, a large supporting cast of supernumeraries with well-differentiated social obligations and social functions in the creation of cultural authority. Given the magisterial position of Shakespeare, the various ministerial agencies for the transfer of his authority must be circumspect in promoting their own claims.

Oddly, though Kittredge was not apparently much interested in theater, he grants full independence of creative authority only to actors, denying similar status to critics and interpreters.

The actor's problem is . . . to energize the character. He must let the conception possess him, so that the two personalities are merged, are as completely coincident as possible; and then, when he has forgotten himself in the part, he must act. . . . The actor, then, is not a puppet, of which Shakspere or some critic pulls the string. He is co-creator with the poet, translating derived impulses into action – but originating impulses too, so that the outcome of it all is Shakspere's man or woman expressed

133

in terms of this actor's art, but also in terms of this actor's nature. . . .
For his embodiment of the character is a fact, an entity, a concrete
denizen of the imaginative world, that wins a right to exist by its own
lifelikeness, its own fidelity to human nature, whether or not it accords in
all particulars with what Shakspere inferentially meant.

(Kittredge 1916: 14)

In this passage Kittredge departs from the somewhat more usual
view of the actor's appropriation of a Shakespeare character. Here
the strong appropriation of the author's word, and the merging of
the character with the actor's individual nature create an entity that
'wins a right to exist' and even to co-exist on an equal footing with
the originary creation itself. The authenticity of a strong and
coherent theatrical performance exceeds anything that might be
achieved by the interpretive critic. The task of interpretation is
defined entirely as a roster of specific duties – to understand, to
expound, and above all to keep the faith (Kittredge 1916: 16).
Authentic creativity and fresh originality is specifically excluded
from the activity of interpretive scholarship, which is defined in
strictly ministerial and fiduciary terms.

The interpretation of Shakespeare demands an understanding of
two primary mediations, both of which are in effect foreign
languages, media of expression that do not lend themselves to direct
communicative intimacy. These mediations are: first, the institutional
setting of the theater, and second, the historically distant context of
Elizabethan language and social custom in which the plays are
embedded. Of these, it is the second that constitutes the major
difficulty. Kittredge evidently saw the 'dramatic medium' as
historically invariant; in any case his analysis seems to imply that
drama is a formal rather than a historical type of mediation.
Elizabethan language represents a more complicated kind of
resistance.

Americans are separated from the immanent experiences of the
Shakespearean context by enormous stretches of socio-cultural time
and space. This is in its own way a kind of intellectual advantage,
providing both cognitive distance and detachment. At the same
time, however, the fact of distance should not be mistaken for a
clean, uncluttered medium of dissemination. The cognitive space
contains various distorting and impure substances that cast
deceptive shadows on the object of investigation. '[D]istance is

deceptive too; and there are clouds between, and some shadows, and much smoke from heretical altars, and the fumes of incense from many ill-swung censers' (Kittredge 1916: 22). The image of an obscuring 'popish' ritual, of distortions and shadows occasioned not only by error, but by a kind of superstition, is both an admonition and a protest against the degradations of a pristine originating word in the routine practices of self-perpetuating institutions. Interpretive knowledge cannot be discovered in such unclean and insubstantial forms. On the contrary, knowledge demands the clearing away of 'smoke' and 'fumes', and the opening up of institutions to greater and more direct interpretive immediacy. Such immediacy is, however, not so easily achieved.

Kittredge regards Shakespeare as an instance of *traditio*, even though, like Emerson, his philosophical position accords primary importance to spontaneous and expressive individual experience. The audience assembled in the Saunders Theater to hear Kittredge's address would certainly have understood themselves to be autonomous individuals and also independent agents with a capacity for powerful social initiative. Kittredge's lecture on Shakespeare, however, identifies an important limitation to the scope and the autonomy of individual understanding, a limitation identified both with the 'Shakespearizing of America' and with the omnipresence of a routine institutional life that obstructs the formation of new thinking.

> We who are assembled in this room today cannot think our own thoughts about Shakspere. We are the unconscious inheritors of a vast array of preconceived ideas – good and bad, clever and stupid, judicious and enthusiastic. Wriggle as we may, we cannot shuffle off our ancestry. We still insensibly regard Shakspere as an untrained miracle of genius, even when we are emphasizing the significance of that best of all training, the training that comes of doing things in competition with one's fellows. (Kittredge 1916: 33)

The accumulation of knowledge is no longer connected with any idea of progress or with the defeat of ignorance or the clearing away of superstition. Knowledge presents itself to Kittredge here as a disorganized and confusing aggregate, a promiscuous admixture of truth and error that no longer possesses any speculative reliability. The pre-emptive Shakespearizing of the subject cannot be distinguished in practice from ideological maladies of every possible description. Kittredge's argument moves from the the decoding of historically distant contexts, to the ineradicable prejudices of the subject. But from this position in which 'smoke gets in your eyes', Kittredge suggests the consoling notion that knowledge is probably not worth having.

In *Shakspere* meaning is objectified in a universe of complex, integral artificial persons who, though they lack physiological embodiments in their own right, can nevertheless be authentic occupants of our own social space and time. These artificial persons or characters define what questions may be asked, and also what might count as answers to those questions. Everything in this constellation expresses and objectifies its own Logos, that is, the personality of Shakespeare, which cannot be inferred from any one speech or any one character. All characters are the objectification of Shakespearean expressivity. Moreover, all characters exist as complete instantiations of that expressivity. Kittredge rejects the principle that the meaning of individual characters is accessible to any kind of typological analysis. Such analysis 'reduces' character to tendentious and mechanical schemata (Kittredge 1916: 53 ff.). On Kittredge's view, characters are not machines for generating meanings that constitute binding imperatives, but rather models of 'human individuality'. The case for this distinction rests on the demonstration that even evidently one-dimensional characters – the examples are Iago and Oswald – possess contradictory traits. Although all characters equally reveal Shakespeare, what is revealed is without content. The invariant meaning of the individual character is the expressive or histrionic ability to be anything. Kittredge's logocentricity is dogmatic and vacuous at the same time; it insists on an expressive autonomy that is absolutely devoid of determinate features of any kind. This is a quasi-religious doctrine of an impassive and unaccountable origin, the literary equivalent of *deus absconditus*. The task of interpretation entails a binding obligation to keep faith with this source, which, however, cannot be known.

> Let us therefore be humble. We may fancy what we choose to fancy, for that is our prerogative. But we have no right to dignify our idle reveries with the name of biographic fact. Shakspere is not Hamlet – neither is he Falstaff or Iago or Edmund or Lear or Touchstone. So much we know. And the lesson should be easy to learn. Perhaps Shakspere is the man of the sonnets – perhaps he is not. Assertion either way is equally fallacious,

> equally presuming. Nor would knowledge either way profit us if we could
> obtain it. For what is any one of us that he should think to read the
> riddle of another's personality. (Kettredge 1916: 53)

The enigmatic character of the social other, and the renunciation of
social knowledge are ethical imperatives in Kittredge's position. But
the 'riddle of personality' before which Kittredge stands mute is not
entirely an inexplicable phenomenon.

The mystery of the social other isolated within a closed, private
subjectivity emerges as a 'natural fact' in bourgeois political
economy. Civil society, the structure of social relations brought into
being by political economy is concerned with ordering relations
between persons who are strangers to one another. This condition is
a presupposition of 'rational' market relations and is inherently
antithetical to all pre-existing modes of solidarity in kinship
networks, or in the co-operative allocation of social labor. Within
this dispensation social order exists only when it has been achieved
through the state apparatus. By hypostatizing the category of the
private subject, it becomes extremely difficult to conceive of society,
except as an asymmetrically allocated and externally imposed
structure of social discipline.

CHARLES MILLS GAYLEY:
THE DISCOURSE OF HEGEMONY

The derivation of principles of social discipline and the necessary
ordering of democratic government from the writings of Shakespeare
is articulated in Charles Mills Gayley's *Shakespeare and the Founders of
Liberty in America*. Gayley develops the thesis that American
democracy, which he characterizes as a system to be administered
by the most fit, is derived from Shakespeare's England, and most
particularly from the small group of liberals who constituted the
Virginia company.[10] Shakespeare was closely connected with this
group, which, according to Gayley, was responsible for establishing
the tradition of English liberty both in New England and in
Virginia.[11] The primary elements of that 'English liberty' correspond to the social forms that have become familiar to everyone in
the 'western democracies', and these are all related to the central
principle of consent of the governed. In fact, few of the principles
Gayley cites are specifically English, but the sense of a unified racial

destiny (there is no other way to describe the position) outweighs the consideration of detailed intellectual or cultural history. Gayley is concerned with a singular intellectual genealogy or line of direct succession from the 'judicious Hooker' to the 'minds of our Revolutionary Fathers'. The pivotal connections, in addition to Shakespeare, are certain of the 'patriots' who obtained various charters from King James for setting up the Virginia Colony.

The patriots of the Virginia Council were determined, according to Gayley, to establish 'liberty' in 'their colony'. The patriots – Southampton, Sandys, and their allies – petitioned King James for redress from the heavy exactions of Elizabeth's reign. They complained primarily about the centralization of governmental functions such as the power of taxation within the Crown administration, and also about royal favoritism. Some of these 'abuses' belong to the 'progressive tendencies' of the Elizabethan monarchy and some to the persistence of an archaic style of personal rule. Opposition to these heterogeneous practices was itself a mixed and confused affair of high ideals and opportunistic rationalizations, but for Gayley the arguments developed by the patriots were to provide a coherent intellectual and documentary basis for the eventual establishment of constitutional government in the United States. James's response to the patriots' demands actually made matters worse. He granted charters to the planters in Virginia, but reserved to himself and his officers the right both to establish the form of government and to control the appointment of magistrates. The patriots fought for a system in which the

> prerogatives of James I should pass to the body politic, and by which ultimately the colonists should compass an independent development. Burdened neither by autocracy nor communism, they were to be secure in the individual enjoyment of prosperity and of civil and religious liberty. (Gayley 1917: 3)

The King evidently failed to understand or to approve these aims; he vacillated and eventually withdrew many of the conditions of the original charter. The patriots were obliged under these circumstances to engage in a long-winded struggle to secure their liberty.

Shakespeare's affiliation with this Elizabethan 'liberal party' and his alignment with the patriots' overall political and social agenda is indicated by his 'admiration' for the Earl of Essex. Gayley also argues for Shakespeare's acquaintance with Sir Henry Neville,

Thomas West, Lord De la Warr, Sir Robert Sidney, and many other adherents of the Essex faction, although the evidentiary support for these supposed connections is tenuous in the extreme. Evidence for Shakespeare's association with members of the Virginia company who were not specifically of the 'Essex provenience' is only slightly better. Quite apart from the difficulty of making a plausible case for Shakespeare's affiliation with this 'party', however, there is a notable peculiarity in Gayley's political interpretation of this group and of the meaning of liberty implicated in their program. The barons of the Essex group were much concerned with their own liberties *vis-à-vis* the encroachments of the Crown, and equally so *vis-à-vis* the competing authority of Commons. In many respects this was an extremely reactionary and parochial faction, however, concerned only with very narrow class interests. The only liberty they could have had in mind was the liberty to exercise *Herrschaft* over their own dependents, tenants, clients, and servants, without interference from state authority. It is clear from the documents cited by Gayley himself that the intent of these 'founders of liberty' was to institute precisely such a system of *Herrschaft* within their own colonial plantations, 'burdened neither by autocracy nor communism'. In other words, the liberals of the Virginia Company demanded, and for a time received, charters of aristocratic liberty. Such liberty is very far from being equivalent to political democracy, and it certainly does not entail anything like a doctrine of political and social equality.

The liberty sought by the Virginia colonists was conceived as the direct empowerment of the original group of adventurers; such an idea of liberty is, however, by no means incompatible with the idea of autocratic government and severe social discipline. After protracted negotiation with the Crown, considerable local autonomy was granted to the body politic of planters and adventurers. The power of democratic consultation and self-direction among the members of the company was primarily deployed to control

laziness, insubordination, and crime due in larger part to the still existing joint-stock provisions stipulated by the King's first charter . . . steps were taken for the abandonment of the system of communal proprietorship: individual allotments were assigned to some of the colonists; and thus were laid the foundations of personal effort and industrial prosperity. This under the governorship of the unjustly

execrated Sir Thomas Dale. 'With great and constant severity,' says the chief founder of our colonial liberties, Sir Edwin Sandys, 'with great and constant severity he reclaimed almost miraculously these idle and disordered people, and reduced them to labor and an honest fashion of life.'
(Gayley 1917: 5)

Liberty thus means, among other things, relentless opposition to communism, popular rule, and to anything that interferes with the rational, that is, profitable economic and social discipline of labor.

The Virginia colony was not, of course, an exclusively economic project, although the expected profit of the plantations was a primary element in attracting supporters, participants, and in the recruitment of a labor force. A religious motive was also of fundamental importance, at least as a legitimation both of the plantation itself, and of the behavior of the colonists towards the native population. In Gayley's text, these two motives are closely linked. Gayley quotes the eulogy for James I from the final scene of *Henry VIII*, probably written by John Fletcher, celebrating James as the maker of new nations.

[L]ittle as the conduct of James justified any encomium, the lines will breathe to all time the confidence of one of Shakespeare's friends in the blessing that England was to confer upon the world: for the plantation of England in Virginia was a Christian crusade as well as a commercial and political undertaking.
(Gayley 1917: 80)

For Gayley, however, liberty has an additional meaning as a binding imperative that links the 'liberal England' of the seventeenth century with its primary successor culture in the United States.

A considerable portion of *Shakespeare and the Founders of Liberty* is devoted to a lengthy analysis of Richard Hooker as the most eloquent and persuasive as well as the most cogent philosopher of 'liberty regulated by law and conserved by delegated authority' (Gayley 1917: 95). In Gayley's argument, Hooker provides the fullest and most coherent political philosophy not only for the founders of the Virginia company and for Shakespeare, but for their successors at the time of the American Revolution. In this argument, particular stress is laid on Hooker's articulation of the principle that a legitimate government is one which enjoys the assent of the governed. Although Hooker makes it clear that such assent may be withdrawn under certain conditions, such a doctrine does not entail any generalized redistribution of political authority. Assent of the governed means only that there is some basis for popular review of the activities of the ruler and his administrative cadres. The popular element, or whatever segment of it is enfranchised, participates only in the ritual acclamation of the lawmaker, not in the activity of lawmaking itself. Democratic accountability, popular sovereignty, consent of the governed, are all interpreted in the same extremely limited way by Gayley, as principles for the selection and the affirmation or disaffirmation of leadership cadres. For Gayley, as for many subsequent commentators on Shakespeare, this principle is identified with the doctrine of the 'specialty of rule'.

Gayley is not the first writer – and he is certainly not the last – to cite the speech of Ulysses in support of a principle of differentiation and political division of labor; John Adams had done something roughly similar much earlier.[12] The aim here is not, however, the general legitimation of hierarchy as a principle of social rationality.

What's really at stake in this argument is not so much the interpretation of Shakespeare, but rather the interpretation of democracy. As with many conservative culture critics, Gayley is committed to a meritocratic and paternalistic conception of the democratic process. The routine affirmation of leadership cadres through the electoral process is valuable not only in preventing the tyranny of inherited power, but even more urgently as the means to forestall the radical and levelling collective will of the mass.[13] At the time Gayley was writing, of course, even this limited exercise of 'democracy' was limited to males, and mostly to white males at that. The extension of suffrage to previously disenfranchised groups has done little to alter the general structure and control of the democratic process that Gayley articulates here. For one thing, the sphere of democracy is still strictly limited to the 'political' domain in the narrow sense. In the economic or industrial domain, the principles of democratic accountability and consent of the governed have no applicability. The democratic process is still conducted within the terms of a general ideological mobilization, in which the activities of the culture industry have paramount importance.

Gayley's insistence on the continuity of a unified Anglo-American culture as well as on the imperial and evangelical mission of that culture is easy to understand in the context of general mobilization at the time his book was published.

In this period of conflict, the sternest that the world has known, when we have joined heart and hand with Great Britain, it may profit Americans to recall how essentially at one with Englishmen we have always been in everything that counts. That the speech, the poetry, of the race are ours and theirs in common, we know – they are Shakespeare.

(Gayley 1917: v)

Although the research presented here is motivated by the need to generate support for the Anglo-American alliance, it would be quite wrong to dismiss this text as a mere temporary aberration. For one thing, both the primary themes of Gayley's general cultural criticism and his linking of Shakespeare with those themes are still not only widely current, they are in fact official policy in the areas of education and international affairs. Furthermore, the position represented by Gayley has been as significant in the constitution of a research agenda for Shakespeare scholarship as that of Kittredge, though to be sure in somewhat more subtle variants.

I have already mentioned one of the reasons for taking Gayley's work seriously, rather than dismissing it as a quaint, outmoded aberration. The argument developed in *Shakespeare and the Founders of Liberty in America* remains current within the wider intelligentsia, even though it may not be taken very seriously by Shakespeare scholars. There is, however, a further reason for giving this work serious consideration, namely that Gayley might be right in the broader outlines of his position, even if the detailed account of Shakespeare's affiliation with the members of the Virginia company is completely untenable. Shakespeare's ideological alignments might indeed fall within the parameters described by Gayley. Marxist and neo-conservative critics have frequently argued that the plays represent the determinate world-consciousness of an aggressive and self-confident entrepreneurial class. This position could be defended, or it could be refuted, through a program of organized historical research. It is precisely its accessibility to the activities of knowledge-seeking that make this position valuable, even if it is both wrong and politically repugnant. The claims advanced by Gayley, and by other representatives of tendentious criticism cannot, however, be addressed either by traditional or by post-modern variants of the expressivist position that simply declare every allocation of determinate meaning to be an 'error' induced by theoretical zeal and by blindness to the special autonomous dimension of the literary object.

142

Gayley's militant and doctrinaire account of Shakespeare seems at first to be deeply incompatible with the much more apparently open, expressivist views of Kittredge. In fact, however, these two positions can co-exist, and have co-existed for decades as the primary elements in the background consensus of Shakespeare scholarship. The emerging historicist research on Shakespeare during the 1930s and 1940s expressly repudiated the doctrine of precocious and anticipatory modernity both in respect of the plays and of the historical context in which they were written. As against Burck-hardt's conception of the Renaissance as the emergence of a revolutionary world-consciousness, scholars like Hardin Craig and Theodore Spencer emphasized the intellectual continuity of Renaissance thought with the dominant world-view of the Middle Ages.

Chapter six

OLD HISTORICISM

'The emancipated individual is the constant object of Shakespeare's concern.'[1] Given the importance of individuality in the hierarchy of ethical, social, and cultural categories elaborated by Emerson and by other American writers of the nineteenth and early twentieth century, this observation could easily be taken as an indigenous American view of Shakespeare's cultural importance. In fact, however, the quotation is taken from an essay by Anatoli Lunacharsky, 'Bacon and the characters of Shakespeare's plays', originally written in Russian and published in 1934. Lunacharsky, who was both an academic and a statesman in the Soviet Union under the regime of Joseph Stalin, thought of Shakespeare as the poet of a proleptic and precocious modernity, no longer aligned with the traditional world-view of declining feudalism and at the same time fascinated by the experience of an autonomous and ethically self-defining subjectivity.

> Shakespeare is imbued with the most profound respect for intellect. He is far from despising, far from detesting even the most cynical 'chevaliers of intellect'. He understands their peculiar freedom, their predatory grace, their incomparable human value which rests in their very contempt for all preconceived opinions.[2]

Lunacharsky acknowledges that his view of Shakespeare is derived from Jakob Burckhardt's studies of the Renaissance as a time of 'tempestuous individualism'. He might also have acknowledged Emerson, whose view of Shakespeare as the poet of a self-defining and self-determining individuality has been summarized in the preceding chapter.

For Lunacharsky the term 'renaissance' has a distinct and atypical semantic inflection. To speak of renaissance is evidently to speak of

144

rebirth, that is of the reanimation and reaffirmation of a distant past. It is also, by implication, to speak of a long decadence or degradation preceding the moment of rebirth. Renaissance writers certainly depicted themselves as 'looking backwards' to classical antiquity as the inspiration for their own efforts. For Lunacharsky, however, 'renaissance' is most important not for what it claimed for itself, namely the revival of the classical past, but rather for the social and political future it anticipated. Given the decidedly Bolshevist orientation of Lunacharsky himself, the radically individualist focus of Shakespearean drama and its articulation of the doctrine 'all is permitted' is viewed with considerable ambivalence. Nevertheless, it is the revolutionary potentiality of Shakespeare's plays that give them value and importance.

IDEAS AND THEIR HISTORIES

American Shakespeare scholars writing at about the same time as Lunacharsky adopt a profoundly contrasting orientation to Shakespeare, to the Renaissance, and most fundamentally to modernity itself. Although this was a period of conflict and of considerable social effervescence, the ideological horizons reflected in the study of the traditional literary canon is primarily conservative.[3] The historicism that emerged in the 1930s is committed to the exposition of a background consensus specific to late medieval and Renaissance culture. Literary texts and other cultural materials are interpreted as expressions of that background consensus which is treated as a normative framework for understanding historically contingent social action. An important substantive element in the historicist orientation is the characterization of this background consensus as a traditional world-view rather than as an ideology. The picture of Shakespeare that results from this research agenda is in sharpest contrast with the progressive, individualistic, future-oriented Shakespeare described by Lunacharsky. In Old Historicism we are presented with Shakespeare as the poet of tradition, of religious orthodoxy, and of a politically conservative view of the individual constrained within the hierarchy of master and servant.

Opponents of Old Historicism have usually identified a fundamental mistaken assumption in this orientation, namely the idea that the literary work is nothing more than a signifier of some authoritative presence, authorial intention, or 'Elizabethan world picture'. The correct view, so the opponents argue, demands acknowledgement of those qualities specific to the medium of literature. A Shakespeare play is not the mere servant of an ideology or of any other kind of cultural *doxa*, but is rather master in its own house. This line of argument usually falls far short of demonstrating the necessity for a doctrine of literary autonomy. It is not immediately self-evident that the absence of any such assumption in Old Historicism should be regarded as a mistake. The privileged notions of 'textuality' and of the 'specifically literary' are themselves assumptions of a discourse, perhaps unjustified assumptions. The idea that all cultural production forms a totality and that literary expression cannot in any meaningful way be segregated from that totality may not be a mistake at all but a perfectly reasonable and even a compelling theoretical axiom.

Traditional historicist research demanded a radical refusal to accept the existing conditions of contemporary society as natural or perdurable manifestations of human nature. The exclusive historicist focus on those aspects of Shakespeare's society specific to the sixteenth century, the disregard for socio-cultural continuity and for struggle was part of a critical strategy of cognitive estrangement. Old Historicism is a 'critical theory' in its own right; in other words its research program aims at a critique of existing conditions accomplished through the historical reconstruction of socio-cultural and spiritual conditions of life other than those presently in force. However, the interests that motivated this orientation were the interests of entrenched and privileged social groups and of the professional cadres affiliated with those groups.

The intellectual orientation of traditional historicist Shakespeare studies cannot be adequately reconstructed without taking into consideration the impact of A. O. Lovejoy's work in a new discipline he called the history of ideas. Lovejoy worked from a somewhat peculiar sense of the historical, but his methodological procedures gave researchers a feeling of rigor and coherence in their own research activity. The history of ideas offered a strong sense of standards and accountability in a field that seemed to consist, at least to some people, of subjective *aperçus* and *ad hoc* value judgements. Traditional historicist research can be said to have 'democratized' access to scholarly careers in that achievement depended on professional skills that presumably anyone could acquire, given the opportunity.[4]

146

Lovejoy set out to establish an academic discipline or research program that would study the historical movement of what he called 'unit-ideas'. The aims and methods of that research program are set forth in the first chapter of *The Great Chain of Being*. The first methodological tactic in this study is the distinction between intellectual history as this is commonly understood and the history of ideas as a new academic discipline. Intellectual history tries to account for contingent historical movements, even when such movements do not possess authentic unity. Lovejoy's example of such a contingent and specious unity is Christianity, which he characterizes as 'a conglomerate bearing a single name and supposed to possess a real unity, [but which was in fact] the result of a historic process' (Lovejoy 1936: 6). Historic process is something to be distinguished from 'real unity'; the operative term here, however, is the notion of 'conglomerate'.

For Lovejoy heterogeneity has a decisive negative importance for critical scholarship and research. It is most often the case that a total body of doctrine, or even the 'systematic' work of a single philosopher, will prove to be a heterogeneous aggregate or 'unstable compound'. Evidently for Lovejoy this condition of impurity, contradiction, the linking of incompatible elements, is inimical both to the truth of a given philosophical or intellectual system, and, more important, to the historical reconstruction of such a system. The history that Lovejoy proposes to write is the history of unit-ideas, in other words the stable and homogeneous elements out of which larger, heterogeneous doctrines may be constructed. For Lovejoy the actual number of distinct philosophical ideas is 'decidedly limited'. The aim of a history of ideas is the identification of these 'distinct philosophical ideas' and an account of their migration from one context to another. It is an important principle in Lovejoy's system that the ideas that migrate in this way do not experience change; their meaning, or intellectual character, is not affected by specific deployment within any contingent historical context. As for any philosophical idealist, homogeneity, self-sameness, resistance to the effects of temporality and historical change are qualities that correspond to basic notions of goodness.

In order to understand the role of 'history' within the history of ideas, it is necessary to consider Lovejoy's specific definition of the unit-ideas that are the primary objects of research. Lovejoy is concerned to distinguish the category of unit-ideas from various implicit assumptions, mental habits, or philosophical motivations which affect the articulation of particular philosophical writings, but which are not themselves 'distinct philosophical ideas'. It is apparent that Lovejoy's conception of unit-ideas is based on the assumption that it is valid to speak of an idea independently of its concrete realization within actual and definite semiotic materials. In other words the being-in-itself of the idea – the idea of the idea as one might say – has no necessary or significant relationship to the social context of any given utterance. As to the being-in-the world of the idea, Lovejoy has very little to say, since it is precisely in the 'fall into social actuality' that ideas lose their coherence, and indeed their very identity as ideas.

Lovejoy's category of unit-ideas is defined so as to suggest that there are many such entities. The choice of 'the great chain of being' as an 'example' is by no means a casual or arbitrary selection from a larger repertoire of equally significant cases in point. 'The great chain of being' is, in the vast empire of ideas, *primus inter pares*, a sovereign and magisterial entity. This conception plays a pivotal role in the research program of traditional historicism, especially in providing a substantive link between a historically specific recon-struction of the background consensus of an age and the cognitive surplus, survivability, or, to use the traditional formulation, the universality of great works of art. By implication the 'great chain of being' has a privileged status as a genuine principle of social rationality, valid in differing socio-historical contexts. It is empha-tically not to be construed as a mere legitimating ideology.

Once he has defined a unit-idea Lovejoy proceeds to describe the activity of the historian of ideas.

> After he has isolated a unit-idea he next seeks to trace it through . . . the provinces of history. If a unit idea is to be understood it must be traced through all the phases of . . . reflective thought. . . . The same idea appears, . . . considerably disguised, in the most diverse regions of the intellectual world. (Lovejoy 1936: 15)

For Lovejoy, the study of ideas does not entail consideration of any concrete elements such as the institutional setting in which ideas are formulated or the social conditions in which they are disseminated. In fact these are precisely the distractions and confusions that the history of ideas is designed to screen out. The historian's focus of attention is to be on an intellectual world which is organized as a great cosmopolitan empire. The domains of history and of literature are colorful and exotic provinces which ideas, and presumably their historians, may visit. During such visits the ideas may perforce adopt some sort of native costume, but their self-identity remains intact despite these surface deformations.

The imagery of tourism, understood sociologically, reflects not so much a method as an ethos of research. Evidently research is disinterested, it can visit the provinces without 'going native', it penetrates disguises, it reveals the self-identity of its object. Serious research also knows how to avoid crowds. This observation is not meant facetiously. For Lovejoy history of ideas reformulates and utterly transforms the category of the historical. His is a history without the noise and confusion of the streets and the public square. This history unfolds in the more tranquil and exclusive surroundings of the archive and the privately owned library. Research into such an idealized displacement of history is equally removed from contingent historical struggle. History of ideas as a mode of intellectual practice is defined by a principal of social exclusiveness or agoraphobia – literally, fear of the *agora* or public meeting place – which is disguised and repositioned as a methodological imperative. The clear advantage is that one avoids the nuisance of actual history both in one's inner life and in the concrete life-world in which one operates.

Lovejoy argued that literary study should not be divided according to national and linguistic boundary lines.

> For there was doubtless more in common in fundamental ideas and tastes and moral temper, between a typical educated Englishman and a Frenchman or Italian of the later sixteenth century than between an educated Englishman of that period and an Englishman of the 1730s.
>
> (Lovejoy 1936: 18)

It would be easy to dispute this proposition by arguing that the idea of a synchronic cultural unity denies or overlooks such factors as cultural lag or uneven development, to say nothing of such divisive factors as wealth, *métier*, or social position. Surely there are important dis-unities to be observed depending on whether an educated Italian is a landowner, a wealthy merchant, or a professional scholar and teacher. For the purposes of my argument, however, I want to stipulate that Lovejoy is perfectly correct to assert that a cosmopolitan elite exists, and moreover that such an elite is united both by common interests and by a common substantive culture. The ethos of traditional historicist research then is best understood as motivated by the interests of just such a cosmopolitan elite. Scholars and university professors then would be seen as the professional cadres of this larger intelligentsia. Whatever one may wish to make of the history of ideas in purely intellectual terms, it is clear that its orientation and structure are not the result of some sort of 'mistake'. The overall shape of Lovejoy's new discipline reflects the operation of careful strategic deliberation.

In order to see the extra-disciplinary factors that have been displaced into an intra-disciplinary research program, it is useful to consider Lovejoy's role in the academic freedom committees of the American Association of University Professors. Lovejoy was the first secretary of this organization, which was founded in 1915 in order to preserve intellectual and professional autonomy for scholars and teachers within the university community.[5] The principle of intellectual autonomy was closely connected both with the idea of 'professional standards' and with the equally significant notion that academics could be counted on to police their own organizations.[6] Obviously the notion of academic freedom would have certain boundary conditions, and Lovejoy played an important role over a period of several decades in defining those boundary conditions.

At the end of the First World War Lovejoy prepared a report entitled 'Academic freedom in wartime'. This recommended that academics should no longer be protected if they showed themselves to be against the war. In 1949 Lovejoy published an article in *American Scholar* entitled 'Communism and academic freedom' which demanded an even more rigorous interdiction of communists from the ranks of university professors. In these publications Lovejoy maintained that war-resisters, pacifists, and above all communists were in violation of *professional* standards. This was not a matter of identifying those professionals who espoused seditious or heretical ideas and turning them over to the 'secular arm'. Lovejoy's position was that even in cases where no law had been violated, communists should not be permitted to hold jobs as university teachers.[7] The logic of this exclusion, which Lovejoy pursued actively in his role as a consultant to universities engaged in dismissal proceedings against left-wing staff members, is powerfully isomorphic with the methodological principles inscribed in the history of ideas.

One of the more frequently reiterated principles in the work of

Lovejoy and of those historicist scholars who adopted some variant of his research program concerns the supposed unity of outlook shared by the 'educated' cadres within a given historical period. This is not actually a matter of empirically supportable *fact* so much as it is a methodological assumption. Nowhere is it maintained that critical opposition to a prevailing *doxa* does not exist, only that such oppositional or transgressive orientations, as the sign of heterogeneity, cannot belong to the historical universe of ideas. The unity of a given world-consciousness is confirmed by this magisterial act of intellectual exclusion. Precisely the same self-confirming circularity as is practiced at the level of the substantive content of research is replicated in the careful policing of institutional membership. The unity and the integrity of the academic profession, its right to professional autonomy, is confirmed by the severity of its exclusions. Spontaneous loyalty to the authority of the state apparatus and to established principles of orderly social differentiation are implicit universalizing principles that link the activities of scholarly research to the objects of that research.

THEODORE SPENCER: THE NATURE OF MAN

The idea that a Shakespeare play is both a historical phenomenon that expresses a specifically Elizabethan world-consciousness and a trans-historical phenomenon that expresses 'human experience as a whole' is the explicitly stated point of departure of Theodore Spencer's *Shakespeare and the Nature of Man*. In addition to the two categories of 'history' and 'human experience as a whole', Spencer proposes 'the artistic medium' to complete his model of historical research. In choosing to organize his research around this intellectual agenda, Spencer was certainly not timid. He was committed to something more than a strictly antiquarian interest in the past, and was in fact pledged not only to a reconstruction of that past, but to the evidently critical objective of 'judging the truth of what is expressed'. Exactly *how* that truth is to be judged, what its cognitive and ethical relationship to our own time might be, what axiological and epistemological assumptions are required in order to carry out such a judgement are all questions that Spencer, and the other traditional historicists, choose to disregard. The reason such evidently crucial problems are overlooked is related to the Old Historicist discomfort with their own times, a discomfort hinted at, sometimes openly expressed, but never analyzed with the same engagement and sympathy given to the reconstruction of the past. Scholarly rigor and thoroughgoingness are reserved for the reconstructed past and, in the case of Shakespeare, for those historical elements within his work that are specific to Jacobean and Elizabethan culture.

Spencer's historiographical assumptions mandate that his reconstruction of the Renaissance dispute over the definition of man's nature must be made up exclusively of elements that are specific to the Renaissance. Long-term continuities between Shakespeare's time and our own – the operation of a money economy, the existence of capital, of a semi-proletarianized labor force, and of a placeless market – are not included on the register of legitimate topics for historical research. Whatever we might share with Shakespeare, the category of 'human experience as a whole' is to be understood as a religious problem. The fundamental question to be addressed in any consideration of the 'nature of man' is whether this generic figure is inherently good or inherently evil.

Spencer ascribes the 'optimistic view' to various neoplatonic writers such as Richard Hooker and Raymond Sebonde. The dignity of man and his place in the cosmic scheme of things is identified with the cosmology of Ptolemy and with the political conservatism of Cicero. The opposite view, that man is inherently evil, belongs to the writings of Montaigne and Machiavelli, and is identified as well with the 'new cosmology' of Copernicus and Galileo. In Spencer's thinking this latter group prefigures certain modern writers whose theories make him distinctly uncomfortable. Montaigne and Machiavelli are stand-ins here for Freud and Marx respectively; they are the critical theorists of the sixteenth century. The critical and emancipatory significance of their writing is not, however, regarded positively here. For Spencer all of this is just plain bad news; indeed such de-idealization of individual motivation and of social order is nothing less than a primary cause of anomie and social badness, not to mention unhappiness. Spencer did not fail to understand that Montaigne and Machiavelli, or Freud and Marx for that matter, were in fact proposing a *diagnosis* of social badness and that nothing in any of their writing could actually be construed either as praise for sinister motivations or as advocacy of bad social behavior. Nevertheless, in so far as pessimistic views describe the facts of man's inherently evil nature without at the same time affirming as an ideal his equally inherent goodness, they do indeed seem to bring about the very effects in social and in spiritual life that they purport to diagnose. Spencer's project, however, is aimed at segregating historical research from such necessarily corrosive and negative programs.

For Spencer the category of 'human experience as whole' is first and foremost a metaphysical pathos, a matter of what we believe to be true. Although the community of believers is left undefined, the substantive elements of a shared belief system, irrespective of its content, can be positioned as the normative framework to evaluate critical theories of human desire and of social organization. Critical theories – pessimistic views of man's place in the cosmos, to use Spencer's terminology – give only half the truth. It is the other half, the 'ideal picture', that Spencer's program of historical research is designed to elucidate.

The normative view of Man is central to the background consensus of Renaissance culture, as far as traditional historicist research is concerned. Given the relationship of 'man' to the state and to the order of the cosmos, the pattern of 'human experience as a whole' can be most adequately and fully represented by a single social type. 'This is the ideal aristocrat, dutiful, learned, religious, temperate, constant, controlling passion with reason, and ruling sense with judgment. It represents the same ideal which Shakespeare was to expound.'[8] Spencer does not claim that any such paragon ever actually existed because his argument is based only on the existence of an ideal *standard* of human self-organization and self-control. Traditional historicist research does not identify this as a specific mode of class-consciousness and still less as a hegemonic ideology. For the Old Historicists, this ideal subject was male, he belonged to the administrative cadres of society, and he either owned wealth or represented those who did.

Old Historicism continually asserts that 'Elizabethans' universally believed in the legitimacy of this absolute social hierarchization. Viewed more critically the Old Historicist argument could be restated as follows: the class consciousness of a landowning aristocracy was constituted as a traditional world view that was both normative and binding for the population at large. This world view was successfully disseminated both as an official political discourse and as a structure of feeling; at the same time it was objectified in the concrete relations of production so that questions of legitimation could be deferred virtually indefinitely. In these terms it becomes clear why the operative terms for the Old Historicists is the abstract and aggregative notion of 'Elizabethans'. This particular totalizing conception proved useful in the way it blocked off research into other historical modes of class-consciousness.

There is another factor that motivates the assertion that the background consensus of Renaissance society is a universally shared world-consciousness rather than an ideology. This is revealed in a casual remark by Spencer.

> In the sixteenth century the combined elements of Aristotelianism, Platonism, Neo-Platonism, Stoicism, and Christianity were almost indistinguishably woven into a pattern which was universally agreed upon. . . . If there was dispute, it was dispute about details; people were concerned as to *how* Christ manifested himself through the Eucharist; they did not ask whether or not he did so at all.
>
> (Spencer 1966: 1)

The choice of the doctrine of the eucharist as the exemplary case of a background consensus is extremely revealing, mainly for what it leaves out. Differences over the philosophical and ontological characterization of the eucharist are called disputes over details, a description that leaves the impression that these were primarily bookish matters worked out in a collegial setting of mutual forbearance and of general solidarity in the 'higher belief'.

Disputes over the details of the eucharist were a good bit more colorful than Spencer suggests here. Protestant rioters, for example, ridiculed their Catholic victims for worshipping a 'god of dough' just before they beat these victims to death to the accompaniment of popular festive laughter.[9] On a larger scale, such 'disputes over details' led to chronic civil war, violent persecution, and the eventual derangement of the social and economic order of Europe during the Thirty Years War. Presumably the emergence of a 'pessimistic view' of man's nature has a significant relationship to this protracted condition of total war, but neither Spencer nor any other traditional historicist critic of Renaissance literature shows much interest in relating literature to any such facts of social and political derangement. By characterizing the interpretation of the eucharist as a dispute over details, Spencer represses whatever knowledge he has of European history during the Renaissance or 'early modern period'.

The reasons for this repression are to be found in part in notions

154

of background consensus itself. Elizabethans, the Old Historicists never tire of reminding us, universally believed in a well-defined constellation of normative concepts, although their insistence on this point is usually shaded and nuanced by certain social qualifications and exclusions. Creditable theorists, reasonable men, responsible and educated individuals – in other words the same cosmopolitan intelligentsia privileged by Lovejoy – fully represent the general category of Elizabethans and express the unity of the 'Renaissance mind'. A more critical description of the situation might be the argument that there was, in the sixteenth century, a cosmopolitan intelligentsia whose objective *interests* were the same irrespective of their affiliation with one side or the other in the wars of religion. Because Old Historicism is committed above all to the idea of a higher order resolution of conflict, research into partisan interests, when it is undertaken at all, is generally referred to a larger normative framework.

The real strategic importance of Spencer's depiction of the 'ideal aristocrat' as the primary agent for guaranteeing the security of such a normative framework becomes clear if this formulation is related to Spencer's immediate context of utterance, in other words to the series of lectures presented at the Lowell Institute in Boston in the spring of 1942. In a social setting of this kind the idea of self-government as first and foremost a matter of private self-regulation has more than antiquarian interest. Such self-regulation is the precondition for assuming social responsibility, something that Spencer's students from Harvard – and Radcliffe as well – would be obligated to accept in due course. Use of a general category like 'Elizabethans' is a way to express the social imperative of a unified national consciousness. Spencer's implicit theory of social organization must be understood in terms of notions of hegemony and the engineering of consent. Such mobilization would be implemented by the exemplary probity of leadership cadres. It is not in the least difficult to understand why Spencer and his audience would be responsive to these conceptions of social control by qualified leaders during the spring of 1942, even though Spencer makes only the most oblique and discrete references to the Second World War.

At the time Spencer delivered his lectures at the Lowell Institute some of his own colleagues at Harvard were exiled and displaced European intellectuals. The idea that their common interests might or should transcend even the massive social and political dislocations of the Second World War was part of Spencer's own concrete social life-world. It certainly had an impact on his self-understanding. The idea of a background consensus, a system of higher belief in which violent social conflict is transformed into collegial disagreement over the interpretation of common ritual experience or the implementation of shared values is a form of political wishful thinking. Like all serious wishful thinking this has elements both of objective cogency and of fundamental misrecognition.

For scholars working within the framework of traditional historicist research, Shakespeare's cultural value is ascribed to his sympathy with the point of view of general humanity. In this respect traditional historicist research in the United States concurs with the orientation set out by Emerson in his discussion of Shakespeare's originality. But in Old Historicism the point of view of general humanity is redefined as a retrospective orientation, rather than as a proleptic understanding of emergent consciousness.

> According to every creditable theorist of [Shakespeare's] time, man had a definite place in the universe, in nature, and in the state; and his relations to God, to the rest of Creation, and to society, were, broadly speaking, universally agreed upon. The picture was quite different from any picture that we have at the present time; a man living in Shakespeare's day was living in almost the last generation that could unquestioningly accept, with all the available evidence before him, the old over-orderly scheme, the scheme which Galileo and Newton in one way, and Bacon and Locke in another, were to rearrange so that its basic assumptions (to our ultimate confusion) could eventually be destroyed.
>
> (Spencer 1966: viii)

In this passage Spencer takes a stand on the purely academic question of how to interpret the period we know as the Renaissance. He rejects the picture elaborated by Burckhardt of a genuine emergence in favor of the view that the Renaissance is a continuation of the Middle Ages. However, it is not this well-known academic controversy that is of primary interest here. Spencer is expressing his feeling of regret, sadness, even recrimination over the disappearance of a stable, and affectively supportive world-consciousness linking the realms of matter and spirit, of natural process and socio-cultural order. Traditional historicist research is specifically motivated by its longing for the conditions of such a totalizing order, and even more by the desire to experience a feeling of unquestioning trust in its validity.

The longing for universal coherence or the 'nostalgia for presence' is a recognizably modernist sentiment.

> [If] a first class writer is to appear in our century he will have to present, in an artistic form that is taken for granted by his audience, the individual experiences of human beings in relation to themselves, to society, and to the larger forces that control them. The best writers of our generation have already recognized this responsibility and any future historian of our time, in considering the work of Thomas Mann, of Proust, of Eliot, Yeats, and Joyce (and there are others besides these), will see that each of them, in various ways, has been seeking for that ordered pattern of relationships which is the only true universality.
>
> (Spencer 1966: 221)

True universality in the form of an ordered pattern of relationships is precisely what is to be found in Shakespeare. The pattern is a social structure with a perfectly rationalized chain of command and a perfectly rationalized division of labor. Orderly differentiation creates a general and organic solidarity. Hierarchical order, which is not, on this view, the same thing as social inequality, does not in and of itself cause conflict. The ideal forms of social life correspond to this stable pattern of universal meanings. Both the ideals themselves and the reality of universal correspondence are embodied in the canonical works of great literature as well as in the exemplary figures within the leadership cadres.

HARDIN CRAIG: THE PERMANENCE
OF THE RENAISSANCE

The unity of the 'Elizabethan mind' as a background for understanding Shakespeare did not originate with Spencer. Hardin Craig, in *The Enchanted Glass* (1936) had already developed a comprehensive overview of that unifying background, a fact that Spencer acknowledges in his discussion of the same ensemble of findings.[10] Craig, like Spencer, insists on two substantive conclusions. First, the Elizabethan mind, or world-view, is unified despite any contingent disunity over the details of belief and practice. Second, this mind must be fully differentiated from 'modern consciousness'. Craig does not merely intend to point out various

157

socio-cultural differences. There is a methodological imperative here requiring a description of the Elizabethan mind that consists exclusively of elements specific to that historical period.

In his *An Interpretation of Shakespeare* of 1948 Craig acknowledges the problematic character of these two theses. The unity of the Elizabethan mind does not reflect anything like uniformity of social experience, much less a universality of interests.

> [L]uxuries . . . were exceptional and were largely confined to the rich. The houses of workmen and agricultural laborers were apt to be very bad indeed, probably by no means so good as the stables in which many modern cows and horses live.[11]

Objective social differences do not seem to have given rise to any specifically inflected class consciousness, or at least not to any form of class consciousness that Craig was prepared to recognize as legitimate. The comparative impoverishment of workmen and agricultural laborers is to be seen either as part of the normal order of things, or possibly as the occasion for rebellion, something that Elizabethans 'always considered horrifying'. Evidently the unprivileged either knew their place or they stopped being Elizabethans when they set out to change society by violent means.

Despite the actual existence of rebellions, Craig maintains that Shakespeare as a writer transcends the partisan allegiances and invidious differentiations of his own time. Craig's position recalls Emerson's discussion of Shakespeare's universal and original genius. The Emersonian echo is most striking in the description of Shakespeare's broad human sympathy.

> Shakespeare's works are appropriate to a man of the kind he seems to have been. His genius, like that of Chaucer and Goethe, was of the normal objective kind. His works are written from the point of view of general humanity, which means that they have in them the minimum of affectation, formalism, dogmatism, egotism, and prejudice. They are about life, about people and about recurrent human situations. His people are lovers, husbands, fathers and sons, mothers and daughters, kings, counsellors and subjects, servants, inn-keepers and soldiers, beggars, tramps, and country people. They are made of ordinary human stuff, and show ordinary human needs, passions, and qualities.
>
> (Craig 1948: 9)

The doctrine of a non-partisan and transcendent world-consciousness of general humanity is related to the notion that recurrent human situations are fully intelligible because they are socially and spiritually invariant. Nevertheless, the complex systems of mediation present in any specific cultural setting tend to obscure the trans-historical unity represented in Shakespeare's plays.

Craig maintains that Elizabethan life and consciousness were radically different from those prevalent in our own time and that this difference requires detailed elucidation. Social and spiritual invariants are indeed fully articulated in Shakespeare's plays, but they are expressed in a foreign language, so to speak. The task of a 'trained historical imagination' is to facilitate the project of translation. Elizabethans, according to Craig, lived very differently from the people of our time, though Craig does not fail to point out continuities. Like us, Elizabethans lived in houses, ate meat, and drank beer. On the other hand they did not wear underwear, take baths, or practice public sanitation.

> Elizabethans were for the most part, active, cheerful country people, living rather eagerly in a fairly primitive way. Those of us who know the lives lived by pioneers, mountaineers, and remote country people in our own land will have little difficulty in comprehending the lives lived by Elizabethans.
>
> (Craig: 1948: 11)

This is a fascinating passage, not least for its autobiographical implications. Hardin Craig's own father was a Scottish immigrant who settled in Kentucky in the mid-nineteenth century. Craig grew up on the family farm and presumably includes himself among those who know what it feels like to be a pioneer. The sense of affective and practical continuity between his own agrarian background and the practical life-world of Elizabethans suggests an interesting research program of its own, one that would focus on the organization of society in transitional economies as a significant context for understanding a sixteenth-century world-consciousness. For Craig, however, neither the social life-world of ordinary people nor the practical consciousness that might reflect that life-world belong to history or to historical research. In order to recuperate the point of view of general humanity expressed in Shakespeare's plays, attention must be directed to the formally articulated general ethos of the times. Craig understands that this means focusing on the objectively top-most strata of society and treating the much larger popular element as marginal. Intellectual history takes precedence over broader-based social history because it is only among the cosmopolitan elite that the substantive doctrines of reason and true religion are adequately represented.

Unlike many other scholars engaged in the traditional mode of historicist research, Craig did not blindly idealize the culture of the Elizabethan and Jacobean period. He takes note of the crowded and filthy living conditions many Elizabethans had to endure. In addition he is careful to point out that the historical reconstruction of the period would entail a 'history of error' as well as a discussion of correspondence, hierarchy, and reason as 'truthful' elements of an Elizabethan belief system. Elizabethans believed in witches, anthropaphagi, and venomous toads. Their medicine was murderous. More important, they affirmed their ideals and their depth of conviction not only in poetry and drama, but also in grisly public tortures and executions.

> Burning a human being alive under conditions of solemnity and in the face of the people is an awful thing to contemplate. Those responsible were sure they were right, and yet they were as wrong and un-Christian as hell itself.

(Craig 1948: 17)

For Craig, the Elizabethan period cannot be adequately described in and through elucidation of the category of order. He is, moreover, willing to differentiate between Elizabethan beliefs and the validity of such beliefs. Any such differentiation implies a critical orientation, a framework that would take historical research beyond the horizons of affirmative culture. And yet, despite the general level of historical awareness evident in a writer like Craig, traditional historicist research remains almost entirely innocent of any critical theory. At times it seems that Old Historicism is committed above all to the defence of its own theoretical innocence. Although these scholars could not have been ignorant of the important critical thinkers of the nineteenth and twentieth centuries, one would never suspect, reading Old Historicist research, that Marx, to name only one of them, had ever existed. Instead of a critical and historical social science, traditional historicism produces substantive doctrines. These doctrines, and the cultural policy agenda that they reinforce, constitute a defense against as well as a substitute for their own quite nebulous understanding of the ambient conditions of 'modernity'.

Hardin Craig's *Freedom and Renaissance*, a collection of essays written in the years 1946–8 and first published in volume form in 1949 sets out an explicit legitimation program derived from the research program of Old Historicism. That political agenda lays considerable stress on the relationship between cultural renaissance and social renewal.[12] Craig's lectures are concerned with the mission of higher education in the immediate post-war period. That mission is understood as primarily religious, a matter of 'saving' America by means of a 'renaissance' of its original purity. The post-war reformation of America entails both a return to a radically fundamentalist Christianity and a restoration of the Anglo-American tradition of freedom and self-government. Not surprisingly this is a counter-normative or radical-return-to-origins view both of historical process and of tradition itself.

It is abundantly clear at the very outset that the notion of freedom for Hardin Craig has nothing to do either with a spirit of social experimentation, or with any kind of social effervescence or anomie. It certainly is not to be understood as any kind of untrammeled individual expressivity. Freedom means above all free assent to higher imperatives, 'obedience to law and respect for the spirit of the laws'. The idea of 'liberty under the law' – as opposed to what he calls barbarian liberty – has, for Craig, a radical and paradoxical meaning.

> Liberty in responsibility and responsibility in liberty mean taking your orders direct from God instead of from other men. . . . There is no doubt that Christianity points the road to the maximum of earthly happiness, that it conforms in this respect to Aristotle's doctrine of happiness, and that it supplements and perfects that doctrine.
>
> (Craig 1949: 4, 10)

There is something absolutely breathtaking in the ease and self-assurance with which Craig proclaims the indubitable and absolute objective superiority of Christianity. This is a recognizably funda-mentalist or revivalist Christianity with a durable power to rejuvenate itself, despite its chronic and continual degradation by institutions that render it 'mythical, ceremonial, and sanctimonious'. Taking orders direct from God does not mean blind conformity with secular institutions that merely reflect the interests of 'other men'. At the same time, however, doubt, skepticism, anything like a critical spirit are evidence of barbarism. Christianity sets the standard for 'civilization', although exactly what content these terms possess is left undefined.

In the standard conservative view of religious and social tradition as it has been articulated by Petrarch, Thomas More, Edmund Burke, and others, the idea of 'taking orders directly from God instead of other men' is characteristic of the most hare-brained and terrifying radicalism. 'Other men' or in other words the accumulated wisdom of customary social practices may not perfectly represent an 'ideal' Christianity, but the best way to approximate conformity to God's will is through the collective intelligence of institutional life. To think otherwise is to assume either that 'other men' are utterly and hopelessly degraded or that God is a malicious deceiver. Craig himself adopts precisely this perspective to denounce the pretentious utopian claims of socialist parties. Liberty under the law, or taking orders directly from God, is not the same thing as usurping God's throne. The operative notion is in taking orders as opposed to giving them. As to the question of exactly how God's orders are transmitted, Craig has a quite definite answer.

Craig can reconcile his denunciation of socialism as a usurpation of God's providential initiative with his idea of liberty as 'taking orders directly from God', by arguing that God's orders are already implemented, though by no means completely, in Anglo-American political institutions.

When I was a student under Woodrow Wilson at Princeton I learned and took into my innermost belief the idea that our British-American form of government is itself a product of evolution and is indeed the working out in practice of the greatest discovery man has ever made in the field of government. . . . Totalitarianism in one form or another was the ancient, established, authoritarian thing in human government. But in the seventeenth century something happened, or began to happen, in the Anglo-Saxon race. . . . They saw that men can govern themselves and that, if men are allowed their natural liberty, they will thrive and prosper in the exercise of it. To this, far more than to any racial trait or special superiority, is due the fact that since the eighteenth century our race has spread over the whole world and has accomplished miracles in colonization and development.

(Craig 1949: 84)

Craig gave his *Freedom and Renaissance* lectures at the University of North Carolina in the late 1940s, when it was still a racially segregated institution. The references to 'our race' are obviously not intended as a mere figure of speech. It would be hard to imagine a more candid or self-congratulatory account of white supremacist politics and of Anglo-American global hegemony, although Craig is careful to credit a kind of institutional genius rather than a 'racial trait' for the 'miracles of development' taking place throughout the world. It is important to keep in mind, however, that this argument occurs in the context of defining a social and cultural role for the larger intelligentsia. The task of professional cadres, or in other words of scholars, is the discovery of legitimations as these are preserved in canonical literary and philosophical texts. Craig maintains that public education must be committed to training and staffing leadership cadres as the fundamental enabling condition of popular democracy. The task of eduction is to produce 'statesmen' so that the people can have 'friends and proponents among the educated classes'.

Craig describes his program as the 'restoration' of Jeffersonian principles. His views represent an interpretation of Jefferson considerably indebted to the theory and practice of American government advocated by Woodrow Wilson. American history proceeds as a counter-normative project or return to origins. The same counter-normative understanding of tradition constitutes the general *telos* of professional intellectual practice.[13]

In the substantive account of Shakespeare given by traditional historicist research the modernist nostalgia for presence is projected backwards through history. It is in Shakespeare that Old Historicist scholars find that absolute trust in a definitive order which they continue to desire for themselves. The Shakespeare that this research program discovers is learned rather than popular or spontaneously expressive. He is a 'man of substance' filled with contempt for the barbarism of the popular element. The value of his writing is in its affirmation of a higher truth-content that comprises both an ideal picture of Man and a series of illustrations of what happens when one fails to live up to the proper ideals. What I have tried to suggest in the preceding account of Old Historicism is a powerful correspondence between the substantive account of Shakespeare and the underlying cultural policy agenda that motivates this substantive account.

The supposed unity of the 'Elizabethan mind' is best understood as a coding for the unified national consciousness felt to be imperative in the highly conflicted social and political environment in which Spencer, Craig, and the other Old Historicist scholars worked. The identification of Shakespeare with order rather than with the 'emancipated individual', the insistence on a traditional world-view rather than on emergent social and spiritual initiatives and events reflect the anxiety and the *ressentiment* of professional cadres and social classes that feel themselves to be in decline, or who fear being engulfed by a 'barbarian' popular element. Craig, like Charles Mills Gayley, viewed the dispensation of 'liberty under the law' as the rational *via media* between the archaic forms of autocratic government, and the menacing degradation of social and cultural life anticipated in a 'baleful' Communism.

Hardin Craig was already in his 70s when the lectures that make up the text of *Freedom and Renaissance* were first delivered, which accounts, at least in part, for his distinctive affective and ideological orientation towards problems of post-war reintegration. Like many Americans, Craig did not see the post-war period as simply a return to business as usual. However, his conception of that reintegration was not based on notions of technical progress, or on wider social access to the 'American standard of living'. It was based instead on the idea of a 'renaissance of spiritual values'. Such a renaissance would be negative in the sense that it would oppose the instrumental values and calculations of self-interest that Craig saw as the dominant forms of modern consciousness. The culture-heroes of the Renaissance could provide what we would now call the 'role-models' for such a cultural project. 'The men of the Renaissance . . . never doubted that this is a world in which something can be done. This contrasts with a nerve-slackening skepticism in the modern world and to an unrecognized hedonism' (Craig 1949: 79). The critique of bourgeois skepticism and of an ideology of private self-interest are particularly striking in the context of the post-war period, especially in the light of a broad consensus that encouraged individuals to seek material compensation for sacrifices made during the war against Fascism. But Craig's argument is not a critique of bourgeois ideology, it is a reaffirmation of some of its characteristic themes. For Craig the enemy to be overcome is never identified as Fascism; it is barbarism, or crackpot utopianism, or sometimes clearly Communism that the post-war renaissance is mobilized against.

Craig's protest against the tyranny of instrumental values and of the increasingly pervasive hegemony of an industrial discipline is made in the name of an agrarian spiritual culture, rather than in solidarity with a progressive social movement of some kind. And in fact the entire text of *Freedom and Renaissance* resonates with echoes of 'the lost cause' and with the idea that the spiritual degradation of America is related to the hegemony of the industrial North.

> It would obviously be a very fine thing if we could now begin a revival of the spirit in America . . . it would be a possible and a very noble achievement if the South, instead of following along in the materialism of the North, would devote a generation or two to the task of saving the nation. (Craig 1949: 81)

The nation would be saved not only from the industrial and commercial materialism of the North, but also from the evils of socialism.

In one of his lectures Craig told his audience that he knew they preferred the 'American system' to Communism, but that he was prepared to enlighten them as to the reasons for this preference. To be opposed to Communism while remaining ignorant of its theoretical and its practical content was a fundamental imperative of the counter-subversive agenda that was already in place long before anyone had heard of Senator Joseph McCarthy. And it was this fundamental and persistent 'innocence' in his audience that Craig found ultimately most reassuring.

For Hardin Craig the immediate post-war period seemed to be the long-awaited moment for a Southern *risorgimento* that would redeem all of American society from a long period of waywardness and error.

> The defeated promise of the First World War, the downfall of Woodrow Wilson's plans for a universal peace, the greedy and piratical business activities of the 1920s, the decay of honest American culture in many people make me hesitant to say that you and I at this moment stand on the threshold of a new life for ourselves and our posterity . . . I am disposed to believe that there is even now the promise of a better world. (Craig 1949: 84–5).

Craig does not mention Fascism, or the massive dislocations of the Second World War, or indeed anything in the experience of recent history outside the United States, among the things that might make him 'hesitate . . . on the threshold of a new life'. Nor does he identify racial segregation as one of the aberrations from the ideal of freedom he proposes for Americans. In any case, for many people who had actually experienced the effects of the war at first hand, it did not seem to contain the 'promise of a better world'. On the other hand, the *desire* for a better world certainly made sense in this context, and it is this desire that is expressed not only in Craig's lectures, but in a number of other formulations of a post-war cultural policy agenda. *Freedom and Renaissance* is a powerful instance of nostalgia, a longing for the restoring of Craig's own lost 'social being'.[14] For the most part, however, post-war scholarship is characterized not by such nostalgia, but by the promise of a more inclusive and ecumenical view of American society that emerged in the doctrines of 'advanced liberalism' during the 1950s.

166

Chapter seven

FROM POLITICS TO SENSIBILITY

The end of the Second World War was an important period of cultural reintegration for the society as a whole. Hardin Craig's fantasy of a Southern *risorgimento* did not grow into a broad cultural consensus, although the counter-subversive and explicitly anti-socialist elements in his agenda were fundamental to the consensus that did in fact emerge. One of the primary social facts to which this cultural consensus was oriented was the reintegration of returning veterans into the peacetime economy. The complex program of demobilization obviously entailed a general settlement of institutional claims touching virtually all constituencies within American society. An important medium for this reintegration was the university system, which was made accessible to a much wider social spectrum than ever before. To facilitate this project it was important to foster a spirit of tolerance, brotherhood, and of mutual respect among various ethnic communities. The domain of learning was to be ecumenical, pluralistic, and open to everyone committed to the 'interests of general humanity'.[1] The immigrants whose presence frightened J. Q. Adams less than a generation earlier were now becoming integrated into the very apparatus that administered the sources of cultural discipline.

Although there were important continuities with the politics of the New Deal in the post-war cultural consensus, the period of the late 1940s could not be described simply as a return to business as usual. The reorganization of a broadly based coalition politics was undertaken in which the fundamental antagonisms in the society would be harmonized.[2] A diverse plurality would emerge around what Arthur Schlesinger called the 'vital center'. Schlesinger was an important spokesman for this cultural policy agenda, but he understood that there would be difficulties in promoting the unified

167

structure of feeling that would generate both a genuine solidarity within particular interest groups, and a diffuse loyalty to the state apparatus.

> We have made culture available to all at the expense of making much of it the expression of a common fantasy rather than of a common experience. We desperately need a rich emotional life, reflecting actual relations between the individual and the community. The cultural problem is but one aspect of the larger problem of the role of independent groups, of voluntary associations in free society. There is an evident thinness in the texture of political democracy, a lack of appeal to those irrational sentiments once mobilized by religion and now by totalitarianism ... a democratic society, based on a genuine cultural pluralism, on widespread and spontaneous group activity, could go far to supply outlets for the variegated emotions of man, and thus to restore meaning to democratic life.[3]

Schlesinger understood that the instrumental values that tended to predominate in democratically organized civil society could not in themselves satisfy affective and expressive needs even when the structures of civil society are reinforced by the 'common fantasies' of the culture industry. Identification with a parochial group or community was essential to the stability of the new 'pluralistic' order, but it was essential to prevent such group identification from emerging as divisive class consciousness. In the ideology of advanced liberalism it was suggested that class struggle had no meaning for American society, because of the background consensus of national unity that permitted a wide range of disparate interests to negotiate and settle their differences. This set of ideas was elaborated more fully in Daniel Bell's *The End of Ideology*, which argued that action-orienting ideologies, of which Marxism was the exemplary case, could no longer play any significant role in a society like the United States. Bell maintained that industrial society in the West had achieved such a high level of technical efficiency, satisfying the demands of the most varied interests, that symbolic legitimations in the form of ideologies were bound to disappear.[4] Nevertheless, as Schlesinger had already pointed out, the technical efficiency of the society, and the necessarily wide accessibility of educational opportunity that went along with this technical efficiency would very likely give rise to corrosive 'cultural contradictions', even if inherent economic contradictions could be managed or deferred more or less indefinitely.[5]

The imperative need for a unified and unifying national consciousness that transcends partisan and parochial interests was widely self-evident during the 1930s and even more so during the war years. The ability to transcend ideology must have seemed particularly valuable to those groups directly affiliated with hegemonic interests, especially when that ideology was subversive, or to put it bluntly, socialist. During the post-war period an even larger social investment in the elaboration of a national consciousness has been required. The spirit of ecumenical tolerance promoted so enthusiastically by Schlesinger carried with it one extremely important stipulation, namely that Communists would have to be excluded from the spectrum of legitimate disagreement. This would entail, among other things, the self-policing of institutions with respect to subversion and subversive elements. Within the academic community this function has usually been accomplished through a disciplinary ideology of pluralism and collegial tolerance.[6]

THE INSTITUTIONAL AUTONOMY OF LITERATURE

In an influential article first published in 1946, and frequently anthologized, Harry Levin set out to analyze 'Literature as an Institution'.[7] Levin's discussion of this topic begins with a consideration of the work of Hippolyte Taine. The earliest movement of a historicist kind was, in Levin's account, the scholarship of Renaissance humanism. Faced with the problem of comparing their own contemporary literature with that of classical antiquity, the humanists resorted to a strategy of historical relativism in order to diminish the force of invidious comparison. The nationalist movements of the early nineteenth century elaborated this doctrine by locating literary production within separate and distinct linguistic communities. Taine, working in the framework of 'scientific positivism', added a sociological dimension to the historical and geographical factors identified in these earlier intellectual movements. According to Levin, Taine's work constituted a link between literary criticism and the social sciences, but this created more problems than it solved. In addition, Taine's own construction of the problem was limited by his privileging of the realist novel as a universal norm for literary achievement.

169

Taine's critical theory is grounded upon the practice of the realists, while their novels are nothing if not critical. His recognition of the social forces behind literature coincides with their resolution to embody those forces in their works. The first to acknowledge Stendhal as a master, he welcomed Flaubert as a colleague and lived to find Zola among his disciples. . . . The social basis of art might thereafter be overlooked, but it could hardly be disputed. . . . On the whole, though critics have deplored the crudity of his analyses and scholars have challenged the accuracy of his facts, his working hypothesis has won acceptance. (Levin 1946: 159)

Levin points out that Taine was unable to apply his own method to the case of Shakespeare, who was characterized as virtually immune to social and environmental factors of any kind. But Levin's critique is less concerned with Taine's various lapses than with his failure to follow up the implications of his own position. The doctrine of environmentalism as enunciated by Taine does not distinguish between personality as a socially contingent and historically limited phenomenon, and art, which cannot be absorbed without remainder into the social milieu.

Sociological criticism, in Levin's view, is finally tangential to the concerns that should typify literary study. Sociological critics are insensitive to the implications of form, to what is specifically literary about literature, because their research demands that literature be subordinated to political ends. Taine had attempted to describe the social factors that determined the production of the literary text. Later sociological critics, such as Georg Brandes, had extended the sociological problematic into the areas of reception and the cultural effect of literary texts. This observation leads to a brief consideration of Levin's colleagues and contemporaries, the American Marxist critics V. L. Parrington and Granville Hicks. In general Levin regards this work as deeply flawed by a Marxist concern with *praxis* so exclusive and narrowly focused that it entails the 'device of discarding artistic standards'. Levin does not engage the implications of Marxist theory that call into question the very existence of independent and autonomous artistic standards. The idea that the aesthetic is itself a social phenomenon, or that literary standards are derivative of social relations is, in Levin's view, simply inadmissible. Literature is a genuine form of existent, it is a phenomenon that carries its own meaning within itself and that is its own reason for being in the world. The claims of sociology and of social history to give an exhaustive account of this phenomenon are simply dismissed in this essay not so much as a mistake but rather as a more pervasive type of obliviousness to a commanding and indubitable type of reality.

Despite his lack of sympathy for the Marxist research agenda, Levin does make a conscientious effort to do justice to this position. He views the sociological orientation as a limited one, but he also concedes that its pertinence has been solidly established.

> Literature is not only the effect of social causes; it is also the cause of social effects . . . it will be judged in the heat of the battle by its polemical possibilities. We need not deny the relevance or significance of such judgements; we need only recognize that they carry us beyond the limits of esthetic questions into the field of moral values. There are times when criticism cannot conveniently stop at the border.
>
> (Levin 1946: 163)

Levin was entirely clear in his own mind that a border actually existed, and that the domains of moral/political struggle and of aesthetic contemplation were each sovereign territories. What's interesting about this formulation is the acknowledgement that boundary disputes may occur, and that the frequency of such disputes is likely to increase over time.

Central to Levin's position is the distinction between a secure past and a problematic future. The identification of literary scholarship with the 'remembrance of things past' rather than with *praxis* is something of a commonplace in post-war literary study, although it is not entirely clear in what sense the past can be regarded as 'secure'. Evidently for Levin, as for many others, there is a point at which historical reality itself becomes a finished object. The contentious and troubling problem of narrating or interpreting is not itself a source of insecurity, since the past *as past* has become an impassive, quasi-aesthetic reality. This sense of the past as safely neutralized, innocuous, devoid of contemporary political effects seems to be as much a matter of forgetting or denying history as it is of understanding the workings of historical reality. It is helpful at this point to recall that 'Literature as an Institution' was written in the immediate post-war period, at a time when many intellectuals cherished the hope that the past could be, if not forgotten, at least consigned to memory and to the archive. 'We shall be safe while we are aware that virtue and beauty are as intimately related as beauty and truth, and as eternally distinct.' (Levin 1946: 164). This expresses as candidly as possible Levin's enduring faith in the doctrines of affirmative culture and of the existence of an autonomous domain of the specifically literary. Despite his desire to inhabit a safe and secure world, a desire for which he could hardly be blamed, Levin does not fail to acknowledge the problems raised for the practice of affirmative culture by the sociological approach.

The existence of a separate and autonomous domain of aesthetic reality does not lead Levin to a denial of the social situatedness of the art work or to the doctrine of art as an autotelic and fully self-justifying practice.

> The truth . . . is that literature has always been an institution. Like other institutions, the church or the law, it cherishes a unique phase of human experience and controls a special body of precedents and devices; it tends to incorporate a self-perpetuating discipline, while responding to the main currents of each succeeding period; it is continually accessible to all the impulses of life at large, but it must translate them into its own terms and adapt them to its peculiar forms. Once we have grasped this fact, we begin to perceive how art may belong to society and yet be autonomous within its own limits, and are no longer puzzled by the apparent polarity of social and formal criticism.
>
> (Levin 1946: 167)

The doctrine that literature has its own 'internal laws of development' has had manifold forms of expression, especially in the period since the end of the Second World War, and literary scholars will be familiar with one or more of its influential variants. The problem with this position is that of identifying a determinate content for the notion of the specifically literary. For Levin, this determinate content is identified as 'convention' though in the loose sense in which it is used here convention can hardly be 'specifically literary'. It is clear that he had reached a satisfactory middle ground here, one that avoided the radical dissolution of literature into an exclusively sociological category, but one that equally avoided the type of radical aestheticism that would de-humanize art in a quite different way.

Levin's discussion of literature as a social institution is actually a veiled political statement, one that hints at a general post-war settlement of institutional claims and functions. Reference has already been made to the openly expressed desire for safety and security here, a desire that was widely shared throughout American society in the years immediately after the end of the Second World War. The strategy selected for fulfilling that desire is hinted at in Levin's account of literature as 'belonging to society' and yet at the same time 'autonomous within its own limits'. This description corresponds very closely to the ideology of interest group politcs within a national consensus that was widely prevalent in the post-war period.

Within the general institution of literature, Shakespeare has a very particular historical position. In the first annual lecture delivered to the newly organized Shakespeare Association of America, Levin argued for the 'primacy of Shakespeare'. The argument begins with a quotation from Levin's antagonist for the occasion, Northrop Frye. In the *Anatomy of Criticism* Frye had argued for the application to literary criticism of a distinction considered basic in North American social science.

> Shakespeare, we say, was one of a group of English dramatists working around 1600 and also one of the great poets of the world. The first part of this is a statement of fact, the second a value judgment so generally accepted as to pass for a statement of fact. But it is not a statement of fact. It remains a value judgment, and not a shred of systematic criticism can ever be attached to it.[8]

In proposing this separation of systematic criticism from the socially inscribed activity of literary evaluation, Frye had in mind the general principle of literary autonomy. And in fact Levin's attack on Frye in this lecture seems quite peculiar, since it is in Frye's *Anatomy* that the general doctrines worked out in Levin's 'Literature as a social institution' appear to have been elaborated in very full detail. Whatever differences they might have, both Levin and Frye are passionate advocates of literary autonomy as a methodological principle, and of the independent existence of the literary domain as an ethical imperative. However, it is evident that Levin wants to situate the 'fact' of Shakespeare's greatness *within* the domain of the specifically literary, unlike Frye, who tended to interpret the inhabitants of the specifically literary universe in a more egalitarian spirit.

Frye's argument could be challenged at the level of the general distinction between facts and values itself, rather than the application of that distinction to literature in general or Shakespeare in particular. The idea that there are any facts at all, especially cultural or social facts, that are not at the same time social values is in itself a very dubious proposition. But Levin does not criticize the philosophical validity of the distinction, only its provenance. In his effort to establish that Shakespeare's 'primacy' or 'greatness' has the status of a fact, Levin presents an overview of the history of Shakespeare's reputation, a procedure that establishes quite emphatically that Frye's assertion is correct. If Shakespeare's 'greatness' is a fact, on the evidence Levin assembles it can only be a historically contingent social fact rather than a determinate feature of the domain of the specifically literary. And even in this respect the history of Shakespeare's reputation is by no means one of unanimous approbation.

'The primacy of Shakespeare' is an essay that demonstrates that Shakespeare's value has been a durable and settled cultural fact since the period of the Enlightenment. The argument concludes with an extremely brief and sketchy summary of the primary reasons for this cultural fact.

> Shakespeare occupies us as much as he does because he offers a principal key to our capacities for speech, and therewith opens access to experience beyond ourselves and our day. Insofar as the past stays alive, it lives through its first-hand communications, rather than the synthetic reconstructions of history . . . the writers' projections and formulations, so long as they last, are the strongest links in the chain of human time.[9]

Levin's argument here, as throughout the essay, is that Shakespeare's greatness may not be construed as a mere social convention. Leaving aside the troubling question of exactly what is meant by 'primacy' or 'greatness' it seems evident that the cultural obligations sedimented in Shakespeare's work cannot be satisfactorily explained as a mere custom. But Levin's attempt to engage with this argument finally ends in a relatively weak reiteration of the humanist faith in expressivity and vicarious experience.

FRYE AND BARBER: THE POLITICS OF RECONCILIATION

Northrop Frye articulated his views on Shakespeare in a series of lectures delivered at Columbia University in 1963. The Brampton Lectures were later published as *A Natural Perspective: the Development of Shakespearean Comedy and Romance.* The first lecture begins by making a broad distinction between critical orientations that privilege the genres of tragedy, realism, and irony, and Frye's own orientation that privileges comedy and romance.

> Many of our best and wisest critics tend to think of literature as primarily instructive. . . . They feel that its essential function is to illuminate something about life, or reality, or experience, or whatever we call the immediate world outside literature. . . . They are attracted to tragedy, to realism, or to irony, because it is in those modes that they find the clearest reflection of what Freud calls the reality principle.[10]

Frye's own alignment is with the literary genres of comedy and romance, which implies an affiliation with something like the pleasure principle or desire as the existential basis of his critical stance. The specific content of that desire, in Frye's exegetical system, is the unity or reconciliation of private subjectivity with a social totality. Literature, on this view, is itself a totality that expresses the various phases of that movement towards the horizon of reconciled wholeness.

Frye argues vigorously that literature is an authentic form of existence, although he does concede that the hierarchy of texts *within* the canon of literature is greatly affected by publicity.

> Shakespeare was more popular than Webster, but not because he was a greater dramatist; Keats was less popular than Montgomery, but not because he was a better poet. Consequently there is no way of preventing the critic from being, for better or worse, the pioneer of education and the shaper of cultural tradition. Whatever popularity Shakespeare and Keats have *now* is equally the result of the publicity of criticism.[11]

On this view the specific existence of literature demands that critics also exist, since it is only critics, and not the poets themselves, who can give an account of the literary work's being-in-the-world. Critics, in other words, do not create the redemptive media, but their work is crucial to the social and political administration of those media.

Because literature is a medium of social reconciliation, a reservoir of 'fables of identity', criticism must *exclude* from its practice the sort of invidious and trivializing judgement that reflects a primarily economic view of literature as cultural consumer goods of some kind.

The first step in developing a genuine poetics is to recognize and get rid of meaningless criticism. . . . [This] includes all casual, sentimental, and prejudiced value judgements, and all the literary chit-chat which makes the reputations of poets boom and crash in an imaginary stock exchange. That wealthy investor Mr Eliot, after dumping Milton on the market, is now buying him again; Donne has probably reached his peak and will begin to taper off; Tennyson may be in for a slight flutter but the Shelley stocks are still bearish. This sort of thing cannot be part of any systematic study, for a systematic study can only progress: whatever dithers or vacillates or reacts is merely leisure-class gossip.

(Frye 1957: 18)

Frye expresses here the idea that literary texts are 'priceless values' that exist in a domain set apart from the exchange values of the marketplace. This has two distinct consequences. First, invidious comparisons between literary works of art are inadmissible, since works of art exist in a kind of egalitarian state, embodying meanings that together constitute an indivisible totality. Second, it is specifically a leisure class appropriation that is expressed in the 'judgement of taste' and the allocation of a cultural 'dollar-value' to literary works of art in the form of lists of great, near-great and not-so-great texts. Frye's work is an effort to achieve a critical valorization of the totality of literature as a form of cultural resistance to this leisure-class appropriation. In that sense it is a rebuke to the programs enunciated by I. A. Richards, F. R. Leavis, and Lionel Trilling, all of whom stressed the element of discrimination as essential to criticism.

The 'priceless' character of the literary work makes the elaboration of value judgements socially invidious and intellectually pointless. The separation of the domain of literary values from political economy is not, in Frye's system, a matter of bidding up the cost of literary experience. To say that literature is a priceless value is not to be construed as meaning that only the rich can afford it. Attempts to systematize the practice of literary discrimination are condemned as illusions in the history of taste. It is in precisely this context that Frye makes the statement that Harry Levin later found so inflammatory, specifically that Shakespeare's greatness could never figure as a valid statement within a systematic – or scientific – criticism. But the argument that Frye actually makes, an argument substantiated by the evidence Levin assembles to refute it, is that literary value judgements are the expression of social interests, and

176

of parochial social interests at that. Aesthetic principles like high seriousness, the hierarchy of genres, decorum, and so forth are primarily expressions of the class structure of society. According to Frye, a scientific criticism, that is, a criticism that actually seeks knowledge instead of affirming any given historical moment in class society, must 'look at art from the standpoint of an ideally classless society'. This is an arresting statement, especially in a critic who would disavow any formal link either with a political or a philosophical Marxism. But Frye's polemic in the *Anatomy* is a protest against an elitist cultural and social policy enunciated through the aesthetic programs of humanist literary criticism that preceded him. The principles of a systematic criticism set forth in the *Anatomy* are an attempt to overcome the class-based and parochial appropriation of literature on behalf of a social totality. This is, however, only vaguely delineated in Frye's own work.

Frye's primary aim is not to articulate the social horizons in which the experience of resistance and reconciliation are to be enacted, but rather to describe the general co-ordinates of the domain of a specifically literary universe. That other world is in its totality – but only in its totality – the negation of the fragmented world of actuality and also an ideal alternative to that world. In this task he is willing to make common cause with T. S. Eliot, in so far as Eliot espouses 'the principle that the existing monuments of literature form an ideal order among themselves' (Frye 1957: 18). But Frye makes it clear that he has no desire to be affiliated with Eliot's cultural politics of Tory nostalgia for order and discrimination. Criticism, on Frye's view, is a type of genuine knowledge, and as such it is supposed to emancipate the subject from his or her own parochial interests. He thus takes issue with critics like Middleton Murry or Eliot himself who assert that critics must set definite standards, and must insist on definite positions or authoritative judgements of literary quality.

> There are no definite positions to be taken in chemistry or philology, and if there are any to be taken in criticism, criticism is not a field of genuine learning. . . . One's definite position is one's weakness, the source of one's liability to error and prejudice, and to gain adherents to a definite position is only to multiply one's weakness .
>
> (Frye 1957: 19)

Frye understands that a science must also be exclusive and intolerant in establishing the boundary between scientific and non-scientific statements, but his argument is concerned with parochial stands *within* the boundaries of a discipline. Knowledge is related both to freedom and to the idea of totality in that it is knowledge that emancipates the subject from particular class or cultural interests.

The broad socio-cultural principles set forth in the opening polemical chapter of the *Anatomy* are fleshed out in a program of readings governed by Frye's own distinctive and idiosyncratic hermeneutics. In that system it is comedy that emerges as the generic master code, because it is in comedy that the movement from *pistis* to *gnosis* is most clearly and most consistently articulated. In Frye's account comedy moves from a situation of rigid, archaic law (*pistis*) – we might characterize this as ideological blindness – to a situation of clarity, freedom, and social harmony based on mutual acceptance of difference. Comedy, on this view, is a utopian movement rather than a reaffirmation of existing social conditions. The unreality of comedy, its dependence on arbitrary plots and unbelievable conventions including the convention of the happy ending, is precisely what constitutes the 'natural perspective' that Frye identifies as the general *telos* of Shakespeare's romantic comedies. These plays provide a proleptic image of that world of reconciled wholeness which is the sovereign meaning shared by all of literature.

Frye's double stress on the reconciliatory social power of literature and on its fundamentally egalitarian character is elaborated in the specific program of hermeneutics for which he is best known. This is the doctrine of a literary and cultural totality unified by a single, overarching myth of a universal human experience.

> The mythical backbone of all literature is the cycle of nature, which rolls from birth to death and back again to rebirth. The first half of this cycle, the movement from birth to death, spring to winter, dawn to dark, is the basis of the great alliance of nature and reason, the sense of nature as a rational order in which all movement is towards the increasingly predictable. . . . Comedy . . . is based on the second half of this cycle, moving from death to rebirth, decadence to renewal, winter to spring, darkness to a new dawn. (Frye 1965: 119, 121)

In *Anatomy of Criticism* these principles are elaborated at length. Shakespeare's comedies provide the richest and most abundant reservoir of examples for the discussion of comedy in the terms described. In the more specialized study of Shakespeare romance, however, the element of *pistis* or repression is described as a necessary condition in the social movement towards emancipatory knowledge.

> . . .[I]rrational law represents the comic equivalent of a social contract, something we must enter into if the final society is to take shape. The irrational law, also, belongs to that aspect of nature which appears, in other contexts, rational, centered in the inevitable movement from birth to death. As the end of the comic action usually reconciles and incorporates its predecessor, what corresponds to the irrational law has been internalized, transformed to an inner source of coherence.
>
> (Frye 1965: 127)

Frye's idea of correspondence between inner and outer coherence, between a self-identity achieved through the internalization of repression and a social harmony achieved by the actual fulfilling of the social contract appears to be a religious rather than an obviously political agenda. Frederic Jameson, whose *Political Unconscious* is a working out of some of these same ideas in the conceptual vocabulary of the Frankfurt School, interprets Frye's doctrine as a primarily social application of religious symbolism.[12] As with earlier thinkers like Feuerbach and Durkheim, Frye discovers in a 'universal' religious symbolism the expression of a *collective* desire for the transcendence of social contradiction, inequality, and exploitation. Frye's 'myth of concern', like Durkheim's 'organic solidarity' is in many respects a socially conservative program in its affirmation of an all-encompassing social totality, but this is not the same thing as an affirmation of actually existing conditions.

The reconciliatory tendency is paramount in all of Frye's writing, but it is strongest and most confident in his discussion of Shakespeare's comedy. In the light of what is obviously an orientation to social integration and to the recuperation of transgressive cultural energy in a 'marriage' of disparate or forbidden social elements, the 'war against Northrop Frye' that was waged for a time by more conventional critics like Harry Levin is a bit puzzling. Frye's program is in many important respects a version of the same affirmative culture that was being actively promoted by Levin, by Lionel Trilling, and by many others. And Frye was certainly in agreement with Levin and others both as to the principle of literary autonomy and the identification of formal convention as the salient feature of the domain of the specifically literary. But the mainstream literary scholars who attacked Frye sensed a hidden agenda in his writing, although they were by and large unable to identify its content. The governing principles of Frye's hermeneutics were generally attacked, though it was the social/cultural agenda motivating that hermeneutics that was the primary source for the indignation and the sense of menace so widely felt by business-as-usual literary scholars during this period. For one thing, Frye's doctrine generally did away with the distinction between literature and popular culture. The same meanings that were present in literature were also present in comic books and in television programs, a fact that eliminated the primary *raison-d'être* of much of the preceding literary criticism. And to make matters worse, the main principles of Frye's hermeneutics could be learned in a matter of days, maybe even hours, by an attentive undergraduate, who would then have a way of decoding any number of literary works without any recourse to particularist research. In this sense Frye was actually in a position to make good his mild-mannered protest against the elitism of literary studies, but he was by no means able to exceed the general political horizons of affirmative culture, and both these effects can be traced to the same structural cause within Frye's program.

There is a fundamental ambiguity in the cultural politics of Frye's project of a systematic literary criticism. He confuses consensus politics, in which legitimate interest groups can negotiate among themselves, with resistance politics, which seeks to organize a coalition within the opposition against inequality and exploitation.

Desipte his avowed intention to develop a systematic criticism with an emancipatory function, Frye's program never developed into anything like a critical social or cultural theory. One reason for this is that Frye's myth-criticism, like any reconciliatory hermeneutics, is very well suited to the goal values of affirmative culture. By insisting on the autonomy of the domain of literature, Frye encouraged a contemplative interpretation of his program, one that focused primarily on inwardness and on an exclusively imaginative and expressive freedom as the ultimate horizon of resistance and social concern. This general routinization of his program was partly a function of its completeness and its coherence as a master code. Frye's great unifying myth provided a plausible answer to an unlimited number of interpretive questions, which made it virtually impossible to find any problems that would constitute a research agenda. Thus, although he was firmly committed to knowledge, and firmly opposed to the primacy of *ad hoc* aesthetic judgements, what Frye's system actually produced was neither science nor scientists, but a quasi-religious *doxa* of a fairly innocuous kind.

The task of administration of the redemptive media is, I have argued, not easy to reconcile with the activity of knowledge seeking. In the work of Northrop Frye the ministerial function is, finally, paramount. Frye's program really is egalitarian and ecumenical in spirit, so much so that it aroused considerable alarm in mainstream literary scholars, but it is also evangelical rather than critical in its epistemological and its social orientation. Reconciled wholeness as dream, or desire, is finally incompatible with the reality principle, or with history, or for that matter with knowledge, which is necessarily repressed in the comedies and the romances of Shakespeare. These plays provide the viewer with a marriage masque or some other ritual affirmation as the achieved resolution of dramatic or narrative tension.

> In a typically festive conclusion all previous conflicts are forgiven and forgotten. In ordinary life this phase is seldom a moral reality, because it is usually a contradiction: to forgive an offense implies that the offense was real; to forget it implies that something in it was not. . . . To forget implies a break in the continuity of memory, a kind of amnesia in which the previous action is put out of our reach.
>
> (Frye 1965: 132)

This amnesia, or better still, cancellation of the past is obviously linked to the doctrine of forgiveness and remission of sins, but it could hardly have any place in a critical theory. Freud would never countenance such 'forgetting', which would figure in psychoanalysis as an infantile regression. And it is precisely the refusal to forget the injuries and the suffering of real history that constitutes the fundamental point of departure for thinkers like Benjamin and Adorno. But for Frye forgetting the past is one of the necessary conditions for the achieving of reconciled wholeness. The reason for this is that in Frye's system of hermeneutics the 'transcendental signified' in the trajectory of desire is the return to a state of innocence.

Frye's description of a structural movement from *pistis* to *gnosis* is a way to accommodate the margin of anomie evident in Shakespeare's comic dramaturgy. An important variant of this position is elaborated by C. L. Barber in an article published in the *Sewanee Review*.[13] This essay attempted to account for certain features of Shakespeare's comedy through notions of 'license' or 'saturnalian release'. Barber's inspiration was unmistakably modernist in its orientation. The idea of a residual persistence of elements of folk-ritual had become familiar to a wide public through the imaginative writings of T.S. Eliot and James Joyce. The work of the 'Cambridge anthropologists' – F. M. Cornford, Jane Harrison, and Gilbert Murray – also contributed to this awareness. Inspired by these writers, Barber was able to sense something positive in the carnivalesque elements, the irreverent speech, disguises, games, and other modes of transgression represented in the plays. Traces of popular festive form in Shakespeare's writing are interpreted as the expression of surplus desire that can be recaptured to serve the interests of repression and rational order. Ludic and popular festive elements may entail genuine risks for the preservation of order, but occasional outbreaks of social effervescence and anomie are valuable in that they augment and enhance the capacity of a repressive social order to legitimate itself at the level of a communal structure of feeling. Order, as Barber conceives it, is dynamic rather than static; stable equilibrium is best achieved not through rigid and coercive insistence on duty, obedience, and knowing one's place, but rather in and through periodic 'release', which permits individuals to submit or accommodate themselves to 'rational' social constraints. Barber cannot offer any guarantee that all the surplus energy of festive release can be recaptured by the repressive regime. In his account of festive anomie, however, recognition of the need for harmonious accommodation occurs naturally in all but a few radically deranged and aberrant individuals. The 'refusal of festivity' is, for Barber, a serious breach of solidarity, one that can justify banishment.

Barber's thesis is certainly a very conservative one, based on the idea of a harmonious nature more or less faithfully replicated in the social division of labor and on an understanding of private human nature most fully realized in rational subordination. The notion of the world's 'hospitality to life' corresponds to the doctrines of the 'end of ideology', though the sustaining abundance that eliminates any need for antagonistic class-consciousness is located not in the sphere of technical efficiency but rather in nature. Nevertheless, his account of festive comedy has been criticized by quite a number of traditional historicist critics as a radical departure from the elaboration and instantiation of order central to Old Historicism. These objections to the Barber thesis are not without cogency. Even though Barber's theory of saturnalian release is fundamentally conservative, both socially and politically, it is also the thin end of the wedge. The idea that 'clarification' – that is accommodation to social order – happens only after a release that itself may entail quite hair-raising transgressions, is a muted but genuine threat to the project of order and to the argument that hierarchical social differentiation is in fact a valid and fully comprehensive principle of social rationality. For one thing Barber opened up the possibility that at least some forms of social anomie might not be dysfunctional. Such a suggestion has a most alarming corollary, because it implies that hierarchical social differentiation entails coercive restraint or at least some element of discomfort and inconvenience, especially for the unprivileged. What is radical in this otherwise conservative perspective is the implication that social badness, that is, discord, violence, suffering, and so on, might not be attributable to wayward desire in every case, but could be a consequence of hierarchy itself. Sacramental kingship, hierarchical social differentiation, the correspondence of social and of cosmic order, in short the whole intellectual apparatus of the Elizabethan world picture is revealed to be that most undignified of thought-forms, an ideology.

Barber did not pursue the issue of ideology in his account of social and dramatic form. Nevertheless, the theory of festive comedy is undoubtedly potentially subversive of the order reconstructed by Old Historicism. Despite its overtly reconciliatory and paternalistic ethos, Barber's work initiated a shift in scholarly orientation both to Shakespeare and to popular festive form. Barber not only brings 'social custom and dramatic form' into significant relation to each other, but also insists on drawing attention to the ludic elements in the theater. Nevertheless, this potentially subversive reorientation does not entail any notion of collective action leading to change.

Subversion, for Barber, remains a strictly private and parochial moment of defiance that in the end affirms the very order it pretends to uncrown or overthrow. The utopian spirit of social acceptance, generosity, and the release of desire is haunted by scattered images of violent exclusion. The saturnalian pattern of release and clarification replicates an element in the political unconscious of 'advanced liberalism', that is, the sparse casualties of the aggressive counter-subversive policy of the 1950s. The story of *Shakespeare's Festive Comedy* is a narrative fantasy, expressed in the genre of scholarly discourse, of a broad and ecumenical program of reconciliation and social healing. But the pattern of release and clarification is a euphemistically described program of surveillance and control of subversive energies.

Although Barber's theory of festive comedy is objectively conservative, the prominence of notions of transgression and desire made his work attractive to an emerging intellectual counter-culture. And in addition to his own work on festive comedy, Barber was extremely important in fostering the emergence of the feminist critique of Shakespeare. But the comic modalities of private transgression and public reconciliation elaborated by Barber and by Northrop Frye were not fully adequate to the problematic implied in their work. Frye attempted to subsume tragedy within a broader and more encompassing theory of comic romance. Barber was more reticent on the problem of the tragic genre. The reason for this is that the tragic problematic is extremely difficult to encompass within the ecumenical cultural and political dispensation envisioned in the various notions of festive comedy. Tragedy presupposes an action undertaken in a world that is finally *inhospitable* to life. The cultural agenda implicit in the criticism of Frye and Barber is utopian, but it is emphatically not action-orienting.

MAYNARD MACK: ACTION AND AMBIGUITY

The problem of social initiative and of action undertaken in a problematic setting is addressed in an influential article on Shakespearean tragedy by Maynard Mack. 'The world of Hamlet' was published in 1952 in *Yale Review*, which gave it a wide audience within the intellectual community, an audience that was considerably broader than the professional community of Shakespeare scholars. This article also formed the basis for Mack's undergraduate lectures on *Hamlet*. The essay begins by establishing the principle of local autonomy for the domain of literature. Like Harry Levin and Northrop Frye, Mack subscribes to the notion that great literature constitutes a world or microcosm that is distinct from actuality in its formal coherence and its semantic plenitude. This microcosm has its own internal principles of organization, but it is a world that matters to us because it is isomorphic with social and existential reality.[14]

Mack's interpretation of *Hamlet* sets aside the traditional problem of Hamlet's 'indecision' and stresses instead the problematic character of the social/existential 'world' that Hamlet must address. That world is structured in the 'interrogative mood'. The analysis of the text that follows from this observation is inflected by the influential work of Mack's 'new critical' colleagues and their stress on poetic ambiguity. Mack's analysis of the world of Hamlet is concerned less with verbal ambiguity, however, than with the more compelling problem of ontological ambiguity.

> Man in his aspect of bafflement, moving in darkness on a rampart between two worlds, unable to reject, or quite accept, the one that, when he faces it, 'to-shakes' his disposition with thoughts beyond the reaches of his soul . . . a world where uncertainties are of the essence.
>
> (Mack 1952: 507)

The universe in which Hamlet is obliged to make decisions is not only inhospitable, it is also undecidable and even grossly unfair in the demands it sets for individual agents. Furthermore, the normative codes elaborated by the human institutions are difficult to translate into any coherent program of actions.

Mack's essay depicts Hamlet as a character forced to accept a universe in which God is silent and may even be absent. But the absence of any kind of onto-theological certainty cannot be compensated for by any resort to social convention or the social contract. The structure of social relations in this play is, in Mack's analysis, constituted primarily in terms of predatory self-interest, meretricious self-fashioning, and a looming sense of individual mortality.

> The ghost's injunction to act becomes so inextricably bound up for Hamlet with the character of the world in which the action must be taken – its mysteriousness, its baffling appearances, its deep consciousness of infection, frailty, and loss. . . . He had never meant to dirty himself with these things, but from the moment of the ghost's challenge to act, this dirtying was inevitable. It is the condition of living at all in such a world. (Mack 1952: 518)

The idea that social reality is dirty or infected, and that even the most scrupulous moral fastidiousness cannot preserve the individual from defilement is prompted by the play. It would be difficult to say

185

that Mack's interpretation of the play is wrong. But this is something more than just an interpretation of 'the play itself', since, as Mack argues in the opening paragraphs, this play, Shakespeare's *Hamlet*, is a model or homologue with the ontological and social undecidabilities faced by his readers and auditors.

The modernist nostalgia for ontological certainty, the grieving over an absent Logos, resonates throughout Mack's essay. This pathos is, in the concluding phases of the argument, focused on the unreliability, the lack of self-identity of private subjectivity.

> Human infirmity – all that I have discussed with reference to instability, infection, loss – supplies the problem with its third phase. Hamlet has not only to accept the mystery of man's condition between the angels and the brutes, and not only to act in a perplexing and soiling world. He has also to act within the human limits – 'with shabby equipment always deteriorating', if I may adapt some phrases from Eliot's 'East Coker', 'In the general mess of imprecision of feeling, Undisciplined squads of emotion.' . . . [Hamlet] learns to his cost how easily action can be lost in 'acting', and loses it there for a time himself.
>
> (Mack 1952: 520)

What's missing from *Hamlet*, of course, is any sense of human solidarity or human social purpose that would constitute an action-orienting philosophy. Or at least that is a pattern of meanings that becomes visible and painfully so in the world of Maynard Mack and his students. What is fascinating about this essay is the way it maps a strategic retreat from ontological and theological certainty through the domain of political and social relations to the sphere of private ethical sensibility. It is on this final ground, on these 'battlements', that the subject must come to terms with something mysterious and unintelligible 'out there' that refuses to give any coherent account of itself.

I want to conclude this discussion of the discourse on Shakespeare that characterized the immediate post-war period by relating Mack's essay to part of its intertext. The article that follows immediately after Mack's 'The world of *Hamlet*' in the *Yale Review* for 1952 is entitled 'Viet Nam: a nation off balance', by Paul Mus.[15] Obviously the positioning of these two articles is a kind of fantastic coincidence, but I would like to attempt a very brief 'reading' of that coincidence here. Mus begins with a general description of Vietnamese society as it has been observed by visitors. This description is remarkable for

186

the way it so easily adopts the normative criteria of 'western civilization' as natural categories.

> No civic spirit, a general lack of foresight, the individual disengaged and alienated from society – such is the dark side of the picture drawn by visitors to Viet Nam. They give us another side, too, but the dark side is worth emphasizing because it presents the most problems, especially the problem of accounting for these faults. Are they to be attributed to some profound lack in the Vietnamese character, or to the way circumstances have shaped Vietnamese life, or to some peculiarity in the attitude of the observers, men of good will though they undoubtedly are?
>
> (Mus 1952: 525)

This essay, written in the period immediately before Dien Bien Phu, still assumes, without the least self-consciousness, that Vietnam is a suitable theater of operations for the 'men of good will' who read the *Yale Review*. What makes this essay chilling, especially in retrospect, is not only the way it reveals an intention to take action 'on behalf of Vietnam' but also in the way it projects and displaces its own 'dark side', its own imbalances and contradictions into Vietnamese society.

Mus interprets Vietnam as a society thrown off balance by the complex transition from a traditional, ritualistic state to a modern political economy. In this transition, according to Mus, it is the Vietnamese who experience a demoralizing sense of anomie and a radically destabilizing pathos of modernity. The modern fate in the form of civil society with its demand for individual responsibility cannot be resisted, though Mus implies that some form of assistance from western society will be absolutely necessary if the transition is to be achieved.

> Viet Nam's lack of balance . . . comes from the irreparable loss of that ancient harmony which gave to life its sense of being natural. . . . The charge to bring against the foreign domination is not that it destroyed time-honored institutions; in so doing the French merely performed an historical function. . . . Their real mistake was that they introduced an economy based on exchange without being sufficiently aware of the need to adjust it to the whole society of the country.
>
> (Mus 1952: 532–3)

Mus's distinctions between the ritualistic village and civil society and his sense of the socially corrosive effects of the exchange

187

economy, correctly identify elements in his own political unconscious, but at the same time disavow these elements of contradiction
by locating them in the 'imbalance' of Vietnam.

There is an eerie resonance in Mus's essay of 'The world of
Hamlet', a resonance within the shared political culture common to
the audience addressed in the two articles. In both these essays the
imperializing, masculine subject of political economy, equipped with
little more than vague good intentions, must commit himself to
action within a setting he cannot hope to understand. The
premonition of disaster in this ominous situation will be confirmed,
but on a much larger scale than the subject anticipates.

Chapter eight

SUBVERSION AND ITS CONTAINMENT

The 'great Shakespeare' was discovered, at least for Americans, by Ralph Waldo Emerson. That same 'great Shakespeare' is the origin and the object of contemporary scholarly and critical discourse. But where Emerson was able to speak of Shakespeare in the broadest general terms, assuming evidently that his readers would be able to derive their own originality directly from the textual source, contemporary writers must engage in the most intense scrutiny of textual detail. The reason for this latter-day requirement of close reading is connected with the problem of sustaining the Emersonian ideal of the autonomous subject in the present historical moment. In Emerson's context that subject was still living the immediate post-revolutionary experience of American society. The economic and political, to say nothing of the geographical, contours of that society were incomplete and unfinished. For someone like Stanley Cavell, or Stephen Greenblatt, or the writer of the present study, however, neither the struggle for national union nor the idea of manifest destiny can still be lived with while putting the same trust in the future that Emerson seemed to have. On the contrary, contemporary Americans are obliged to live the idea of manifest destiny in the context of Vietnam and of an interventionist Central American policy, and it is in respect of these real historical events that Emersonian confidence vanishes. In its place there is a sense of anomie which can not be made good by appeals to social order or even common sense.

STANLEY CAVELL: THE DEFENCE AGAINST SKEPTICISM

In 1952, when Maynard Mack published 'The world of Hamlet', the 'imbalance' of Vietnam was still on the next page. Fifteen years later, Vietnam breaks through in the midst of an interpretive essay on *King Lear* by the philosopher and literary theorist Stanley Cavell. This remarkable passage, which is presented here in full, was first published in *Must We Mean What We Say?* It is all the more striking in that Cavell is not primarily identified with militant protest of any kind, nor is the essay itself oriented in any obvious way to the aim of social or political criticism.

[Of] the great modern nations which have undergone tragedy, through inexplicable loss of past or loss of future, or self-defeat of promise, in none is tragedy so intertwined with its history and its identity as in America. It is cast with uncanny perfection for its role, partly because its power is so awe-inspiring, partly because its self-destruction is so heartbreaking . . . its knowledge is of indefeasible power and constancy. But its fantasies are those of impotence, because it remains at the mercy of its past, because its present is continuously ridiculed by the fantastic promise of its origin and its possibility, and because it has never been assured that it will survive. . . . Those who voice politically radical wishes for this country may forget the radical hopes it holds for itself, and not know that the hatred of America by its intellectuals is only their own version of patriotism. It is the need for love as proof of its existence which makes it so frighteningly destructive, enraged by ingratitude and by attention to its promises rather than to its promise.

Since it asserted its existence in a war of secession and asserted its identity as a war against secession it has never been able to bear its separateness. *Union* is what it wanted. And it has never felt that union has been achieved. Hence its terror of dissent which does not threaten its power but its integrity. So it is killing itself and killing another country in order not to admit its helplessness in the face of suffering . . . it turns toward tyranny to prove its virtue. It is *the* anti-Marxist country, in which production and possession are unreal and consciousness of appreciation and of its promise is the only value.[1]

This passage, which comes towards the conclusion of a very long essay, seems completely unmotivated; it would be difficult to anticipate, reading through some hundred pages or more of very close textual analysis, that Cavell's intellectual trajectory is leading to this extraordinary rhetorical outburst.

The Preface to *Disowning Knowledge in Six Plays of Shakespeare,* where this essay is reprinted as the *first* chapter, appears to disavow these words. The Vietnam oration is described as a scar, or as an aside, something not really integral to the body of the essay. And yet in the republished version that trace of Vietnam has not been effaced. I believe that these 'scars of our period in Vietnam' are of fundamental importance not only for understanding where Stanley Cavell is coming from, but also for delineating a number of other contemporary transformations within the contemporary cultural dispensation.

In a recent article in *Critical Inquiry*, Cavell describes a sequence of events at a recent conference in which a 'senior scholar' denounced the educational reforms of recent decades and urged the reassertion of values enshrined in the literature of the Renaissance.[2] Later that same day a 'young professional' denounced the 'senior scholar' and, in Cavell's version of events, maintained that Shakespeare's writings were inessential to the delineation of our values. In this dialogue of Youth and Age, it is the opinions of Youth that are made to seem a bit more unsettling, but the main intention here is not to take sides in this debate, but to explicate it from the position of a relative outsider. For Cavell what this encounter means is that a field where two such positions can appear to coexist must be in a state of paradigm crisis.

Following Thomas Kuhn, Cavell also observes that such a state of crisis might be precisely the condition of business-as-usual within the humanities.[3] The essay does not, however, consider the argument, made by Kuhn and others, that paradigm crisis in the sciences is correlated with structural changes and re-orientations in the socio-cultural sphere, and that the very idea of a paradigmatically rigorous 'science' is inseparable from the historical emergence of bourgeois political economy.[4] But the wider implications of Kuhn's work are not pursued here; in order fully to appreciate the sense of crisis articulated in this essay, it is necessary to return to Cavell's massive parapraxis in his analysis of *King Lear*.

Cavell's work on Shakespeare is an attempt to address the problem of philosophical skepticism, which he sees emerging in the text of the plays. From the perspective of philosophy these plays are themselves interpretations of skepticism, and, at the same time, susceptible of interpretation *by means of* a complex linguistic and ontological skepticism. Because this project assumes that the skeptical problematic is already fully inscribed within Shakespeare's *oeuvre*, it necessarily troubles the boundary between philosophy and literature as professional disciplines, but this is exactly the effect Cavell wants to produce.

Disowning Knowledge is written in a highly self-conscious style that recalls the rather less systematic writing of Ralph Waldo Emerson, and it is indeed with Emerson that Cavell most wishes to be identified. Like Emerson's, Cavell's is a philosophy of intuition, or more precisely, one organized around the dialectic of intuition and tuition. This is a difficult position to defend, or even to state, because it must not only defend itself against skepticism, but equally against knowledge, at least in the sense that knowledge is understood from the perspective of the Enlightenment.

> In calling my guiding theme an intuition I am distinguishing it from a hypothesis. Both intuitions and hypotheses require what may be called confirmation or continuation, but differently. A hypothesis requires evidence and it must say what constitutes its evidence. . . . An intuition, say that God is expressed in the world, does not require, or tolerate, evidence but rather, let us say, understanding of a particular sort.
>
> (Cavell 1987: 4)

This 'understanding' is itself a type of 'enlightenment', though of a spiritual rather than a cognitive type. In the 'scientific' meaning of enlightenment – which describes a social effect – knowledge is something achieved through a particular kind of labor; enlightenment is the consequence or 'product' of that labor. In the philosophy of intuition, you have to 'see the light' first; epistemological labor is linked here with notions of domination and possession.

The ancestral burden, obligation, or gift that we know as Shakespeare is a powerful instance of this intuitive – as opposed to possessive – knowing. The argument here develops Emerson's distinction between the primary act of intuition and the ensuing of that primary act in a tuition or putting into words. Evidently intuition is something that befalls or happens to someone, it is not an action, cannot be achieved through strategic deliberation. This is why Shakespeare is a 'creature' of certain wordings which themselves can function as tuitions leading to fresh intuitions. All of this actually runs against the grain of any determinate knowing.

> Epistemology will demonstrate that we cannot know, cannot be certain of, the future, but we don't believe it. We anticipate, and so we are always wrong. Even when what we anticipate comes to pass we get the wrong idea of our powers and of what our safety depends upon, for we

imagine that we *knew* this would happen. . . . Nietzsche thought the metaphysical consolation of tragedy was lost when Socrates set *knowing* as the crown of human activity. . . . Bacon and Galileo and Descartes were contemporary [with Shakespeare]. We will hardly say that it was *because* of the development of the new science and the establishing of epistemology as the monitor of philosophical inquiry that Shakespeare's mode of tragedy disappeared. But it may be that the loss of presentness . . . is what works us into the idea that we can save our lives by knowing them.   (Cavell 1987: 93–4)

The alarm expressed in the historical coinciding of Shakespeare with Bacon, Galileo, and Descartes echoes the sentiments expressed some thirty years earlier by Cavell's predecessor at Harvard, Theodore Spencer. But of course Stanley Cavell is the legitimate successor of a long line of 'transcendental subjects' located in Cambridge, Mass., a line of descent that converges very powerfully in the writings of Emerson and that powerfully reasserts itself in this remarkable discussion of *King Lear*.

When Stanley Cavell speaks of Shakespeare's 'medium of drama' he is not thinking of a historically determinate social and economic institution, but rather of a complex genre of spiritual awareness expressed through an equally complex genre of verbal representation. Shakespeare's interpretation of skepticism, his representation of the knowing subject's loss of ontological certainty and the defection of God, reveal the close connection between the violence implicit in the project of objectifying knowledge, and the destructiveness implicit in skepticism. These two antagonists or opponents of 'presentness' are actually one and the same. Since presentness is, in today's context of philosophical discourse, a very loaded expression, it is important to distinguish precisely what force it is intended to have here.

The 'presentness' to which *Disowning Knowledge* is committed derives from notions of ordinary language and the social interactions that such notions imply. Skepticism must be opposed as an irresistible power to isolate and to excommunicate; the objection here is not to philosophical wrongfulness, but to the socially destructive character of the skeptical orientation.

My work begins with philosophical defenses of the procedures of ordinary language philosophy, of appeals to the ordinariness of our attunements in words as responses to the skeptical threat. In recent years

I have identified what philosophy thus calls the ordinary or everyday with what in literature is thematized as the domestic, or marriage. . . . the paradox of marriage (two becoming one) is the paradox of the ordinary (the union of public and private).

(Cavell 1987: 29)

The ground of knowing is in the immediacy of interpersonal relations, which is also the ground of ethical determinations. It becomes clear in the interpretation of *King Lear*, however, that the sphere of personal relationships is not a foundational knowledge in the usual meaning of this expression, though it is an authentic standpoint from which to resist the onslaught of skepticism. The social other – lover, child, friend, or colleague – is not an *object* to be known, but rather a subject to be *known by*. To suffer another to know you is, apparently, the basis for Cavell's notion of love.

In his reading of *King Lear*, Cavell stresses Lear's violent struggles to avoid being recognized or known, to ward off the 'the shame of exposure, the threat of self-revelation'. This manoeuver appears to be the obverse of skepticism, or in other words it is the desire that one would not be known, not be objectified for the knowledge of another. The self and its deepest desires are a secret that must be kept at all costs. Thus, in Cavell's reading of the first scene,

Lear knows it is a bribe he offers, and – part of him anyway – wants exactly what a bribe can buy: (1) false love and (2) a public expression of love. That is, he wants something he does not have to return *in kind*, something which a division of his property fully pays for.

(Cavell 1987: 61)

This bribe or *quid pro quo* is a way to maintain the concealment of self, to keep it not only intact and inviolate, but unknowable. The hypostatizing of 'personal integrity', the insistence on closed and inaccessible individuality, is, for Cavell, the 'avoidance' of love that ensues in the catastrophic horrors that the play depicts. Lear keeps himself secret so as to avoid the shame of exposure, but the result of this commitment is to permit others to constitute him as mere object and to compel his utter social abjection. With a slight shift in vocabulary we might describe Lear's 'avoidance of love' as a 'refusal of solidarity'. This slight shift would indicate a possible further direction for Cavell's analysis to follow, but it would also signal that this direction is 'the road *not* taken'. The point I wish to stress here is that Cavell's analysis must perforce lead him to consideration of *social relations*, or in other words to the oration on Vietnam, but his philosophical position makes it impossible to speak of the social except in terms of a private, affective dimension of interpersonal relationships.

To speak of 'solidarity' as opposed to 'love' is an attempt to grasp the primary social bond as something other than an extension of family connection or the need for intimacy. This is a move that Cavell does not want to make. His own construction of the social bond is clear in his summary of the interpretation of *King Lear*.

> Suppose we see in the progress of Lear's madness a recapitulation of the history of civilization or of consciousness: from the breaking up of familial bonds and the release of offenses which destroy the social cosmos, through the fragile replacement of revenge by the institutions of legal justice, to the corruption of justice itself and the breaking up of civil bonds. (Cavell 1987: 76)

The violent derangement that *King Lear* forces us to witness may be grasped as the history of civilization *or* of consciousness. Cavell recognizes in this material that the psychoanalytic trajectory is already present in Shakespeare's dramaturgy, which presents us with a self-enclosed and highly self-conscious subject isolated within the heart of the family romance. Here the family is no longer a kinship network that confers identity and helps to sustain it, so much as it is a perpetually destructive struggle for ascendancy – or personal integrity. What this analysis cannot discover, however, is that the psychoanalytic subject *and* the family romance which is his *mise-en-scène* are both historically related to the mode of subjectivity brought into being by bourgeois political economy and the elaboration of civil society.

Cavell identifies the opening scene of *King Lear* with the idea of a bribe or *quid pro quo*, but he does not discuss at length the relationship between notions of payment or exchange, and the notion, evidently central to his interpretation of Lear's character, of a desire for personal integrity and closure so hyperbolically outrageous that it demands an absolute refusal of love. In the civil society that is brought into existence by the bourgeois revolutions at the end of the eighteenth century, the protocol of social relations is circumscribed by the requirements of 'rational exchange' between autonomous economic agents. These revolutions dismantled an *ancien regime*, intending to abolish not only all hierarchical relations of *Herrschaft*, but equally and at the same time, all collegial relations of *Genossenschaft*. The 'freeing' of the subject from the constraints of a traditional social order or social ethos exacts a price, however, and it is this pathos of the autonomous private subject that Cavell, and others, have discovered within the plays of Shakespeare. I should add here that it is my conviction that this exceptional subject is 'really there', though it could not become visible for critical understanding until the structure of social relations made some degree of critical empathy with these extraordinary characters possible.

The dilemma created for Cavell by the challenge of skepticism can be resolved by a certain loyalty to canonical texts, and above all to Shakespeare. Instead of seeking to know the text, however, it seems that the subject must be known by the text, or, in Emerson's words, 'Shakespearized'. The transcendental subject of Emerson's philosophy must redefine his social and political horizons in accordance with private ethical sensibility. Cavell reads 'the Great Shakespeare' from this stance of civil privatism, but even this last redoubt of reliable tuition seems threatened by the general disaffection not only of the uneducated mass, but also and more disturbingly of those same 'young professionals' who would normally have continued to promote an affective bonding of new generations with Shakespeare, and with other canonical writers.

There is pervasive anomie and latent instability within the present social dispensation, though the source of these phenomena is not a small handful of dissident intellectuals or wayward 'young professionals'. For those who share the outlook articulated in *Disowning Knowledge*, however, the failure to achieve and to sustain successful social integration cannot be attributable to structural contradiction or ambiguity in the sphere of political and economic organization. The eternal supremacy of autonomous individuality within the 'rationality' of the marketplace is the *alpha* and *omega* of this position, even when it has not been explicitly articulated. In the light of this imperative, then, the management and control of redemptive media take on an extraordinary importance. Venerable themes of falling away, the return to origins, and the counter-normative reaffirmation of traditional values come powerfully back into play.

Cavell's orientation to the authority of canonical text is complex; he does not rely on unsupported assertions about the priceless value

196

of literature or the affirmation of western achievements. Literary texts are not exactly knowledge in the commonsense meaning of that expression, but they are part of the philosophical trajectory that Cavell relates to the historical struggle for knowledge. This orientation is motivated, not by a desire for a scientific integration of theory and practice, but rather by what I have called the counter-normative movement of tradition. Cavell wants to bring himself into relation with Shakespeare as significant other; although he understands that this can never be an unmediated relation, he nevertheless tends to move towards the horizon of a return-to-origins. Fidelity to the text remains a fundamental tenet in the practice of many literary scholars.

RICHARD LEVIN: AGAINST READING

Within the practice of business-as-usual literary scholarship there is a powerful counter-normative movement of tradition expressed not so much in a will to absolute origins, but rather in the idea of the being-in-itself of the art work as the general *telos* towards which all critical activity is oriented. This orientation has been fundamental to the background consensus of literary debate. This attitude may entail a denunciation of interpretation in favor of affirmation of the thing in itself, the art work as a priceless aesthetic value, or as the sedimented expressivity of an individual artist. Judged by this standard, all interpretation can be indicted both for its effrontery in seeking to provide a substitute for 'the real thing' and for its repressive 'institutionalization' of the artist. This account of literary interpretation or 'reading' as both an excessive private egoism *and* as a diffuse mode of socially conventional repression is not an entirely paradoxical position when these ideas are viewed within a counter-normative orientation to tradition.

The counter-normative agenda is perennially active in the study of Shakespeare and of other Renaissance dramatists; it is given elaborate formal and rhetorical articulation in Richard Levin's challenge to the institutional centrality of reading. This challenge is set forth in Levin's much cited *New Readings vs. Old Plays*, which attempts a broad synoptic overview of critical writing about Renaissance drama from about 1950 through the mid-1970s. In general Levin raises the question 'Why is there interpretation?' or 'What do we need interpretations for?' and then proceeds to a

197

critique of certain contemporary models of exegesis that seem, to him at least, to add little to anyone's knowledge of the original material. The normative criteria used by Levin to demonstrate this fact are unclear in the opening assault on the tyranny of 'readings'. Levin's reconstruction of the principles of reading does not distinguish between notions of interpretation as 'supplements' of the text and notions of interpretation as 'semantic models' or 'concretization of indeterminacies'.[5] Despite this lack of theoretical clarity, however, he does identify an implicit claim central to every reading, namely that reading distinguishes between apparent and non-apparent meaning. Since Levin is himself committed to the task of separating good interpretations from bad ones, he takes this claim very seriously, but finds it unwarranted in almost every case. Reading, on this account, belongs mainly to the history of cultural error, and in some cases it represents something worse, like willfully meretricious distortion or even malicious deception. In any case it is clear that the attack on the primacy of reading is a protest against routine institutional scholarship and the encouragement it offers to opportunistic seekers after professional reputations. Levin's own position insists not only on the absolute supremacy of the text, but equally on the transparency of that text as against interpretive distortion or mystification.

One of the more influential articulations of this counter-normative return to origins has been Susan Sontag's essay 'Against interpretation'. Sontag's point of departure for her argument is a notion of the primordial condition of art as an experience fully integrated with the larger spiritual life of a community. 'Art . . . was incantatory, magical . . . an instrument of ritual.' The notion of a primordial cultic status for the artist is important for establishing that an artist does something. The idea that an artist 'means something' in the sense of a paraphrasable discursive content is a refusal or even betrayal of 'the real thing'. On this view the concreteness of an art object is the residual form of an originating act. Attention must be directed to that act if the art object is to do its work. Since the ephemeral gesture is crystallized in a durable object, one that is easy to conserve in a curatorial setting, the sense of immediacy is gradually lost, and so interpretation, initially a compensatory function, gradually insinuates itself into the place of the art work. Routine institutional life becomes a substitute for an experience of immediacy in the encounter with what is radically other.

This notion of the interpretive adulteration of the art work, or the obscurantism of every interpretation, is common to all writers working within a counter-normative agenda. For Sontag what is at stake is not the purification or reform of religious authority, but rather 'transparency [as] the highest and most liberating value in art – and in criticism'.[6] This encompasses the affirmation of the art work, as well as the experience of sensuous immediacy and libidinal gratification that such work offers to a responsive subject. On this account reception should be guided not by a hermeneutics but by an erotics.[7]

It would probably astonish Richard Levin to learn that in his critique of reading as vitiated institutional scholarship he makes common cause with Susan Sontag. Nevertheless, the attack on 'reading' is a reprise of many of Sontag's themes, and in some cases appears to be a near paraphrase. The close family resemblance between Sontag's 'Against interpretation' and Levin's attack on 'reading' is puzzling, given the apparent ideological divergence in their respective outlooks. But the convergence of these two positions does reflect a situation of 'neighboring differences' within a broader counter-normative orientation. Both sets of ideas are motivated by similar utopian longing for radical undifferentiation of definitive personal authority and the nurturing, sensuous immediacy of a pre-industrial social life-world. That longing imagines a disappearance of alienating institutional forms and the return of communicative intimacy and affective fullness. Sontag's ultimate horizon is that of expressive, antinomian individualism and thus an existential refusal of routine institutional life. On this view the art work embodies such a refusal of the routine and the conventional, its value derives from transgression and even violence. For Levin, however, art is seen, not as transgressive, monstrous, or subversive, but as a fund of commonsense meanings that can be kept in general circulation without the mediation of any specialized theoretical discourse.

Levin privileges what he calls the 'apparent meaning' as a normative standard, a notion that corresponds very closely to Sontag's 'clear meaning'. The practitioners of reading are taken to task for their effrontery in displacing the clear or apparent meaning for a new one of their own invention. Levin concentrates for the most part on the shabby egoism, and the foolish competitiveness of reading as a discursive practice. But the illustrative material assembled here suggests a somewhat different conclusion. Implicit in

Levin's evidence is the inference that *every reading is in principle irrefutable*. The voluminous compilation of examples gradually reveals that a reading is a performative genre that traces a private act of cognition. Every reading, in other words, is implicitly framed by the statement 'I interpret the play *this* way' or 'This is *my* reading of the text'. As a report of a subjective experience or phenomenological description such discourses cannot be false, unless their authors are lying about what they see in the text.

The claim that readings 'distort the text' is not wrong – it is basically meaningless. The real question to be raised in respect of reading is to ask exactly what *interest* any such private cognition can have for another interpreting subject. Even more pertinent would be the problem of the social function of an institutional practice that circulates but does not attempt to co-ordinate this affluence of private meaning. The normative or co-ordinating standard that Levin proposes is the apparent or the established meaning, which should enjoy absolute authority in the field of interpretation.

The equation of 'apparent meaning' with 'established meaning' raises some difficult problems with the phenomenon of ideology, but Levin is not much concerned with the possibility that meaning could become established as the result of a diffuse misrecognition of social relations. His notion of established meaning is derived from a model of the social process of authorial production and the reception of the authorial meaning or intention. The model is based on the following assertions:

1 The dramatist wanted to be understood by his audience.

2 The dramatist was competent, he had the ability to achieve the objective stated in (1)

3 We can trust not only the playwright's candor and his competence, but also the response that his writing has evoked in most viewers and readers.

These assumptions, and the model of communication that they imply, are crucial to understanding Richard Levin's implicit cultural agenda. The general protocol set forth here, however, contains several intractable difficulties.

To begin with, it is by no means reasonable to assume that authors want to be understood. Under conditions of censorship and persecution, conditions that occur more often than not in historically concrete socio-cultural settings, it is not at all self-evident that dramatists want to be understood.[8] Even under the relatively more

200

pleasant conditions of liberal society, guile and perversity may figure in any account of an author's desire. Leo Strauss has demonstrated that the social fact of persecution must always be taken into account in any consideration of writing, even in the case of expository discourse.[9] In the case of Elizabethan *drama*, where clowns, devils, and other marginal figures are constantly present, the unexamined assumption that we can proceed from an author's simple and honest desire to be understood seems completely disingenuous. It amounts to denying that there could have been anything subversive in the material, anything that might need shielding from official surveillance, censorship, and the monitoring of cultural production by the state apparatus.[10]

Levin's stipulation of the author's competence is proposed as a purely notional suggestion that writers are able to do whatever it is that they do. However, there is a more precise sense of linguistic and communicative competence that ought to be considered in this context. Linguistic competence is a social and a historical phenomenon; a writer's communicative competence presupposes a *specific* community of native speakers. The features of a language – usage, vocabulary, etc. – are not, however, either socially or historically invariant. For this reason the specific communicative competence of a writer is oriented to a specific group of native speakers. Any writer is increasingly likely to be misunderstood as the social and historical distance from that community of native speakers increases. The idea of an obvious meaning generated from a historically invariant and abstract competence must be predicated on an equally abstract – and equally naïve – conception of the social context of communication.

The communicative model adopted by Levin represents an idyllic – or utopian – situation characterized by absolute candor, trust, and openness between the parties to a singular communicative action that can be exactly reproduced under any and all social conditions with exactly the same cognitive and affective results. Such a view requires an extremely idealized view of communicative agents with exactly matching competence operating within invariant linguistic/communicative codes. It also requires an absolutely uncluttered communicative space. On this view communicative interference and the circulation of perverse misinterpretations are purely contingent phenomena, motivated by discursive and political malevolence.

The apparent naïveté of Levin's communicative theory is quite misleading. In fact this is essentially a political doctrine to the effect that consensus and common accord are natural, easily reached, and stable over time. Values, purposes, social imperatives, do not change, though various contingent historical factors may interfere with the easy circulation of such established meanings. This is the view that in matters of social, cultural, or political discussion everything is out in the open, the debate is clear, honest, and participants are uncoerced. Things as they are reflect both reason and common accord, or at least they would if there were not active conspiracies that aim at the overthrow of a durable natural order. Levin's position then is programmatic in its aims. The counter-normative impulse is also a counter-subversive program. The return to the 'original' object – in this case it happens to be an 'old play' – is linked up with a cultural policy that repudiates routine, conventional institutional life in favor of the re-affirmation of a long-lost tradition. In this context, however, tradition has a primarily instrumental meaning as the means by which subversion and the usurpation of discursive sovereignty may be opposed.

The established interpretations privileged as normative entities in Richard Levin's research program are not social agents. Interpretations cannot actually do things like make decisions, or read and evaluate manuscripts; those tasks must be carried out by human decision-makers. In Levin's program the practical agenda-setting or gate-keeper function is discreetly positioned behind the scenes while 'established interpretations' stand guard over critical discourse. In this situation intellectual standards can be made to serve the purposes of a profoundly anti-intellectual cultural policy. Under the socio-cultural regime mandated by Levin's established interpretations, the gate-keepers – senior scholars, editors, etc. – achieve a monopoly of knowledge that is absolutely self-legitimating. Established meanings would have the enormous advantage of being considered true until proven false. But it is never made clear who would have the authority to determine whether a constellation of meanings is or has become established. In an institutional organization of this type, critical knowledge would be disempowered. No benefit of the doubt or presumption of innocence can be accorded to non-established interpretations; these privileges are reserved to interpretations already enshrined in a substantive culture.

The model of scholarly research proposed by Levin is not really concerned with knowledge production, however, but with the reproduction of substantive culture or the administration of redemptive media, which is quite another matter. In Levin's proposal, absolute primacy is given to established views. New ideas are charged with a full 'burden of disproof'. Since Levin gives no account of scholarly jurisprudence, it is never made clear how one might disprove an established interpretation. What – or who – would determine such things as the admissibility of evidence or the even more important matter of just what is to count as a legitimate scholarly question? The task of separating the good interpretations from the bad ones takes on a particular urgency for Levin, because his overall project is motivated by a repressive 'will to solidarity' or 'will to consensus'. Despite the frequently acrimonious and divisive tone of his language, the substratum of this work is characterized by longing for a deep common accord. The idea of intellectual police action to guarantee unanimity within established interpretations shows a fundamental failure to recognize the conditions for achieving any genuine community of interests.

Anyone who allocates such a privileged position to 'established meanings' is open to the accusation of blindly defending the social and cultural status quo. Levin's position is a good bit more complex, however, than such an inference would suggest. A complex nostalgia is operative here, in which consensus and discursive mutuality is coupled with 'remembrance of things past'. This is a traditional intentionalist hermeneutics, which is unusual by virtue of its militant stance and by the exacerbated rancor of its presentation. These affective strains and tensions reveal a considerable uneasiness with the business-as-usual scholarship Levin criticizes in *New Readings vs. Old Plays*. The aim here is manifestly a reformist one, in which various adjustments in the relations of scholarly production will facilitate the integration of young scholars into research institutions and at the same time inoculate those institutions against heterodoxy and subversion.

STEPHEN GREENBLATT: SUBVERSION AND CONTAINMENT

The problem of subversion and its containment is now openly discussed within Shakespeare criticism, and in the writing of Stephen Greenblatt the topic has become a dominant concern. Greenblatt is identified with a group which has designated itself

New Historicist, and the work produced under this banner has been subjected to intense scrutiny in the professional literature. [11] This controversy has produced many confused notions of the New Historicist project, and a few useful assessments of its achievement. Part of the problem is, however, that it is not yet clear whether New Historicism ought to be regarded as a research program, a theory of a substantive type, or simply as a general predilection for the by now familiar range of topics – social abjection, colonization, spectacle, sexuality and its surveillance. The primary concern in this ensemble of critical practices is with the possibility of resistance to coercive authority or, more succinctly, with subversion.

In ordinary usage the idea of subversion seems to be that of an unwanted and unintended effect of power, a mode of conscious resistance to manifestations of power felt to be inimical to the interests of the subversives. Such a view would imply that there is at least a relatively and provisionally rational character to subversion. For Greenblatt, however, subversion is not an unintended effect but rather an instrument and also a sign of power itself.

The idea that subversion is produced by power and that it serves the interests of the powerful seems at first completely counter-intuitive. Subversion might *turn out* to be in the interests of entrenched power because subversives are maladroit, or lack adequate resources. But it is not immediately obvious why a legitimated power structure would find it useful to generate subversiveness where none actually existed. Greenblatt suggests that this production of subversive elements within a power structure is due to the paradoxical nature of power itself.

> But why, we must ask ourselves, should power record other voices, permit subversive inquiries, register at its very center the transgressions that will ultimately violate it? The answer may be in part that power . . . is not perfectly monolithic and hence may encounter and record in one of its functions materials than can threaten another of its functions; in part that power thrives on vigilance, and human beings are vigilant if they sense a threat; in part that power defines itself in relation to such threats or simply to that which is not identical with it. [12]

If the primary *raison-d'être* of the state is the surveillance of its enemies, then the existence of real enemies would appear to be a perpetual necessity rather than merely an localized epiphenomenon. The argument recalls the persistent rumor, widely circulated among the New Left, that a large number of members of subversive organizations were actually FBI agents and informants, and indeed that 'subversive organizations' were as likely as not entrapment devices of law enforcement. And perhaps, considering the apparent persistence of a counter-subversive orientation in American political life, the rumor has a certain cogency as an intuition as to the nature of contemporary state power.

For Stephen Greenblatt, the central fact to be addressed in any consideration of Renaissance culture is the rapid expansion of state power and the growth of the state apparatus. That this growth is not a 'natural fact' is indicated by his emphasis on theatricality and on the grandiose fantasies enacted in political spectacle. New Historicist critics have become notorious for their preoccupation with cultural practices that are marginal, *outré*, and even, some would say, positively disgusting. In the work of Greenblatt this is an effort of cognitive estrangement that has as its strategic objective a delineation of the objective reality of contemporary state power. The psychologically and intellectually difficult task of self-estrangment from the everyday normalness of that environment is undoubtedly facilitated by a deliberately cultivated fascination with the strained and perverse imaginative life of monarchs, their attendants, and their enemies.

In the work of Greenblatt and his associates, the official or hegemonic culture is described as an elaborate masquerade that is simultaneously self-aggrandizing and self-uncrowning. Marginal forms of social effervescence and local refusals of official power are theorized as part of the broad and complex strategies of subversion and containment through which state power confirms and legitimates itself. Subversion is primarily a form of verbal or symbolic transgression, a matter of saying forbidden things about authority. Power recuperates the transgressive energy of subversive social desire by setting up a heads-I-win-tails-you-lose situation. In other words power reveals itself both in its tolerance and in its intolerance of any and all forms of cultural anomie or of organized social resistance.

The history of Elizabethan and Jacobean England that emerges in the criticism of Stephen Greenblatt is a narrative of concrete objectifications of power. Power is everywhere, it is insidious, it has a million disguises. Like Hegelian 'spirit' or for that matter like the Old Historicist 'order' it works inexorably and continuously towards

205

its own historical self-realization. Behind the manifold forms of appearance of power in the Renaissance is a ghostly entity, infused with will and intelligence, that is at once *telos* and unmoved mover. That coercive and dominating will is actualized in the highly developed theatricality of royal authority.

> Elizabethan power is manifested to its subjects as in a theatre, and the subjects are at once absorbed by the instructive, delightful, or terrible spectacles, and forbidden intervention or deep intimacy. The play of authority depends upon spectators . . . but the performance is made to seem entirely beyond the control of those whose 'imaginary forces' actually confer upon it its significance and force.
>
> (Greenblatt 1985a: 44)

Greenblatt understands that power depends on a good deal more than mere theatrical illusion, that it exists somewhere else than in the 'minds of the spectators'. The Tudors made extensive use of pageantry and of theatrical display to augment their power, but they also confiscated the monasteries.

Greenblatt is right to point out that, by contrast with the development of the state apparatus in late capitalist society, Queen Elizabeth had relatively weak institutional means at her disposal for the administration of her kingdom. Nevertheless the assertion that the Queen's power was 'constituted in theatrical celebrations of royal glory and theatrical violence visited upon the enemies of that glory' is finally a quite fantastical notion. Queen Elizabeth certainly realized, as did her associates and colleagues, that her ability to project royal authority into the hinterland of England, to say nothing of the more recently assimilated territories of Scotland, Wales, and Ireland, could not possibly be founded on episodes of street pageantry, no matter how extravagant. New Historicism seems weakest in its attempt to present an account of state power by means of a cultural poetics. The justification for this orientation is, however, that the categories of the aesthetic reveal the primary mediations between the order of social constraints and the experience of individual subjectivity.

The preoccupation with the aesthetics of a poorly defined, ghostly conception of power is related to a concern with the singular subject and to the phenomenon of 'self-fashioning'. New Historicism has been concerned less with formally articulated Elizabethan beliefs and more with descriptions of what it probably felt like to be an

Elizabethan. It would appear from reading Greenblatt that the structure of feeling was predominantly anxious and hostile. Self-fashioning was not much fun in the sixteenth century, and it became increasingly uncertain and strained in the presence of conflicting imperatives.

> If we say that there is a new stress on the executive power of the will, we must say that there is the most sustained and relentless assault upon the will; if we say that there is a new social mobility we must say that there is a new assertion of power by both family and state to determine all movement within the society; if we say that there is a heightened awareness of the existence of alternative modes of social, theological, and psychological organization, we must say that there is a new dedication to the imposition of control.[13]

The argument developed in *Renaissance Self-Fashioning* cuts against the grain of a number of long-standing idealizations of Renaissance culture. Greenblatt's analysis takes away both the idea of Renaissance society as a harmonious structure or division of labor and the equally attractive view of the exceptional subject as an autonomous center of initiative and creativity.

Greenblatt's 'Renaissance man' is repressed, neurotic, and continually menaced by a deeply irrational social order. Such a view was not, of course, likely to attract much support from a traditional scholarly constituency with a deep libidinal investment in a sentimental view of the Renaissance as a great cultural 'flowering'. On the traditional account the subject was self-contained, self-controlled, fully capable of living up to certain ideals of *noblesse oblige* and of deference. Because of this 'Renaissance man' enjoyed a life of expressive and artistic fullness. *Renaissance Self-Fashioning* denies the existence of 'Renaissance man' in this sense. Greenblatt challenges the deeply held conviction that there is 'privileged sphere of individuality' operative in the situated subjects of sixteenth-century England. Self-fashioning is not autogenesis, the growth and efflorescence of some stable core of identity; it is rather autopoeisis, the internalization of various socially inscribed gestures and discursive turns. The self so produced consists of a repertoire of histrionic aptitudes and stage props. Such a subject is, in the last analysis, a purely meretricious tissue of fictive and opportunistic responses to contingent social moments.

The dissolution of stable social identity and the histrionic reconstitution of the subject in the sixteenth century is linked to changes in the social relations of production. In the social structure of feudal estates, social inequality was marked by a kind of taboo against contact. As the money economy expands, however, social mobility increases and some means for controlling that mobility becomes necessary. The demand for a coercive state apparatus capable of policing the economy of exchange diminishes the force of that traditional interdiction. Greenblatt explains these connections in a discussion of the killing of Jack Cade in Shakespeare's *Henry VI, Part 2*.

> [S]tatus relations . . . are being transformed before our eyes into property relations, and the concern . . . for maintaining social and even cosmic boundaries is reconceived as a concern for maintaining freehold boundaries. Symbolic estate gives way to real estate. And in this revised context, the context of property rather than rank, the fear of stain in the representation of an unequal social encounter vanishes.[14]

The connection between the historical appearance of the autopoetic or histrionic subject and the omnipresence of state power is indeed connected with the appearance of 'real estate' as a social phenomenon, though this term can lead to confusion if it is not treated with some precision.

What's 'real' about real estate is not the solid materiality of a piece of land, but the fact that such land is an exchange value. The peasant freeholder who kills Jack Cade does not belong to the land, as in a traditional manorial economy. He owns the land, which he can exploit as a source of production, but which he can also alienate in the abstract 'placeless' market of bourgeois political economy. The 'freedom' to alienate use values, and the 'rationalization' of exchange in the placeless market are correlated with the appearance of an 'autonomous' social agent or 'artificial person' fully empowered to participate in exchange, and with no 'irrational', that is, personal or social constraint on his actions.[15]

Notions of autonomy, organic integrity, and of autopoeisis are first articulated in the life sciences, which attempt to describe biological organisms as bounded sites of homeostatic or self-regulating processes. It is the apparently self-directed character of living things that helps to promote the related notion of a self-directed or autonomous art.[16] Such organicist notions of self-organization and closure can be interpreted as an attempt to ground the economic autonomy of the abstract agents operative of the placeless market in nature. The free, economic agent of political economy is not bound up in a network of arbitrary traditional obligations and duties and he is therefore free to constitute a 'natural' identity from a general fund of freely circulating cultural signifiers. Such a naturally self-constituted subject would be able to achieve the transcendental state of Self-Reliance.[17]

The autopoetic subject is assembled out of diverse social materials, and appears as a temporary image or repertoire of images in a local *mise-en-scène*. Under these conditions the reality of collective life becomes increasingly attenuated. Social life is now experienced as alien, strange, and violent; its form becomes visible only in moments of spectacle. The range of subject positions defined by the spectacle of power is limited to compliance or to an equivocal resistance. In Greenblatt's account of subversion and containment, the more 'subversive' a writer like Shakespeare is in unmasking the fraud and coercive force that sustains power, the more such a writer invites 'the celebration of that power'. This conclusion expresses a political hopelessness that stems from seeing an urgent need for rational political and social change without seeing any credible agency for achieving that purpose.

To criticize the work of Stephen Greenblatt on the grounds that it concludes in bleakness and political paralysis would be an instance of 'blaming the messenger'. The importance of this work is not that it is a 'good interpretation' of Shakespeare or a 'correct interpretation' of the Renaissance. Greenblatt is an extremely sensitive reader whose scholarship very acutely registers certain very deep rifts and contradictions in our cultural dispensation. This is equally true of Stanley Cavell and of Richard Levin. Nor is it in any way surprising that these contradictions should be felt within the institutional construction and administration of Shakespeare as a fundamental cultural authority. That authority is still felt to be somehow binding, but it no longer contains any sense of openness to the future.

REMEMBRANCE OF THINGS PAST

In an essay entitled 'Shakespeare, the Renaissance, and the Age of the Barocco', written in 1946, A. A. Smirnov declares:

The view of Shakespeare as an apologist of the ideology of the nobility has been rejected, as has the definition of Shakespeare as a representative of the humanist values of the middle classes. Shakespeare's claim to the title of a people's poet and an exponent of the folk tradition consisted in the fact that he expressed the progressive tendencies of the democratic strata of society, even though in his views on society, he never adopted a revolutionary outlook. This affiliation with the popular tradition is evident from the way in which Shakespeare's art absorbs all that is finest in the national culture of England. It finds expression in the immediate democracy of the writer, whose plays are clearly intended for a popular audience.[18]

To scholars and other observers in Western Europe and North America, assertions of this kind routinely provoke an exasperated and indignant response, partly because the Soviet Union, even after Stalin, is certainly not a popular democracy, at least not within the range of meanings for this term in circulation in the West. The celebration of Shakespeare's 'democratic tendencies' is seen both as naïve and as intolerable effrontery. Such objections do not, however, really address in any way the substance of these remarks on Shakespeare's identification with the positive aspirations or with the mode of life sedimented within popular culture. Are these descriptions of Shakespeare's 'democratic tendencies' the expression of deluded but persistent hope that the thwarted expectations of the October Revolution will at some future date be fulfilled? Is this simply matter of complicity in the evils of Stalinism, not the least of which is the composition of faked or distorted cultural history? Or is a truthful and far-sighted intuition as to the historical meaning of Shakespeare here?

The idea that Shakespeare's writing has an oppositional force, that he was oriented not to the affirmation of a traditional world view or even to its subversion, but rather to an emancipatory overthrow of the manifold structures of domination that continue to structure collective life, has gained increasing currency and acceptance among western scholars in recent years. It is not altogether clear why notions of popular democracy and energetically utopic, anti-authoritarian modes of social desire should count as 'subversive' in the critical discourse of the western democracies. It is easier to understand why these same notions would have been part of the official party line, even under Stalin, since the achieved social being of the Russian Revolution was still thought of as a valid promissory note. Nevertheless, ideas of popular democracy, social progress, and revolution have a problematic status within the hegemonic societies of late capitalism.

The writers whose work is surveyed in this chapter differ from their immediate predecessors in Anglo-American Shakespeare scholarship in the very high level of uneasy self-consciousness that their work exhibits. That self-consciousness is expressed in a series of complex meditations on 'the Great Shakespeare', the Emersonian reconstruction of the Elizabethan playwright in which the possibilities of expressive autonomy are so richly documented. It is evidently not very easy to achieve the condition of personal sovereignty or self-reliance inscribed somehow in the Shakespearean tuition. Nor is it easy for any of these writers to discover in Shakespeare an image of reconciled wholeness that might reveal the horizon of a new cultural/social dispensation. In all three of the writers discussed here Shakespeare has become the discursive site for investigating a split or division that can no longer be repressed either by an intransigent will to social order or by ecumenical wishful thinking. Reflections on Shakespeare are more emphatically than ever before construed as a remembrance of things past. This is no less evident in Greenblatt's historicism than in Cavell's faith in 'the canonical' or Levin's in 'established meaning'.

Shakespeare is perhaps best thought of as the poet of 'a complete exit from the present order of life'. Emerson's discovery of 'the Great Shakespeare' was linked to his other discoveries of the autopoetic subject capable of functioning equally well, both in a political economy of exchange and a spiritual economy of expenditure. But Emerson's 'Great Shakespeare' belongs, for Americans at least, to a moment whose historical truth has been exhausted. The autopoetic subject, the isolated, self-determining consciousness that must always interact only with strangers has lost its social being; the critics I have discussed reveal very clearly that there is no longer any question of idealizing that subject. A cultural/intellectual dispensation oriented to the conservation of that experience of private autopoeisis cannot envision any future for itself.

NOTES

1 A version of *Hamlet* has been performed on an episode of *Gilligan's Island*, and by Fonzie in an episode of *Happy Days*.

2 This is the main caption of a widely circulated advertisement for an organization known as the Business Committee for the Arts. Shakespeare's success as a 'top-notch salesmen' stems from the decision of a realty company to offer subscriptions to the Alabama Shakespeare Festival to purchasers of their condominium units.

3 Louis Hartz, *The Founding of New Societies* (New York: Harcourt, Brace, 1964); Sacvan Bercovich, *The Puritan Origins of the American Self* (New Haven: Yale Univ. Press, 1975); Alwin Thaler, *Shakespeare and Democracy* (Knoxville: Univ. of Tennessee Press, 1941).

4 Ralph Waldo Emerson, 'Shakespeare: or the poet', in *Representative Men: Seven Essays*, in *The Complete Works of Ralph Waldo Emerson: Centenary Edition*, 12 vols (New York: AMS Press, 1968), 4, pp. 187–220, see p. 211. (First published Boston: Riverside Press, 1903). Further citations of Emerson will all be given in the text.

5 Bertolt Brecht, *Messingkauf Dialogues*, trans. John Willett (London: Eyre Methuen Ltd 1965); Catherine Belsey, *The Subject of Tragedy: Identity and Difference in Renaissance Drama* (London: Methuen & Co. Ltd, 1985).

6 Anthony Giddens, *The Constitution of Society: Outline of the Theory of Structuration* (Cambridge, Mass.: Polity Press, 1984), p. 24.

7 Peter Burger, *Theory of the Avant Garde*, trans. Michael Shaw (Minneapolis: Univ. of Minnesota Press, 1984), pp. 3–15; See also David Held, *Introduction to Critical Theory: Horkheimer to Habermas* (Berkeley: Univ. of California Press, 1980); Raymond Geuss, *The Idea of a Critical Theory* (Cambridge: Cambridge Univ. Press, 1981); Jurgen Habermas, *Knowledge and Human Interests*, trans. Jeremy Shapiro (Boston: Beacon Press, 1971); Thomas McCarthy, *The Critical Theory of Jurgen Habermas* (Cambridge: MIT Press, 1978).

8 Rosalie Colie, *Shakespeare's Living Art* (Princeton: Princeton Univ. Press, 1974); Madeleine Doran, *Endeavors of Art: A Study of Form in Elizabethan Drama* (Madison: Univ. of Wisconsin Press, 1954).

9 Sandra Harding, *The Science Question in Feminism* (Ithaca: Cornell Univ. Press, 1986); Nancy Hartsock, 'The feminist standpoint: developing the ground for a specifically feminist historical materialism', in Sandra Harding and Merill B. Hintikka (eds) *Discovering Reality: Perspectives on Epistemology, Metaphysics, Methodology, and Philosophy of Science* (Boston: D. Reidel, 1983), pp. 283–310; Evelyn Fox Keller, *Reflections on Gender and Science* (New Haven: Yale Univ. Press, 1984).

212

10 Sandra Harding, 'Why has the sex-gender system become visible only now?', in *Discovering Reality*, op. cit., pp. 312 ff.

11 Allan Bloom, 'Liberty, equality, sexuality', *Commentary* (83) April, 1987, pp. 24–30.

12 Max Horkheimer, 'Traditional and critical theory', in *Selected Essays*, trans. M.J. O'Connell (New York: Continuum, 1972), pp. 188–244; Janet Wolff, *The Social Production of Art* (London: Macmillan, 1981); *Aesthetics and the Sociology of Art* (London: George Allen & Unwin, 1983), pp. 11–27.

13 See for example Coppelia Kahn, *Man's Estate: Masculine Identity in Shakespeare* (Berkeley: Univ. of California Press, 1981); Carolyn Ruth Swift Lenz, Gayle Greene, and Carol Neely (eds) *The Woman's Part: Feminist Criticism of Shakespeare* (Urbana: Univ. of Illinois Press, 1980); Linda Bamber, *Comic Women, Tragic Men: A Study of Gender and Genre in Shakespeare* (Stanford: Stanford Univ. Press, 1982); Mary Beth Rose, *The Expense of Spirit: Love and Sexuality in English Renaissance Drama* (Ithaca: Cornell Univ. Press, 1988); Margaret Ferguson, Nancy Vickers, Maureen Quilligan (eds) *Rewriting the Renaissance* (Chicago: Univ of Chicago Press, 1986); Peter Erickson, *Patriarchal Structures in Shakespeare's Drama* (Berkeley: Univ. of California Press, 1985).

14 Richard Levin, 'Feminist thematics and Shakespearean tragedy', *PMLA* (*Publications of the Modern Language Association*) 103 (1988), pp. 125–38.

15 Martin Jay, *The Dialectical Imagination: A History of the Frankfurt School and the Institute for Social Research, 1923–1950* (Boston: Little, Brown, & Co., 1973).

16 Geuss, *The Idea of a Critical Theory*, op. cit., pp. 4–45.

17 Emile Durkheim, *The Elementary Forms of Religious Life*, trans. J. Swain (New York: The Free Press, 1967). See also Dominick La Capra, *Emile Durkheim: Sociologist and Philosopher* (Chicago: Chicago Univ. Press, 1985).

18 Cornelius Castoriadis, 'The imaginary: creation in the social-historical domain', in P. Livingston (ed.) *Disorder and Order: Proceedings of the Stanford International Symposium, Stanford Literary Studies*, I (Saratoga, Cal.: Anima Libri, 1984), pp. 146–61; John B. Thomson, 'Ideology and the social imaginary: an appraisal of Castoriadis and Lefort', in *Studies in the Theory of Ideology* (Berkeley: Univ. of California Press, 1984), pp. 16–42.

19 Karl Marx, *Contribution to the Critique of Hegel's Philosophy of Right* (Cambridge: Cambridge Univ. Press, 1970), pp. 131 ff. See also Burger, *Theory of the Avant Garde*, op. cit., pp. 6 ff.

20 This subject has been addressed in several books and collections of essays. See for example Jonathan Dollimore and Alan Sinfield (eds) *Political Shakespeare: New Essays in Cultural Materialism* (Ithaca: Cornell Univ. Press, 1985); Terry Eagleton *William Shakespeare* (Oxford: Basil Blackwell, 1986); Terence Hawkes, *That Shakespeherian Rag: Essays on a Critical Process* (London: Methuen & Co. Ltd, 1986); Graham Holderness and Christopher McCullough (eds) *The Shakespeare Myth* (Manchester: Manchester Univ. Press, 1987).

21 David Bevington and Jay L. Halio (eds) *Shakespeare: Pattern of Excelling Nature*: *Shakespeare Criticism in Honor of America's Bicentennial*, The International Shakespeare Association Congress, Washington, DC, April 1976 (Newark: Univ. of Delaware Press, 1978). See in particular Alistair Cooke, 'Shakespeare in America' pp. 17–26, and Stephen J. Brown. 'The uses of Shakespeare in America: a study in class domination', pp. 230–41. See also Don Wayne, 'Power politics and the Shakespearean text: recent criticism in England and the United States', in Jean E. Howard and Marion F. O'Connor (eds) *Shakespeare Reproduced* (London: Methuen & Co. Ltd, 1987), pp. 47–67, and Lawrence Levine,

213

Highbrow/Lowbrow: The Emergence of Cultural Hierarchy in America (Berkeley: Univ. of California Press, 1986).

1 DOING SHAKESPEARE

1 Peter Burger, *Theory of the Avant-Garde*, trans. Michael Shaw (Minneapolis: Univ. of Minnesota Press, 1984), pp. 35–55; Janet Wolff, *The Social Production of Art* (London: Macmillan,1981); *Aesthetics and the Sociology of Art* (London: George Allen & Unwin, 1983), pp.11–27.

2 Gerald Graff, *Professing Literature: An Institutional History* (Chicago: Univ. of Chicago Press, 1987), pp. 1–18; Anthony Grafton and Lisa Jardine, *From Humanism to the Humanities: Education and the Liberal Arts in Fifteenth- and Sixteenth-Century Europe* (Cambridge: Harvard Univ. Press, 1986).

3 O. B. Hardison, *Toward Freedom and Dignity: The Humanities and the Idea of Humanity* (Baltimore: The Johns Hopkins Univ. Press, 1984).

4 Emmanuel Levinas, 'Humanism and An-archy', in *Collected Philosophical Papers*, pp. 127–40. (First published in *Revue Internationale de Philosophie*, 85–6 (1968), 323–37)

5 Hans-Georg Gadamer, *Truth and Method* (New York: Seabury Books, 1975), pp. 12–13.

6 Levinas, 'No identity', in *Collected Philosophical Papers*, trans. A. M. Lingis (Dordrecht: Martinus Nijhoff Publishers, 1987), pp. 141–52. (First published in French in *L'Ephémère* 13 (1970), pp. 27–44)

7 Michel Foucault, 'What is an author?', in *Language, Counter-Memory, Practice*, trans. Donald F. Bouchard and Sherry Simon (Ithaca: Cornell Univ. Press, 1973).

8 In passing, it is perhaps worth observing that the Anti-Stratfordian camp continues to play a complex role in helping to constitute the legitimate institutions of Shakespeare scholarship. Anti-Stratfordianism is Shakespeare scholarship's 'other'. More specifically, it is a position whose existence tends to forestall investigation of the actual modes of cultural production applicable to an understanding of Shakespeare. To imply, as I have just done, that Shakespeare is not the author of his works in the 'natural' sense of these terms is to have begun the drift towards the topsy-turvy land of Anti-Stratfordian pseudo-scholarship. See Marjorie Garber, *Shakespeare's Ghost Writers: Literature as Uncanny Causality* (London: Methuen & Co. Ltd., 1987).

9 Emile Durkheim, *The Elementary Forms of the Religious Life*, trans. J. W. Swain (New York: The Free Press, 1965), pp. 464–5. (First published George Allen & Unwin, 1915)

10 Fredric Jameson, *The Political Unconscious: Narrative as a Socially Symbolic Act* (Ithaca: Cornell Univ. Press, 1981).

11 Jonathan Dollimore, *Radical Tragedy: Religion, Ideology, and Power in the Drama of Shakespeare and His Contemporaries* (Chicago: Univ. of Chicago Press, 1984), pp. 249–72.

12 Herbert Marcuse, 'The affirmative character of culture', in *Negations: Essays in Critical Theory*, trans. Jeremy Shapiro (Boston: Beacon Press, 1968), p. 95.

13 Jean-Christophe Agnew, *Worlds Apart: The Market and the Theater in Anglo-American Thought, 1550–1750* (Cambridge: Cambridge Univ. Press, 1986), pp. 6–7.

14 Raymond Geuss, *The Idea of a Critical Theory* (Cambridge: Cambridge Univ. Press, 1981) pp. 4–26.

15 Ann Jennalie Cook, 'Detours and directions in fifty years of Shakespeare

scholarship', in Georgianna Ziegler (ed.) *Shakespeare Study Today: The Horace Howard Furness Memorial Lectures* (New York: AMS Press, 1986), pp. 93–126.

16 Richard Levin, *New Readings vs. Old Plays: Recent Trends in the Reinterpretation of English Renaissance Drama* (Chicago: Univ. of Chicago Press, 1979), pp. 196 ff.

17 Richard Whitley, *The Intellectual and Social Organization of the Sciences* (Oxford: Clarendon Press, 1984), pp. 168–70.

18 ibid., p. 243.

19 Sandra Harding, *The Science Question in Feminism* (Ithaca: Cornell Univ. Press, 1986).

20 Paisley Livingston, *On Literary Knowledge: Theory, Epistemology, and the Philosophy of Science* (Ithaca: Cornell Univ. Press, 1988).

21 Theodor Adorno and Max Horkheimer, 'The culture industry', in *Dialectic of Enlightenment*, trans. John Cumming (New York: The Seabury Press, 1972).

2 TRADITION AS SOCIAL AGENCY

1 William Bennett, 'Lost generation: why America's children are strangers in their own land,' *Policy Review*, 33 (1985), pp. 43–5; 'To reclaim a legacy', *American Educator*, 21 (1985), pp. 1–4; Allan Bloom, *The Closing of the American Mind* (New York: Simon & Schuster, 1987).

2 Stephen H. Balch and Herbert London, 'The tenured Left', *Commentary*, 82 (4) (October, 1986), pp. 41–50. The argument is anything but novel. See, for example, Sidney Hook, 'Academic freedom and "the Trojan horse" in American Education', *AAUP (American Association of University Professors) Bulletin*, 25 (5) (Dec. 1939), p. 555; Arthur O. Lovejoy, 'Communism and academic freedom', *American Scholar* 18 (3) (Summer, 1949), p. 335; Daniel Bell, *Cultural Contradictions of Capitalism* (New York: Basic Books, 1976).

3 Jurgen Habermas, 'Neo-conservative culture criticism in the United States and West Germany: an intellectual movement in two political cultures', in Richard J. Bernstein, (ed.) *Habermas and Modernity* (Cambridge: MIT Press, 1985); see also Margaret Ferguson, 'Afterword', in Jean Howard and Marion O'Connor (eds) *Shakespeare Reproduced: The Text in History and Ideology* (London: Methuen & Co. Ltd., 1987), pp. 273–83; Stanley Aronowitz and Henry A.Giroux, *Education under Siege: The Conservative, Liberal and Radical Debate over Schooling* (South Hadley, Mass.: Bergin & Garvey, 1985); Samuel Bowles and Herbert Gintis, *Schooling in Capitalist America* (New York: Basic Books, 1976); Richard Ohmann, *English in America: A Radical View of the Profession* (New York: Oxford Univ. Press, 1976).

4 Allan Bloom, 'Liberty, Equality, Sexuality', *Commentary* 83 (April, 1987), pp. 24–30.

5 Jurgen Habermas, 'The university in a democracy: the democratization of the university', in *Towards a Rational Society: Student Protest, Science, and Politics*, trans. Jeremy Shapiro (Boston: Beacon Press, 1970), pp. 2–3.

6 These issues have been extensively rehearsed in the debate between Hans-Georg Gadamer and Jurgen Habermas. See Gadamer,'On the scope and function of hermeneutical reflection', in *Philosophical Hermenuetics*, trans. David E. Linge (Berkeley: Univ. of California Press, 1976), pp. 18–43; Habermas, 'On systematically distorted communication', *Inquiry* 13 (1970), pp. 205–18; see also A. M. Hjort, 'The conditions of dialogue: approaches to the Habermas Gadamer debate', *Eidos*, 4 (1985), 11–37; Thomas McCarthy, *The Critical Theory of Jurgen Habermas*, (Cambridge: MIT Press, 1978), pp. 187–93.

7 Anthony Giddens, *The Constitution of Society: Outline of the Theory of Structuration*

(Cambridge: Polity Press, 1984), pp. 200–7; Edward Shils, *Tradition* (London: Faber & Faber, 1981).

8 Marcel Mauss, *The Gift*, trans. Ian Cunnison, with an introduction by E. E. Evans-Pritchard (New York: W. W. Norton & Company, 1967), pp. 50–1.

9 See for example, Jacques Derrida , ' . . . That Dangerous Supplement . . . ', in *Of Grammatology*, trans. Gayatri Spivack (Baltimore: The Johns Hopkins Univ. Press, 1976), pp. 141–57.

10 See for example, Jacques Derrida, 'Structure sign and play in the discourse of the human sciences' in *Writing and Difference* trans. Alan Bass (Chicago: Univ. of Chicago Press, 1978); Emmanuel Levinas, 'Reality and its Shadow', in *Collected Philosophical Papers*, trans. Alphonso Lingis (Dordrecht: Martinus Nijhhoff, 1987) pp. 1–15.

11 Samuel Belkin, *In His Image: The Jewish Philosphy of Man as Expressed in Rabbinic Tradition* (London: Abelard Schuman, 1966); Boaz Cohen, *Law and Tradition in Judaism: A Historical Presentation* (New York: Ktav Publishing House, 1969); Samuel C. Heilman, *The People of the Book: Drama, Fellowship, and Religion* (Chicago: Univ. of Chicago Press, 1983); Emmanuel Levinas, *Difficile liberté: essais sur le judaïsme*, 3rd ed. (Paris: Albin Michel, 1976).

12 Emmanuel Levinas, *Quatre Lectures Talmudiques* (Paris, Editions de Minuit, 1968); Moses Mielziner, *Introduction to the Talmud*, 4th ed. (New York: Bloch Publishing Co., 1968 (Originally published 1894); Hermann L. Strack, *Introduction to the Talmud and Midrash*, (New York: Atheneum, 1969).

13 Gershom Scholem, *Major Trends in Jewish Mysticism*, 3rd ed. (New York: Schocken Books, 1954).

14 Gershom Scholem, 'Religious authority and mysticism', in *On the Kabbalah and Its Symbolism*, trans. Ralph Mannheim (New York: Schocken Books, 1969), pp. 5–32.

15 Gerald Bruns, 'Canon and power in the Hebrew Scriptures', *Critical Inquiry*, 10 (1984), pp. 462–80.

16 Harold Innis, *The Bias of Communications* (Toronto: Univ. of Toronto Press, 1951), pp. 33–61.

17 Scholem, 'Religious authority and mysticism' op. cit.; *Major Trends in Jewish Mysticism* op. cit.; Harold Bloom, *Kaballah and Criticism* (New York: Continuum Books, 1983).

18 Charles Taylor, *Hegel and Modern Society*, (Cambridge: Cambridge Univ. Press, 1979), pp. 83 ff.

19 Friedrich Nietzsche, *Daybreak: Thoughts on the Prejudices of Morality*, trans. R. J. Hollingdale (Cambridge: Cambridge Univ. Press, 1982), p. 10.

20 ibid., p. 11.

21 ibid., p. 12.

22 Pierre Bourdieu, *Distinction: A Social Criticism of the Judgement of Taste*, trans. Richard Nice (Cambridge: Harvard Univ. Press, 1984).

23 *The Journals and Papers of Soren Kierkegaard*, ed. and trans. Howard V. Hong and Edna H. Hong, 6 vols. (Bloomington: Indiana Univ. Press, 1967), 1, p. 86.

24 Hans-Georg Gadamer, *Truth and Method* (New York: Seabury Books, 1975) pp. 244–53.

25 Esther Cloudman Dunn, *Shakespeare in America* (New York: Macmillan, 1939).

26 The speech of Ulysses from *Troilus and Cressida* is very much associated with Tillyard, but in fact the strategic use of this passage has a long history in the critical discourse on Shakespeare in the United States. Charles Mills Gayley (1917), Esther Cloudman Dunn (1930), Hardin Craig (1936), Theodore Spencer (1940) all build the same argument around this speech. Tillyard's appropriation

of this passage and his effacement of his predecessors is a further instance of the remarkable success of *The Elizabethan World Picture* in the field of academic and intellectual publicity.

27 John Adams, *Diary*, in *The Works of John Adams, Second President of the United States*, 6 vols (New York: AMS Press, 1971) 3, p. 393; (originally published Boston: Little, Brown, 1851). The *Diary* referred to in the text as 1971a.

28 Jean Christophe Agnew, *Worlds Apart: The Market and the Theater in Anglo-American Thought, 1550–1750* (Cambridge: Cambridge Univ. Press, 1986).

29 John Adams, *Discourses on Davila: A Series of Papers on Political History* in *The Works of John Adams*, op. cit., 6, p. 232. Further citations will be given in the text, as 1971b.

30 Rene Girard, *Deceit, Desire and the Novel*; Jean-Pierre Dupuy and Paul Dumouchel, *L'enfer des choses: René Girard et la logique de l'économie* (Paris: Seuil, 1979). See also Agnew, *Worlds Apart*, op. cit., pp. 177 ff.

31 Louis D. Hartz, *The Liberal Tradition in America: An Interpretation of American Political Thought Since the Revolution* (New York: Harcourt, Brace, and World, Inc.: 1955); See also Antonio Gramsci, 'Americanism and Fordism', in *Selections from the Prison Notebooks*, trans. Quintin Hoare and Geoffrey Nowell Smith (New York: International Publishers, 1971), pp. 277–320; Samuel Weber, 'Capitalizing History: *The Political Unconscious*', in *Institution and Interpretation* (Minneapolis: Univ. Minnesota Press, 1987), pp. 40–58.

32 Raymond Williams, *The Long Revolution*, (Harmondsworth: Penguin Books, 1965); see also Gerald Graff, *Professing Literature; An Institutional History* (Chicago: Univ. of Chicago Press, 1987); Richard Ohmann, *English in America: A Radical View of the Profession* (New York: Oxford Univ. Press, 1976).

33 Stephen J. Brown, 'The uses of Shakespeare in America: a study in class domination', in David Bevington and Jay L. Halio *Shakespeare: Pattern of Excelling Nature Shakespeare Criticism in Honor of America's Bicentennial*, The International Shakespeare Association Congress, Washington, DC, April 1976. (Newark: Univ. of Delaware Press, 1978) pp. 230–41.

3 THE FUNCTION OF THE ARCHIVE

1 E. P. Thompson, *The Making of the English Working Class* (Harmondsworth: Penguin Books, 1968); Raymond Williams, *The Long Revolution* (Harmondsworth: Penguin Books, 1965), pp.177–95.

2 Jesse Hauck Shera, *Foundations of the Public Library: The Origins of the Public Library Movement in New England* (Chicago: Chicago Univ. Press, 1949) pp. 54 ff.

3 James M. Gibson, 'Horace Howard Furness: book collector and library builder', in Georgianna Ziegler (ed.) *Shakespeare Study Today* (New York: AMS Press, 1986), pp. 169–91.

4 See Gerald Graff, *Professing Literature: An Institutional History* (Chicago: Univ. of Chicago Press, 1987). pp. 36–55.

5 Henry L. Savage, 'The Shakespeare Society of Philadelphia' *Shakespeare Quarterly*, 3 (1952), 341–52. See also Georgianna Ziegler, Introduction to *Shakespeare Study Today*, op. cit.

6 David Laird, 'Horace Howard Furness', *Dictionary of Literary Biography*, 64 (1987), pp. 66–70.

7 ibid., p. 69.

8 Gibson, op. cit., p. 171.

9 Bernard Quarritch, letter to Horace Howard Furness, 25 April 1871, the Horace

Howard Furness Memorial Library, Philadelphia Pennsylvania. All further references to the Horace Howard Furness Correspondence will be as *HHF*.

10 Woodrow Wilson, letter to Horace Howard Furness, 6 October 1902, *HHF*.

11 Sir Walter Raleigh, letter to Horace Howard Furness, 3 April 1911, *HHF*.

12 ibid.

13 Charles Taylor, *Hegel and Modern Society* (Cambridge: Cambridge Univ. Press, 1979), pp. 111 ff.

14 Gibson, op. cit., p. 187.

15 Graff, op. cit., pp. 1–14. Richard Ohmann, *English in America: A Radical View of the Profession* (Oxford: Oxford Univ. Press, 1976), pp. 257. ff.

16 Betty Ann Kane, *The Widening Circle: The Story of the Folger Shakespeare Library and its Collections* (Washington. DC: The Folger Shakespeare Library, 1976).

17 Henry Clay Folger, letter to Horace Howard Furness, 29 September 1892, *HHF*.

18 ibid.

19 Samuel Parkes Cadman, 'Prayer and Discourse at Mr. Folger's Funeral' in *Henry C. Folger* (New Haven: privately printed, 1931), p. 15.

20 Thomas Le Duc, *Piety and Intellect at Amherst College: 1865–1912* (New York: Columbia Univ. Press, 1946), pp. 54 ff.

21 Henry Clay Folger, letter to Herbert Putnam, 19 January 1928, unpublished correspondence of Henry Clay Folger, the Folger Shakespeare Memorial Library, Washington, DC. Further reference to these materials will be cited as Folger Correspondence.

22 Herbert Putnam, letter to Henry Clay Folger, 2 January 1928, Folger Correspondence.

23 Robert Luce, letter to Henry Clay Folger, 19 April 1928, Folger Correspondence.

24 William Slade, 'The significance of the Folger Shakespeare Memorial: an essay towards an interpretation' in *Henry Clay Folger* (New Haven: privately printed, 1931), pp. 41–2.

25 Slade, op. cit., p. 43.

26 Slade, op. cit., pp. 54 ff.

27 Stanley King, *Recollections of the Folger Shakespeare Library* (Ithaca: Cornell Univ. Press, 1950), published for the Trustees of Amherst College, pp. 28 ff.

28 These changes appear to have been related to a quiet and discreetly waged power struggle for administrative control between Emily Jordan Folger and the Trustees, led by Stanley King. King refers to this very tactfully in his own account, indicating that Mrs Folger didn't understand the kind of professional qualifications that were most necessary in the administrative personnel for the Folger Shakespeare Memorial to achieve the goals envisioned by the founder. Mrs Folger was, of course, herself a founder, but her side of the story is harder to discover. See King, op. cit., pp. 34 ff.

29 Joseph Quincy Adams, 'The Folger Shakespeare Memorial dedicated: April 21, 1932: Shakespeare and American culture', *Spinning Wheel* 12, 9–10 (June–July 1932), pp. 212–13, 229–321.

30 Joseph Quincy Adams, *The Folger Shakespeare Memorial Library: A Report of Progress, 1931–1941* (Brattleboro, Vermont: Published for the Trustees of Amherst College, 1942), p. 43.

31 Frederick Hard, *Louis B. Wright: A Bibliography and an Appreciation* (Charlottesville: Univ. press of Virginia, 1968).

32 Louis B. Wright, *Of Books and Men* (Columbia, SC: Univ. of South Carolina Press, 1976), pp. 73 ff.

33 See Carl Cannon, *American Book Collectors and Collecting from Colonial Times to the Present* (New York: H.W. Wilson Co., 1941); John Carter, *Taste and Technique in*

Book Collecting: With an Epilogue (London: Private Libraries Association, 1970).
34 Wright, op. cit., pp. 62–4.
35 Louis B. Wright, 'An obligation to Shakespeare and the Public', *Shakespeare Survey* 16 (1963), pp. 1–9.
36 Wright, 'An Obligation to Shakespeare', p. 3. The Ambassador named was almost certainly John Hay Whitney, who had important interests in the fields of journalism and publishing.
37 O. B. Hardison, '"Put Money in Thy Purse": Supporting Shakespeare' in *Shakespeare Studies Today*, pp. 153–69.
38 O. B. Hardison, op. cit. See also *Toward Freedom and Dignity: The Humanities and the Idea of Humanity* (Baltimore: The Johns Hopkins Univ. Press, 1984).
39 Gregor McLennan, *Marxism and the Methodologies of History* (London: Verso Editions, 1981); Peter Burger, *Theory of the Avant-Garde*, trans. Michael Shaw (Minneapolis: Univ. of Minneapolis Press, 1984), pp. 15–27; Frederic Jameson, *The Political Unconscious: Narrative as a Socially Symbolic Act.* (Ithaca, NY: Cornell Univ. Press, 1981), pp. 26–50 *et passim*.

4 EDITING THE TEXT

1 John Guillory, 'Canonical and non-canonical: A critique of the current debate', *A Journal of English Literary History* 54 (1987), pp. 483–529.
2 Jerome McGann, *A Critique of Modern Textual Criticism* (Chicago: Univ. of Chicago Press, 1983).
3 See David Bevington 'Determining the indeterminate: the Oxford Shakespeare', *Shakespeare Quarterly*, 38 (1987), pp. 501–19.
4 Stephen Orgel, 'The authentic Shakespeare', *Representations*, 21 (1988), pp. 5 ff. See also Leah Marcus, *Puzzling Shakespeare: Local Reading and its Discontents* (Berkeley: Univ. of California Press, 1988), pp. 2–15.
5 Elizabeth Eisenstein, *The Printing Revolution in Early Modern Europe* (Cambridge: Cambridge Univ. Press, 1983). See also Joseph Loewenstein, 'The script in the marketplace', in Stephen Greenblatt (ed.) *Representing the Renaissance*, (Berkeley: Univ. of California Press, 1988), pp. 265–78.
6 Moshe Weinfeld, *Deuteronomy and the Deuteronomic School* (Oxford: Clarendon Press, 1972); Gerald Bruns, *Inventions: Writing, Textuality, and Understanding in Literary History* (New Haven: Yale Univ. Press, 1982); Brevard S. Childs, *Introduction to the Old Testament as Scripture* (Philadelphia: Fortress Publications, 1979).
7 Gerald L. Bruns, 'Canon and power in the Hebrew Scriptures', *Critical Inquiry*, 10 (1984), pp. 462–80.
8 See Gerald Eades Bentley, *The Profession of Dramatist in Shakespeare's Time* (Princeton: Princeton Univ. Press, 1971).
9 Richard Burt, 'Ben Jonson and the politics of early Stuart theatre', *ELH* (*A Journal of English Literary History*), 54 (1987), pp. 529–57.
10 Jonas Barish, *The Antitheatrical Prejudice* (Berkeley: Univ. of California Press, 1981).
11 Harold Innis, 'The problem of space' in *The Bias of Communication* (Toronto: Toronto Univ. Press, 1951), pp. 92–132.
12 See M. Bristol '*The Two Noble Kinsmen*: Shakespeare and the problem of authority', in Charles Frey (ed.) *Shakespeare, Fletcher and the Two Noble Kinsmen* (Columbia: Univ. of Missouri Press, 1989).
13 Pierre Bourdieu, *Distinction: A Social Critique of the Judgement of Taste*, trans.

Richard Nice (Cambridge, Mass: Harvard Univ. Press, 1984), pp. 260–95; Alan Sinfield, 'Give an account of Shakespeare and education . . .' in Jonathan Dollimore and Alan Sinfield (eds) *Political Shakespeare* (Ithaca: Cornell Univ. Press, 1985), pp. 134–58.

14 Barbara Packer, 'Origin and authority: Emerson and the higher criticism', in Sacvan Bercovitch, (ed.) *Reconstructing American Literary History* (Cambridge: Harvard Univ. Press, 1986), pp. 67–92; See also Charles Taylor, *Hegel and Modern Society* (Cambridge: Cambridge Univ. Press, 1979), pp. 1–23.

15 Ralph Waldo Emerson, *Representative Men: Seven Lectures*, in *The Complete Works of Ralph Waldo Emerson: Centenary Edition*, 12 vols (New York: AMS Press, 1968), 4, 193–4.

16 *The Sacred Books of the Old and New Testaments: A New English Translation*, ed. by Paul Haupt with the assistance of H. H. Furness, 6 vols (New York: Dodd, Mead, 1898).

17 The primary contribution is Charlton Hinman's massive *The Printing and Proof-Reading of the First Folio of Shakespeare*, 2 vols (Oxford: Oxford Univ. Press, 1963); for a reappraisal of the achievements of textual editors see Hinman, 'Shakespearian textual studies: seven more years', in Clifford Leech and J. M. R. Margeson (eds) *Shakespeare 1971: Proceedings of the World Shakespeare Congress: Vancouver, August 1971* (Toronto: Univ. of Toronto Press, 1972), pp. 37–50.

18 Fredson Bowers, *On Editing Shakespeare* (Charlottesville: University of Virginia Press, 1966) see also F. P. Wilson, 'Shakespeare and the New Bibliography' *The Bibliographical Society* (London: printed for the Bibliographical Society, 1945), pp. 76–135.

19 W. W. Greg, *The Editorial Problem in Shakespeare* (Oxford: Oxford Univ. Press, 1942); 'The rationale of copy-text', *Studies in Bibliography* 3 (1950), pp. 19–36; R. B. McKerrow, *Prolegomena for the Oxford Shakespeare* (Oxford: Oxford Univ. Press, 1939); A. W. Pollard, *Shakespeare's Folios and Quartos* (London: 1909); Fredson Bowers, 'Greg's rationale of copy text revisited', *Studies in Bibliography* 31 (1977), pp. 91–161.

20 Fredson Bowers, *Bibliography and Textual Criticism* (Oxford: Oxford Univ. Press, 1964), p. 2.

21 Fredson Bowers, 'Established texts and definitive editions', *Philological Quarterly* 41 (1962), pp. 1–17.

22 Fredson Bowers, 'Textual criticism and the literary critic', in *Textual and Literary Criticism* (Cambridge: Cambridge Univ. Press, 1959).

23 Bowers, *Textual and Literary Criticism* op. cit., p. 125.

24 See for example, G. Thomas Tanselle, 'The editorial problem of final authorial intention', in *Selected Studies in Bibliography* (Charlottesville: Univ. Press of Virginia, 1979), pp. 309–55; Jerome McGann, *A Critique of Modern Textual Criticism* (Chicago: Univ. of Chicago Press, 1983), pp. 37–51.

25 Bowers, *Textual and Literary Criticism*, op. cit., p. 123.

26 ibid. p. 120.

27 ibid. p. 5.

28 G. E. Bentley, *The Profession of Dramatist in Shakespeare's Time* (Princeton: Princeton Univ. Press, 1971); see also M. Bristol, *Carnival and Theater: Plebeian Culture and the Structure of Authority in Renaissance England* (London: Methuen & Co., 1985), pp. 111–25.

29 Jonathan Haynes, 'Festivity and dramatic economy in Jonson's *Bartholomew Faire*', *ELH*, 51 (1984), pp. 635–58.

30 Michel Foucault, 'What is an author?' in Donald F. Bouchard (ed.) *Language, Counter-Memory, Practice*, (Ithaca: Cornell Univ. Press, 1977); Stephen Orgel, 'What is a text?' *Research Opportunities in Renaissance Drama*, 24 (1981), pp. 3–6.

220

31 Anne Mette Hjort, 'The interests of critical editorial practice', *Poetics*, 15 (1987), p. 268.
32 Michael J. Warren, 'Quarto and Folio *King Lear* and the interpretation of Albany and Edgar', in David Bevington and Jay L. Halio (eds) *Shakespeare: Pattern of Excelling Nature* (Newark: Univ. of Delaware Press, 1978), p. 96.
33 Steven Urkowitz, *Shakespeare's Revision of* King Lear (Princeton: Princeton Univ. Press, 1980), p. 149.
34 This argument is developed at length in David Wiles, *Shakespeare's Clown: Actor and Text in the Elizabethan Playhouse* (Cambridge: Cambridge Univ. Press, 1987).
35 Jonathan Goldberg, 'Textual properties', *Shakespeare Quarterly* 37 (1986), p. 216.
36 ibid.
37 Orgel, 'The authentic Shakespeare', op. cit, p. 7.

5 SHAKESPEARE IN THE AMERICAN CULTURAL IMAGINATION

1 Marjorie Garber, *Shakespeare's Ghost Writers: Literature as Uncanny Causality* (London: Methuen & Co. Ltd, 1987). See also Alexis de Tocqueville, *Democracy in America, with a Critical Appraisal of Each Volume by John Stuart Mill*, trans. Henry Reeve, 2 vols (NY: Schocken Books, 1961); Louis D. Hartz, *The Founding of New Societies* (New York: Harcourt, Brace, 1964); Sacvan Bercovitch, *The Puritan Origins of the American Self* (New Haven: Yale Univ. Press, 1975).
2 Esther Cloudman Dunn, *Shakespeare in America* (New York: Macmillan, 1939). See also Charles Frey, 'Teaching Shakespeare in America', in *Experiencing Shakespeare* (Columbia: Univ. of Missouri Press, 1988); Louis Marder, *His Exits and His Entrances: The Story of Shakespeare's Reputation* (NY: Lippincott, 1963).
3 Virginia Woolf, *A Room of One's Own* (London: Granada, 1977); Mikhail Bakhtin, 'Response to a question from *Novy Mir*' in *Speech Genres and Other Late Essays*, trans. Vern McGee (Austin: Univ. of Texas Press, 1986), pp. 1–10.
4 Harold Bloom, 'Emerson and Whitman: the American sublime', in *Poetry and Repression: Revisionism from Blake to Stevens* (New Haven: Yale Univ. Press, 1976), pp. 235–67. See also Sharon Cameron, 'Representing grief', *Representations*, 15 (1986), pp. 15–41.
5 Max Weber, *The Theory of Social and Economic Organizations*, trans. E. M. Henderson and Talcott Parsons, ed. by Talcott Parsons (New York: The Free Press, 1964).
6 Barbara Packer, 'Origin and authority: Emerson and the higher criticism', in Sacvan Bercovitch (ed.) *Reconstructing American Literary History* (Cambridge: Harvard Univ. Press, 1986), pp. 67–92.
7 Richard A. Grusin, '"Put God in Your Debt": Emerson's Economy of Expenditure', *PMLA* 103 (1988), 35–44; Howard Horwitz, 'The Standard Oil Trust as Emersonian hero', *Raritan Review* 6 (1987), pp. 97–119; Michael T. Gilmore, *American Romanticism and the Marketplace* (Chicago: Univ. of Chicago Press, 1985).
8 Harry Levin, 'Introduction', in *Shakespeare and the Revolution of the Times: Perspectives and Commentaries* (New York: Oxford Univ. Press, 1976), pp. 13–17.
9 George Lyman Kittredge, *Shakspere: An Address Delivered on April 23, 1916 in Saunders Theatre at the Request of the President and Fellows of Harvard College* (Cambridge: Harvard Univ. Press, 1930). First published 1916. Further reference to this book will be given in the text as Kittredge 1916.

10 Charles Mills Gayley, *Shakespeare and the Founders of Liberty in America* (New York: Macmillan Company, 1917), p. v. Further reference to this book will be given in the text as Gayley 1917.

11 This argument is reviewed by Charles Frey, '*The Tempest and the New World*', in *Experiencing Shakespeare* (Columbia: Univ. of Missouri Press, 1988), pp. 48–62. See also E. P. Kuhl, 'Shakespeare and the founders of America: *The Tempest*', *Philological Quarterly* 41 (1962), pp. 123–46; Stephen Greenblatt, 'Learning to curse: aspects of linguistic colonialism in the sixteenth century', in Fredi Chiappelli (ed.) *First Images of America: The Impact of the New World on the Old*, 2 vols (Berkeley: Univ. of California Press, 1976), 2, pp. 568–76.

12 Gayley anticipates Tillyard, the scholar most commonly associated with the emphatic privileging of Ulysses' speech from *Troilus and Cressida*. It would be interesting to write the history of the citation of this speech. Such a history would show the importance of Gayley's work in establishing a theme within culture criticism and the use of the Ulysses speech within theme. This tactic has been in wide circulation in American Shakespeare criticism throughout the twentieth century, and its appearance in Tillyard should probably be regarded as a routine intellectual commonplace.

13 Jurgen Habermas, *Legitimation Crisis*, trans. Thomas McCarthy (Boston: Beacon Press, 1975); Richard Hofstadter, *The Age of Reform* (New York: Alfred Knopf, 1955); Walter Lippman, *An Inquiry into the Principles of the Good Society* (New York: Little, Brown, 1937).

6 OLD HISTORICISM

1 Anatoli Lunacharsky, 'Bacon and the characters of Shakespeare's plays', in *Shakespeare in the Soviet Union*, trans. Avril Pyman (Moscow: Progress Publishers, 1966), p. 25.

2 ibid. p. 26.

3 Richard Pells, *Radical Visions, American Dreams: Culture and Social Thought in the Depression Years* (Middletown: Wesleyan Univ. Press, 1984); James Burkhart Gilbert, *Writers and Partisans: A History of Literary Radicalism in America* (New York: John Wiley & Sons, 1968).

4 Gerald Graff, *Professing Literature: An Institutional History* (Chicago, Univ. of Chicago Press, 1987), pp. 183–95.

5 Ellen Schrecker, *No Ivory Tower: McCarthyism and the Universities* (Oxford: Oxford Univ. Press, 1986), pp. 19–23.

6 Walter P. Metzger, *Academic Freedom in the Age of the University* (New York: Columbia Univ. Press, 1961).

7 Arthur O. Lovejoy, 'Communism and academic freedom', *American Scholar* 18 (3) Summer, 1949; Sidney Hook, 'Academic freedom and "The Trojan Horse" in American education', *AAUP (American Association of University Professors) Bulletin*, 25 (5) Dec. 1939, p. 555.

8 Theodore Spencer, *Shakespeare and the Nature of Man* (New York: Collier Books, 1966), p. 81. (First published by Macmillan, 1942)

9 Natalie Z. Davis, 'The rites of violence: religious riot in sixteenth-century France', *Past and Present* 50 (1971), pp. 49–75.

10 Hardin Craig, *The Enchanted Glass: The Elizabethan Mind in Literature* (New York: Oxford Univ. Press, 1936).

11 Hardin Craig, *An Interpretation of Shakespeare* (Columbia: Lucas Bros, 1948), p. 10. Further citations of this book will be given in the text, as Craig 1948a.

12 Hardin Craig, *Freedom and Renaissance* (Chapel Hill: Univ. of North Carolina Press, 1949). Further citations of this book will be given in the text, as Craig 1948.

13 Hardin Craig, *Literary Study and the Scholarly Profession* (Seattle: Univ. of Washington Press, 1944).

14 Pierre Bourdieu, *Distinction: A Social Critique of the Judgement of Taste*, trans. Richard Nice (Cambridge: Harvard Univ. Press, 1984), p. 111.

7   FROM POLITICS TO SENSIBILITY

1 Gerald Graff, *Professing Literature: An Institutional History* (Chicago, Univ. of Chicago Press, 1987); Don Wayne, 'Politics and the Shakespearean text: recent criticism in England and the United States', in Jean E. Howard and Marion F. O'Connor (eds) *Shakespeare Reproduced* (London: Methuen & Co. Ltd 1987), pp. 47–67; Frank Lentricchia, *Criticism and Social Change* (Chicago: Univ. of Chicago Press, 1983).

2 Serge Guilbaut, *How New York Stole the Idea of Modern Art: Abstract Expressionism, Freedom, and the Cold War*, trans. Arthur Goldhammer (Chicago, Univ. of Chicago Press, 1983). See also John Morton Blum, *V Was for Victory: Politics and American Culture During World War II* (New York: Harcourt, Brace, Jovanovitch, 1972); Paul Carter, *Another Part of the Fifties* (NY: Columbia Univ. Press, 1983); George Lipsitz, *Class and Culture in Cold War America* (South Hadley, Mass: J. F. Bergin, 1982); Richard Pells, *The Liberal Mind in a Conservative Era* (NY: Harper & Row, 1985); Michael Ryan, *Marxism and Deconstruction: A Critical Articulation* (Baltimore: The Johns Hopkins Univ. Press, 1982).

3 Arthur M. Schlesinger, Jr. *The Vital Center: The Politics of Freedom* (London: André Deutsch, 1970), pp. 252–3 (first published as *The Politics of Freedom*, 1950).

4 Daniel Bell, *The End of Ideology; On the Exhaustion of Political Ideas in the Fifties*, revised ed. (NY: The Free Press, 1965).

5 Daniel Bell, *Cultural Contradictions of Capitalism* (New York: Basic Books, 1976); see also Jurgen Habermas, *Legitimation Crisis*, trans. Thomas McCarthy (Boston: Beacon Press, 1975).

6 Ellen Rooney, 'Who's left out? A rose by any other name is still red: or, the politics of pluralism', *Critical Inquiry* 12 (1986), 550–64.

7 Harry Levin, 'Literature as an institution', *Accent* 6 (1946), 159–68. This article was anthologized several times, notably in Mark Schorer, J. Miles, G. McKenzie (eds) *Criticism: The Foundations of Modern Literary Judgement* (New York: Harcourt Brace, 1958), pp. 546–53, and in Morton Dauwen Zabel, *Literary Opinion in America: Essays Illustrating the Status, Methods, and Problem of Criticism in the United States in the Twentieth Century* (Gloucester, Mass: P. Smith, 1962). A fuller version of this essay served as the introduction to Levin's own *The Gates of Horn: Studies in the Novels of Five French Realists* (New York: Oxford Univ. Press, 1963).

8 Northrop Frye, *Anatomy of Criticism: Four Essays* (Princeton: Princeton Univ. Press, 1957), p. 4. Cited by Levin in 'The Primacy of Shakespeare', *Shakespeare Quarterly*, (26), 1975 and reprinted in *Shakespeare and the Revolution of the Times: Perspectives and Commentaries* (NY: Oxford Univ. Press, 1976), pp. 235–61.

9 Harry Levin, 'The Primacy of Shakespeare', op. cit., pp. 259–60.

10 Northrop Frye, *A Natural Perspective: The Development of Shakespearean Comedy and Romance* (Columbia Univ. Press, 1965).

11 Frye, *Anatomy of Criticism* op. cit., p. 4. Further citations of this books will be given in the text as Frye 1957.

12 Frederic Jameson, *The Political Unconscious: Narrative as a Socially Symbolic Act* (Ithaca, NY: Cornell Univ. Press, 1981). pp. 103–50.

13 C. L. Barber, 'The saturnalian pattern in Shakespeare's comedy', *Sewanee Review*, 59 (1951), pp. 593–611. See also 'The use of comedy in *As You Like It*', *Philological Quarterly*, 21 (1942), pp. 353–67.

14 Maynard Mack, 'The World of Hamlet' *Yale Review* 41, (1952), p. 502.

15 Paul Mus, 'Viet Nam: a nation off balance', *Yale Review*, 41 (1952), pp. 524–33.

8 SUBVERSION AND ITS CONTAINMENT

1 Stanley Cavell, *Disowning Knowledge in Six Plays of Shakespeare* (Cambridge: Cambridge Univ. Press, 1987), pp. 115–16. Further citations of this book will be given in the text.

2 Stanley Cavell, 'The division of talent', *Critical Inquiry*, 11 (1985), pp. 519–39.

3 Thomas Kuhn, *The Structure of Scientific Revolutions*, 2nd ed. (Chicago: Univ. of Chicago Press, 1970).

4 Richard Whitley, *The Intellectual and Social Organization of the Sciences* (Oxford: Clarendon Press, 1984); Sandra Harding, *The Science Question in Feminism* (Ithaca: Cornell Univ. Press, 1986); Max Horkheimer, 'Notes on science and the crisis', trans. Matthew J. O'Connell, in *Critical Theory: Selected Essays* (NY: Continuum Books, 1972), pp. 3–10; see also Horkheimer's 'Traditional and critical theory' in the same volume.

5 On supplementarity see Jacques Derrida, *Of Grammatology*, trans. Gayatri Spivack (Baltimore: The Johns Hopkins Univ. Press, 1976); *Writing and Difference*, trans. Alan Bass. (Chicago: Univ. of Chicago Press, 1978). On the problem of concretization see Roman Ingarden, *The Literary Work of Art*, trans. George C. Grabowicz (Evanston: Northwestern Univ. Press, 1973); Wolfgang Iser, *The Act of Reading: A Theory of Aesthetic Response* (Baltimore: The Johns Hopkins Univ. Press, 1978).

6 Susan Sontag, 'Against Interpretation', in *Against Interpretation and Other Essays*, (New York: Delta, 1967), p. 13.

7 ibid., p. 14.

8 Annabel Patterson, *Censorship and Interpretation: The Conditions of Writing and Reading in Early Modern England* (Madison: Univ. Of Wisconsin Press, 1984).

9 Leo Strauss, *Persecution and the Art of Writing* (Chicago: Univ. of Chicago Press, 1950).

10 Stephen Mullaney, *The Place of the Stage: License, Play, and Power in Renaissance England* (Chicago: Univ. Of Chicago Press, 1987); Michael D. Bristol, *Carnival and Theater: Plebeian Culture and the Structure of Authority in Renaissance England* (London: Methuen & Co. Ltd, 1985).

11 See for example, Jean Howard, 'The New Historicism in Renaissance studies', *English Literary Renaissance*, 16 (1986), pp. 13–43.

12 Stephen Greenblatt, 'Invisible bullets: Renaissance authority and its subversion, *Henry IV* and *Henry V*', in Jonathan Dollimore and Alan Sinfield, *Political Shakespeare: New Essays in Cultural Materialism* (Manchester: Manchester Univ. Press, 1985), p. 26. Further citations of this article will be given in the text.

13 Stephen Greenblatt, *Renaissance Self-Fashioning: From More to Shakespeare* (Chicago: Univ. of Chicago Press, 1980), pp. 1–2.

14 Stephen Greenblatt, 'Murdering peasants: status, genre, and the representation of rebellion', in *Representing the English Renaissance* (Berkeley: Univ. of California Press, 1988), p. 25.

15 Jean-Christophe Agnew, *Worlds Apart: The Market and the Theater in Anglo-American Thought, 1550–1750* (Cambridge: Cambridge Univ. Press, 1986), pp. 101–48.

16 Paisley Livingston, 'On the specificity of literature', unpublished MS, 1986.

17 Richard A. Grusin, '"Put God in Your Debt": Emerson's Economy of expenditure', *PMLA* 103 (1988), pp. 35–44; Barbara Packer, *Emerson's Fall: A New Interpretation of the Major Essays* (NY: Continuum Books, 1982); Sharon Cameron, 'Representing grief', *Representations*, 15 (1986), pp. 15–41.

18 A. A. Smirnov, 'Shakespeare, the Renaissance, and the Age of the Barroco', in *Shakespeare in the Soviet Union*, trans. Avril Pyman (Moscow: Progress Publishers, 1966) p. 59.

SELECT BIBLIOGRAPHY

ACLS Committee on Research Libraries (1967) *On Research Libraries*, Cambridge: MIT Press.

Adams, John (1971) *The Works of John Adams, Second President of the United States*, 6 vols, New York: AMS Press; (originally published Boston: Little, Brown, 1851).

Adams, Joseph Quincy (1942) *The Folger Shakespeare Memorial Library: A Report of Progress , 1931–1941*, Brattleboro, Vermont: published for the Trustees of Amherst College.

Adorno, Theodor (1967) *Prisms: Cultural Criticism and Society*, trans. Samuel and Shierry Weber. London: Verso.

—— and Max Horkheimer (1972) *The Dialectic of Enlightenment*, New York: The Seabury Press.

Agnew, Jean-Christophe (1986) *Worlds Apart: The Market and the Theater in Anglo-American Thought, 1550–1750*, Cambridge: Cambridge University Press.

Althusser, Louis (1977) *For Marx*, trans. Ben Brewster, London: New Left Books.

Aronowitz, Stanley and Henry A. Giroux (1985) *Education under Siege: The Conservative, Liberal and Radical Debate over Schooling*, South Hadley, Mass: Bergin & Garvey.

Balch, Stephen H. and Herbert London (1986) 'The tenured Left', *Commentary* 82 (4): 41–50.

Bamber, Linda (1982) *Comic Women, Tragic Men: A Study of Gender and Genre in Shakespeare*, Stanford: Stanford University Press.

—— (1951) 'The saturnalian pattern in Shakespeare's comedy', *Sewanee Review* 59: 593–611.

Barber, C.L. (1963) *Shakespeare's Festive Comedy: A Study of Dramatic Forms and its Relation to Social Custom*, New York: Meridian Books.

Barish, Jonas (1981) *The Antitheatrical Prejudice*, Berkeley: University of California Press.

Belkin, Samuel (1966) *In His Image: The Jewish Philosphy of Man as Expressed in Rabbinic Tradition*, London: Abelard Schuman.

Bell, Daniel (1965) *The End of Ideology; On the Exhaustion of Political Ideas in the Fifties*, revised ed., New York: The Free Press.

—— (1976) *Cultural Contradictions of Capitalism*, New York: Basic Books.

Belsey, Catherine (1985) *The Subject of Tragedy*, London: Methuen & Co.

Bennett, William (1985a) 'Lost generation: why America's children are strangers in their own land', *Policy Review*, 33: 43–5.

—— (1985b) 'To reclaim a legacy', *American Educator* 21.

Bentley, G. E. (1971) *The Profession of Dramatist in Shakespeare's Time*, Princeton: Princeton University Press.

Bevington, David and Jay L. Halio (eds) (1978) *Shakespeare: Pattern of Excelling Nature: Shakespeare Criticism in Honor of America's Bicentennial*, The International Shakespeare Association Congress, Washington, DC, April 1976, Newark: University of Delaware Press.

Bloom, Allan (1987a) *The Closing of the American Mind*, New York: Simon & Schuster.

—— (1987b) 'Liberty, equality, sexuality', *Commentary* (83): 24–30.

Bloom, Harold (1976) *Poetry and Repression: Revisionism from Blake to Stevens*, New Haven: Yale University Press.

—— (1983) *Kaballah and Criticism*, New York: Continuum Books.

Blum, John Morton (1972) *V Was for Victory: Politics and American Culture during World War II*, New York: Harcourt, Brace, Jovanovitch.

Bourdieu, Pierre (1984) *Distinction: A Social Critique of the Judgement of Taste*, trans. Richard Nice, Cambridge: Harvard University Press.

Bowers, Fredson (1959) *Textual and Literary Criticism*, Cambridge: Cambridge University Press.

—— (1962a) 'Established texts and definitive editions', *Philological Quarterly* 41: 1–17.

—— (1962b) 'What Shakespeare wrote', *Shakespeare Jahrbuch* 98: 24–50.

—— (1964) *Bibliography and Textual Criticism*, Oxford: Oxford University Press.

—— (1966) *On Editing Shakespeare*, Charlottesville: University of Virginia Press.

—— (1972) 'Multiple authority, new problems and concepts of copytext', *Library* 27: 81–115.

—— (1977) 'Greg's rationale of copy text revisited', *Studies in Bibliography* 31: 91–161.

Bowles, Samuel and Herbert Gintis (1976) *Schooling in Capitalist America*, New York: Basic Books.

Brecht, Bertolt (1965) *The Messingkauf Dialogues*, trans. John Willett, London: Eyre Methuen Ltd.

—— (1964) 'A short Organum for the Theatre', in *Brecht on Theatre* ed. John Willett, New York: Hill and Wang.

Bristol, Michael D. (1985) *Carnival and Theater: Plebeian Culture and the Structure of Authority in Renaissance England*, London: Methuen & Co. Ltd.

Brown, Stephen J. (1978) 'The Uses of Shakespeare in America: A Study in Class Domination', in David Bevington and Jay L. Halio (eds) *Shakespeare: Pattern of Excelling Nature: Shakespeare Criticism in Honor of America's Bicentennial*, The International Shakespeare Association Congress, Washington, DC, April 1976, Newark: University of Delaware Press, 1978: 230–41.

Bruns, Gerald (1984) 'Canon and power in the Hebrew Scriptures', *Critical Inquiry* 10: 462–80.

Burger, Peter (1984) *Theory of the Avant-Garde*, trans. Michael Shaw, Minneapolis: University of Minnesota Press.

Cameron, Sharon (1986) 'Representing grief', *Representations*, 15: 15–41.

Cannon, Carl (1941) *American Book Collectors and Collecting from Colonial Times to the Present*, New York: H. W. Wilson Co.

Carter, John (1970) *Taste and Technique in Book Collecting: With an Epilogue*, London: Private Libraries Association.

Carter, Paul (1971) *The Spiritual Crisis of the Gilded Age*, De Kalb, Ill.: Northern Illinois University Press.

—— (1983) *Another Part of the Fifties*, New York: Columbia University Press.

Castoriadis, Cornelius (1984a) *Crossroads in the Labyrinth*, trans. Kate Sooper and Martin H. Ryle, Cambridge: MIT Press.

—— (1984b) 'The imaginary: creation in the social-historical domain', in P. Livingston (ed.) *Disorder and Order: Proceedings of the Stanford International Symposium*, *Stanford Literary Studies* I, Saratoga, Cal.: Anima Libri, 1984.

Caute, David (1973) *The Fellow Travelers – A Postscript to the Enlightenment*, New York: Macmillan.
—— (1978) *The Great Fear*, New York: Simon & Schuster.
Cavell, Stanley (1976) *Must We Mean What We Say: A Book of Essays*, London: Cambridge University Press.
—— (1985) 'The division of talent', *Critical Inquiry* 11: 519–39.
—— (1987) *Disowning Knowledge in Six Plays of Shakespeare*, Cambridge: Cambridge University Press.
Cheyfitz, Eric (1981) *The Transparent: Sexual Politics in the Language of Emerson*, Baltimore: The Johns Hopkins University Press.
Childs, Brevard S. (1979) *Introduction to the Old Testament as Scripture*, Philadelphia: Fortress Publications.
Cohen, Boaz (1969) *Law and Tradition in Judaism: A Historical Presentation*, New York: Ktav Publishing House.
Cohen, Walter (1982) '*The Merchant of Venice* and the possibilities of historical criticism', *ELH* (A Journal of English Literary History) 49: 765–89.
Colie, Rosalie (1974) *Shakespeare's Living Art*, Princeton: Princeton University Press.
Cook, Ann Jennalie (1986) 'Detours and directions in fifty years of Shakespeare scholarship', in Georgianna Ziegler (ed.) *Shakespeare Study Today: The Horace Howard Furness Memorial Lectures*, New York: AMS Press: 93–126.
Craig, Hardin (1936) *The Enchanted Glass: The Elizabethan Mind in Literature*, New York: Oxford University Press.
—— (1944) *Literary Study and the Scholarly Profession*, Seattle: University of Washington Press.
—— (1948) *An Interpretation of Shakespeare*, Columbia: Lucas Bros.
—— (1949) *Freedom and Renaissance*, Chapel Hill: University of North Carolina Press.
Davis, Natalie Z. (1971) 'The rites of violence: religious riot in sixteenth-century France', *Past and Present* 50: 49–75.
De Tocqueville, Alexis (1961) *Democracy in America, With a Critical Appraisal of Each Volume by John Stuart Mill*, 2 vols, trans. Henry Reeve, New York: Schocken Books.
De Grazia, Margareta (1988) 'The essential Shakespeare and the material book', *Textual Practice* 2: 69–86.
Derrida, Jacques (1978) *Writing and Difference*, trans. Alan Bass, Chicago: University of Chicago Press.
Dollimore, Jonathan (1985) 'Transgression and surveillance in *Measure for Measure*', in *Political Shakespeare: New Essays in Cultural Materialism*, Manchester: Manchester University Press, pp. 72–88.
—— (1984) *Radical Tragedy: Religion, Ideology, and Power in the Drama of Shakespeare and his Contemporaries*, Chicago: University of Chicago Press.
—— and Alan Sinfield (eds) (1985) *Political Shakespeare: New Essays in Cultural Materialism*, Manchester: Manchester University Press.
Domhoff, G. William (1967) *Who Rules America?*, Englewood Cliffs: Prentice-Hall Inc.
Drakakis, John (ed.) (1985) *Alternative Shakespeares*, London: Methuen & Co.
Dumouchel, Paul and Jean-Pierre Dupuy (1979) *L'enfer des choses: René Girard et la logique de l'économie*, Paris: Seuil.
Dunn, Esther Cloudman (1939) *Shakespeare in America*, New York: Macmillan.
Durkheim, Emile (1965) *The Elementary Forms of Religious Life*, trans. J. Swain, New York: The Free Press.
—— (1973) *On Morality and Society*, ed. Robert N. Bellah, Chicago: University of Chicago Press.
Eisenstein, Elizabeth (1983) *The Printing Revolution in Early Modern Europe*,

Cambridge: Cambridge University Press.

Emerson, Ralph Waldo (1968) *Representative Men: Seven Lectures*, in *The Complete Works of Ralph Waldo Emerson: Centenary Edition*, 12 vols, New York: AMS Press.

Erickson, Peter (1985) *Patriarchal Structures in Shakespeare's Drama* Berkeley: University of California Press.

Ferguson, Margaret 'Afterword' (1987) in Jean Howard and Marion O'Connor (eds) *Shakespeare Reproduced: The Text in History and Ideology*, London: Methuen & Co: 273–83.

Ferguson, Margaret, Nancy Vickers, and Maureen Quilligan (eds) (1986) *Rewriting the Renaissance*, Chicago: University of Chicago Press.

Folger, Henry Clay, Correspondence, in the Folger Shakespeare Memorial Library, Washington, DC.

Foucault, Michel (1977) 'What is an author?', in *Language, Counter-Memory, Practice*, trans. Donald F. Bouchard and Sherry Simond (eds) Ithaca: Cornell University Press.

Frye, Northrop (1957) *Anatomy of Criticism*, Princeton: Princeton University Press.

—— (1965) *A Natural Perspective: The Development of Shakespearean Comedy and Romance*, New York: Harcourt, Brace, and World.

Furness, Horace Howard, collection of unpublished correspondence in the Horace Howard Furness Memorial Library, Philadelphia, Penn.

Gadamer, Hans-Georg (1975) *Truth and Method*, New York: Seabury Books.

—— (1976) *Philosophical Hermeneutics*, trans. David E. Linge, Berkeley: University of California Press.

Garber, Marjorie (1987) *Shakespeare's Ghost Writers: Literature as Uncanny Causality*, London: Methuen & Co.

Gardner, Helen (1982) *In Defence of the Imagination*, Cambridge: Harvard University Press.

Gayley, Charles Mills (1917) *Shakespeare and the Founders of Liberty in America*, New York: Macmillan Company.

Geuss, Raymond (1981) *The Idea of A Critical Theory: Habermas and the Frankfurt School*, Cambridge: Cambridge University Press.

Gibson, James M. (1986) 'Horace Howard Furness: book collector and library builder', in Georgianna Ziegler (ed.) *Shakespeare Study Today*, New York: AMS Press: 169–91.

Giddens, Anthony. *The Constitution of Society: Outline of the Theory of Structuration*, Cambridge, Mass.: Polity Press.

Gilbert, James Burkhart (1968) *Writers and Partisans: A History of Literary Radicalism in America*, New York: John Wiley & Sons.

Gilmore, Michael T. (1985) *American Romanticism and the Marketplace*, Chicago: University of Chicago Press.

Girard, Rene (1965) *Deceit, Desire and the Novel: Self and Other in Literary Structure*, trans. Yvonne Freccero, Baltimore: The Johns Hopkins University Press.

Goldberg, Jonathan (1986) 'Textual properties', *Shakespeare Quarterly* 37: 216.

Graff, Gerald (1987) *Professing Literature: An Institutional History*, Chicago: University of Chicago Press.

Grafton, Anthony and Lisa Jardine (1986) *From Humanism to the Humanities: Education and the Liberal Arts in Fifteenth- and Sixteenth-century Europe*, Cambridge: Harvard University Press.

Gramsci, Antonio. (1971) *Selections from the Prison Notebooks*, trans. Quintin Hoare and G. N. Smith New York: International Publishers.

Greenblatt, Stephen (1976) 'Learning to curse: aspects of linguistic colonialism in the sixteenth century', in Fredi Chiappelli (ed.) *First Images of America: The Impact* of the New World on the Old, 2 vols., Berkeley: University of California Press, 2: 568–76.

—— (1980) *Renaissance Self-Fashioning: From More to Shakespeare*, Chicago: University of Chicago Press.

—— (1985a) 'Invisible bullets: Renaissance authority and its subversion, *Henry IV* and *Henry V*', in Jonathan Dollimore and Alan Sinfield (eds) *Political Shakespeare: New Essays in Cultural Materialism*. Manchester: Manchester University Press.

—— (1985b) 'Shakespeare and the exorcists', in Patricia Parker and Geoffrey Hartman (eds) *Shakespeare and the Question of Theory*, London: Methuen and Co.

—— (1987) *Shakespearean Negotiations*, Berkeley: University of California Press.

—— (1988) 'Murdering peasants: status, genre, and the representation of rebellion', in *Representing the English Renaissance*, Berkeley: University of California Press.

Greg, W. (1942) *The Editorial Problem in Shakespeare*, Oxford: Oxford University Press.

—— (1950) 'The rationale of copy-text', *Studies in Bibliography* 3: 19–36.

Grusin, Richard A. (1988) '"Put God in your debt": Emerson's economy of expenditure', *PMLA* 103: 35–44.

Guilbaut, Serge (1983) *How New York Stole the Idea of Modern Art: Abstract Expressionism, Freedom, and the Cold War*, trans. Arthur Goldhammer, Chicago: University of Chicago Press.

Guillory, John (1987) 'Canonical and non-canonical: a critique of the current debate', *ELH* 54: 483–529.

Habermas, Jurgen (1970) *Towards a Rational Society: Student Protest, Science, and Politics*, trans. Jeremy Shapiro, Boston: Beacon Press.

—— (1971) *Knowledge and Human Interests*, trans. Jeremy Shapiro, Boston: Beacon Press.

—— (1975) *Legitimation Crisis*, trans. Thomas McCarthy, Boston: Beacon Press.

—— (1979) *Communication and the Evolution of Society*, trans. Thomas McCarthy, Boston: Beacon Press.

—— (1985) 'Neo-Conservative culture criticism in the United States and West Germany: an intellectual movement in two political cultures', in Richard J. Bernstein (ed.) *Habermas and Modernity*, Cambridge: MIT Press.

Hard, Frederick (1968) *Louis B. Wright: A Bibliography and an Appreciation*, Charlottesville: University press of Virginia.

Harding, Sandra (1983) 'Why has the sex-gender system become visible only now?', in Sandra Harding and Merill B. Hintikka (eds) *Discovering Reality: Perspectives on Epistemology, Metaphysics, Methodology, and Philosophy of Science*, Boston: D. Reidel: 312 ff.

—— (1986) *The Science Question in Feminism*, Ithaca: Cornell University Press.

Hardison, O. B. (1984) *Toward Freedom and Dignity: The Humanities and the Idea of Humanity*, Baltimore: The Johns Hopkins University Press.

—— '"Put money in thy purse": supporting Shakespeare' in *Shakespeare Studies Today*, Philadelphia: AMS Press, 153–69.

Hartsock, Nancy (1983) 'The feminist standpoint: developing the ground for a specifically feminist historical materialism', in Sandra Harding and Merill B. Hintikka (eds) *Discovering Reality: Perspectives on Epistemology, Metaphysics, Methodology, and Philosophy of Science*, Boston: D. Reidel; 283–310.

Hartz, Louis (1955) *The Liberal Tradition in America: An Interpretation of American Political Thought since the Revolution* New York: Harcourt, Brace.

—— (1964) *The Founding of New Societies*, New York: Harcourt, Brace.

Hawkes, Terence (1986) *That Shakespeherian Rag: Essays on a Critical Process* (London: Methuen & Co.

Haynes, Jonathan. (1984) 'Festivity and dramatic economy in Jonson's *Bartholomew Faire*', *ELH* 51: 635–58.

Heilman, Samuel C. (1983) *The People of the Book: Drama, Fellowship, and Religion*, Chicago: University of Chicago Press.

Held, David (1980) *Introduction to Critical Theory: Horkheimer to Habermas*, Berkeley: University of California Press.

Hinman, Charlton (1963) *The Printing and Proof-Reading of the First Folio of Shakespeare*, 2 vols, Oxford: Oxford University Press.

—— (1972) 'Shakespearian textual studies: seven more years', in Clifford Leech and J. M. R. Margeson (eds) *Shakespeare 1971: Proceedings of the World Shakespeare Congress: Vancouver, Aug. 1971*, Toronto: University of Toronto Press: 37–50.

Hjort, Anne-Mette (1987) 'The interests of critical editorial practice', *Poetics* 15: 259–77.

Holderness, Graham, and Christopher McCullough (eds.) (1987) *The Shakespeare Myth*, Manchester: Manchester University Press.

Hook, Sidney (1939) 'Academic freedom and "The Trojan Horse" in American education', *AAUP Bulletin* 25 (5): 555.

Horkheimer, Max (1972) 'Traditional and critical theory' and 'Notes on science and the crisis', in *Critical Theory: Selected Essays*, trans. M. J. O'Connell, New York: Continuum Books.

Horwitz, Howard (1987) 'The Standard oil Trust as Emersonian hero' *Raritan Review* 6: 97–119.

Howard, Jean (1986) 'The New Historicism in Renaissance studies', *English Literary Renaissance*, 16: 13–43.

Innis, Harold (1951) *The Bias of Communications*, Toronto: University of Toronto Press.

Jameson, Frederic (1971) *Marxism and Form: Twentieth Century Dialectical Theories of Literature*, Princeton: Princeton University Press.

—— (1981) *The Political Unconscious: Narrative as a Socially Symbolic Act*, Ithaca, New York: Cornell University Press.

Jay, Martin (1973) *The Dialectical Imagination: A History of the Frankfurt School and the Institute for Social Research, 1923–1950*, Boston: Little, Brown, and Co..

Kahn, Coppelia (1981) *Man's Estate: Masculine Identity in Shakespeare*, Berkeley: University of California Press.

Kane, Betty Ann (1976) *The Widening Circle: The Story of the Folger Shakespeare Library and its Collections*, Washington DC: The Folger Shakespeare Library.

Keller, Evelyn Fox (1984) *Reflections on Gender and Science*, New Haven: Yale University Press.

King, Stanley (1950) *Recollections of the Folger Shakespeare Library* Ithaca: Cornell University Press, published for the Trustees of Amherst College.

Kittredge, George Lyman (1930) *Shakespere: An Address Delivered on April 23, 1916 in Saunders Theatre at the Request of the President and Fellows of Harvard College*, Cambridge: Harvard University Press; (first published 1916).

Kuhl, E. P. (1962) 'Shakespeare and the founders of America: "*The Tempest*"', *Philological Quarterly* 41: 123–46.

Kuhn, Thomas (1970) *The structure of Scientific Revolutions*, 2nd ed., Chicago: University of Chicago Press.

La Capra, Dominick (1985) *Emile Durkheim: Sociologist and Philosopher*, Chicago: Chicago University Press.

Laird, David (1987) 'Horace Howard Furness', *Dictionary of Literary Biography*, 64: 66–70.

Le Duc, Thomas (1946) *Piety and Intellect at Amherst College: 1865–1912* New York:

Columbia University Press.

Lentricchia, Frank (1983) *Criticism and Social Change*, Chicago: University of Chicago Press.

Lenz, Carolyn Ruth Swift, Gayle Greene, and Carol Neely (eds) (1980) *The Woman's Part: Feminist Criticism of Shakespeare*, Urbana: University of Illinois Press.

Levin, Harry (1946) 'Literature as an institution', *Accent* 6: 159–68.

—— (1959) *The Question of Hamlet*. New York: Oxford Univ. Press.

—— (1975) 'The primacy of Shakespeare', *Shakespeare Quarterly* 26: 99–112.

—— (1976) *Shakespeare and the Revolution of the Times: Perspectives and Commentaries*, New York: Oxford University Press.

Levin Richard (1979) *New Readings vs. Old Plays: Recent Trends in the Reinterpretation of English Renaissance Drama*, Chicago: University of Chicago Press.

—— (1988) 'Feminist thematics and Shakespearean tragedy', *PMLA* 103: 125–38.

Levinas Emmanuel (1963) *Difficile Liberté: Essais sur le Judaïsme*, 3rd ed. Paris: Editions Albin Michel, 1963.

—— (1968) *Quatre Lectures Talmudiques*, Paris: Editions de Minuit.

—— (1987) *Collected Philosophical Papers*, trans. Alphonso Lingis, Dordrecht: Martinus Nijhoff.

Lippman, Walter (1937) *An Inquiry into the Principles of The Good Society*, Boston: Little, Brown.

Lipset, Seymour Martin (1959) *Social Mobility in Industrial Society*, Berkeley: University of California Press.

Lipsitz, George (1982) *Class and Culture in Cold War America*, South Hadley, Mass: J. F. Bergin.

Livingston, Paisley (1988) *Literary Knowledge: Humanistic Inquiry and the Philosophy of Science*, Ithaca: Cornell University Press.

Lovejoy, Arthur O. (1936) *The Great Chain of Being: A Study of the History of an Idea*, New York: Harper Torchbooks.

—— (1949) 'Communism and academic freedom', *American Scholar* 18 (3).

Loewenstein, Joseph (1988) 'The script in the marketplace', in Stephen Greenblatt (ed.) *Representing the Renaissance*, Berkeley: University of California Press: 265–78.

Lowenthal, Leo (1961) *Literature, Popular Culture and Society*, Palo Alto, Cal.: Pacific Books.

Lunacharsky, Anatoli (1966), 'Bacon and the characters of Shakespeare's plays', *Shakespeare in the Soviet Union*, trans. Avril Pyman, Moscow: Progress Publishers.

Lyotard, Jean-Francois (1977) 'Jewish Oedipus', trans. Susan Hanson *Genre* 10: 395–411.

Mack, Maynard (1952) 'The world of Hamlet' *Yale Review* 41: 502.

—— (1965) *King Lear in Our Time*, Berkeley: University of California Press.

Marcuse, Herbert. *Negations: Essays in Critical Theory*, Boston: Beacon Press.

Marx, Karl (1973) *Grundrisse: Introduction to the Critique of Political Economy*, trans. Martin Nicolaus, New York: Vintage Books.

Marowitz, Charles (1988) 'Reconstructing Shakespeare, or harlotry in bardolatry', *Shakespeare Survey* 40: 1–10.

Mauss, Marcel (1967) *The Gift*, trans. by Ian Cunnison, with an Introduction by E. E. Evans-Pritchard, New York: W. W. Norton & Company.

McCarthy, Thomas (1978) *The Critical Theory of Jurgen Habermas*, Cambridge: MIT Press.

McGann, Jerome (ed.; (1983) *A Critique of Modern Textual Criticism*, Chicago: University of Chicago Press.

—— (1985) *Textual Criticism and Literary Interpretation*, Chicago: University of Chicago Press.

McKerrow, R. B. (1939) *Prolegomena for the Oxford Shakespeare*, Oxford: Oxford University Press.

Metzger, Walter P. (1961) *Academic Freedom in the Age of the University*, New York: Columbia University Press.

Mielziner, Moses (1968) *Introduction to the Talmud*, 4th ed., New York: Bloch Publishing Company (Originally published 1894).

Mus, Paul (1952) 'Viet Nam: a nation off balance', *Yale Review*, 41: 524–33.

Nietzsche, Friedrich (1982) *Daybreak: Thoughts on the Prejudices of Morality*, trans. R. J. Hollingdale, Cambridge: Cambridge University Press.

Ohmann, Richard (1976) *English in America: A Radical View of the Profession*, New York: Oxford University Press.

Orgel, Stephen (1981) 'What is a text?', *Research Opportunities in Renaissance Drama* 24: 3–6.

—— (1988) 'The authentic Shakespeare', *Representations* 21: 5ff.

Packer, Barbara (1982) *Emerson's Fall: A New Interpretation of the Major Essays*, New York: Continuum Books.

—— (1986) 'Origin and authority: Emerson and the higher criticism', in Sacvan Bercovitch (ed.) *Reconstructing American Literary History*, Cambridge: Harvard University Press: 67–92.

Patterson, Anabel (1984) *Censorship and Interpretation: The Conditions of Writing and Reading in Early Modern England*, Madison: University of Wisconsin Press.

Pells, Richard (1984) *Radical Visions, American Dreams: Culture and Social Thought in the Depression Years*, Middletown: Wesleyan University Press.

—— (1985) *The Liberal Mind in a Conservative Era*, New York: Harper & Row.

Rooney, Ellen (1986) 'Who's left out? A rose by any other name is still red: or, the politics of pluralism', *Critical Inquiry* 12: 550–64.

Rose, Mary Beth (1988) *The Expense of Spirit: Love and Sexuality in English Renaissance Drama*, Ithaca: Cornell University Press.

Savage, Henry L. (1952) 'The Shakespeare Society of Philadelphia', *Shakespeare Quarterly* 3: 341–52.

Schlesinger, Arthur (1970) *The Vital Center: The Politics of Freedom*, London: André Deutsch. (first published as *The Politics of Freedom*, 1950).

Scholem, Gershom (1954) *Major Trends in Jewish Mysticism*, 3rd ed., New York: Schocken Books.

—— (1969) 'Religious authority and mysticism', in *On the Kabbalah and Its Symbolism*, trans. Ralph Mannheim, New York: Schocken Books.

Schrecker, Ellen W. (1986) *No Ivory Tower: McCarthyism and the Universities*, Oxford: Oxford University Press.

Shera, Jesse Hauck Shera (1949) *Foundations of the Public Library: The Origins of the Public Library Movement in New England*, Chicago: University of Chicago Press.

Shils, Edward (1981) *Tradition*, London: Faber & Faber.

Smirnov, A.A., (1966) 'Shakespeare, the Renaissance, and the Age of the Barocco', in *Shakespeare in the Soviet Union*, trans. Avril Pyman, Moscow: Progress Publishers.

Sontag, Susan (1967) *Against Interpretation and Other Essays*, New York: Delta.

Spencer, Theodore (1966) *Shakespeare and the Nature of Man*, New York: Collier Books.

Stallybrass, Peter and Allan White (1986) *The Politics and Poetics of Transgression*, London: Methuen & Co.

Strack, Hermann (1969) *Introduction to the Talmud and Midrash*, New York: Atheneum.

Strauss, Leo (1950) *Persecution and the Art of Writing*, Chicago: University of Chicago Press.

Sweezey, Paul. A. (1953) *The American Ruling Class: The Present as History*, New York:

Monthly Review Press.

Tanselle, G. Thomas (1979a) 'Bibliography and science' in *Selected Studies in Bibliography*, Charlottesville: University Press of Virginia, 1979: 1–37.

—— (1979b) 'The editorial problem of final authorial intention', in *Selected Studies in Bibliography*, Charlottesville: University Press of Virginia.

—— (1987) 'Historicism and critical editing', *Studies in Bibliography* 39: 1–47.

Taylor, Charles (1979) *Hegel and Modern Society*, Cambridge: Cambridge University Press.

Thaler, Alwin (1941) *Shakespeare and Democracy*, Knoxville, University of Tennessee Press.

Thompson, E.P. (1968) *The Making of the English Working Class*, Harmondsworth: Penguin Books.

Thomson, John B. (1984) *Studies in the Theory of Ideology*, Berkeley: University of California Press.

Urkowitz, Steven (1980) *Shakespeare's Revision of King Lear*, Princeton: Princeton University Press.

Walzer, Michael (1987) *Interpretation and Social Criticism*, Cambridge: Harvard University Press.

Warren, Michael J. (1978) 'Quarto and Folio *King Lear* and the interpretation of Albany and Edgar', in David Bevington and Jay L. Halio (eds) *Shakespeare: Pattern of Excelling Nature: Shakespeare Criticism in Honor of America's Bicentennial*, The International Shakespeare Association Congress, Washington, DC, April 1976, Newark: University of Delaware Press.

Wayne, Don (1987) 'Politics and the Shakespearean text: recent criticism in England and the United States' in Jean E. Howard and Marion F. O'Connor (eds) *Shakespeare Reproduced*, London: Methuen & Co. 47–67.

Weber, Max (1964) *The Theory of Social and Economic Organizations*, trans. E. M. Henderson and Talcott Parsons, ed. Talcott Parsons, New York: The Free Press.

Weber, Samuel (1987) *Institution and Interpretation*, Minneapolis: University of Minnesota Press.

Weinfeld, Moshe (1972) *Deuteronomy and the Deuteronomic School*, Oxford: Clarendon Press.

Whitley, Richard (1984) *The Intellectual and Social Organization of the Sciences*, Oxford: Clarendon Press.

Wiles, David (1987) *Shakespeare's Clown: Actor and Text in the Elizabethan Playhouse*, Cambridge: Cambridge University Press.

Williams, Raymond (1965) *The Long Revolution*, Harmondsworth: Penguin Books.

—— (1977) *Marxism and Literature*, Oxford: Oxford University Press.

Wilson, F. P. (1945) 'Shakespeare and the New Bibliography', *The Bibliographical Society*, London: printed for the Bibliographical Society: 76–135.

Wolff, Janet (1981) *The Social Production of Art*, London: Macmillan.

—— (1983) *Aesthetics and the Sociology of Art*, London: George Allen & Unwin.

Wright, Louis B. (1963) 'An obligation to Shakespeare and the public', *Shakespeare Survey* 16: 1–9.

—— (1976) *Of Books and Men*, Columbia, SC: University of South Carolina Press.

Ziegler, Georgianna (ed.) (1986) *Shakespeare Study Today*, New York: AMS Press.

INDEX